HMONG ANIMISM

A Christian Perspective

LONG KHANG

Copyright © 2015 by Long Khang

HMONG ANIMISM
A CHRISTIAN PERSPECTIVE
by Long Khang

Printed in the United States of America

ISBN 9781498433655

All rights reserved solely by the author. The author guarantees all contents are original and do not infringe upon the legal rights of any other person or work. No part of this book may be reproduced in any form without the permission of the author. The views expressed in this book are not necessarily those of the publisher.

Unless otherwise indicated, scripture quotations are taken from The New International Version (NIV) of the Holy Bible. Copyright © 1973, 1978, 1984, 2011 by Biblica, Inc. from Biblegateway.com. Used by permission. All rights reserved.

www.xulonpress.com

ACKNOWLEDGMENT

To my father, Xao Doua Khang and mother,
Lah Yang who are now home with the Lord;
My wife, Yee, whose support and encouragement
are the sources of my strength and perseverance;
My children: Nkaujnaag, Yuepeng, Kaoly, Fuabcua,
and Yelemi, who are my motivators;
And my Lord and Savior whose knowledge
and wisdom I endeavor to learn.

Special thanks to Dr. Timothy T. Vang, my pastor and friend, who allowed me to use many of his books and Dissertation as reference sources for this project. I'm also thankful to many people who allowed me to use their stories to be part of this book. Finally, I'm thankful to Judith Lewis for editing part of the project, my daughter, Nkaujnaag, for proof reading, and my wife for everything that she has done.

Lord, I thank you for giving me the courage, knowledge, and opportunity to write this most sensitive subject to advance your Kingdom.

TABLE OF CONTENTS

Preface ix

Chapter 1
A Short History of the Hmong 13

Chapter 2
Introduction to Hmong Animism 29

Chapter 3
Cosmology of Hmong Animism According
to the Showing the Way Chant 41

Chapter 4
The Belief that Satan (*Ntxwngyoog*)
is the Evil Deity 83

Chapter 5
The Belief in the Reincarnation of the Spirit
Definition of Soul and Spirit 92

Chapter 6
Cosmology of Hmong Animism
According to Hmong Shamanism 138

Chapter 7
Worship of the Household Demons 193

Chapter 8
Ancestral Worship 212

Chapter 9
Worship of the Wild Demons 231

Chapter 10
Is God a Strange God? 241

Chapter 11
Oppression and Persecution Impacting
Hmong Christians 266

Bibliography 287

About the Author 295

PREFACE

Throughout history, Hmong animism has been the only belief system the Hmong ever knew and practiced. The Hmong in Laos did not see the light of the Lord until early 1950s. Hmong have since steadily accepted Christ as their Lord and Savior, but the majority of the Hmong are still in the dark and being controlled by Satan and his demons. The following assumptions were made to guide this book and to provide a framework in which the findings of the research will be explained.

1. Hmong animism is Satanism. Hmong animists worship ancestors, demons, Satan, natural and created objects. They believe that demons live in the forest, in the rocks, trees, rivers, mountains, and so on. Hmong animists rely on these demons for protection, blessings, or even to inflict harm or death to another person. They believe that when people die, their spirits become demons. For this reason, Hmong animists are fearful of the dead.
2. Though Hmong animists believe that the spirit becomes demon when the body dies, they also believe that the spirit reincarnates. The spirit that resides in one's body now may already have resided

in hundreds or thousands of bodies in the past. The spirit only borrows the body as a temporary shelter.
3. Hmong animists believe that each person has at least three major spirits and many minor spirits. The minor spirits will die or simply disappear when the body dies, but the major spirits continue to live on. One of the spirits will remain with the body at the grave. The second spirit is guided to the world of darkness, or in other words, the demon world and stays there forever with its ancestors. The third spirit is guided to Satan (*Ntxwgnyoog*) or to God (*Yawmsaub*), as some groups of Hmong animists believe, to ask for a new letter of provision for a new life, to be reincarnated as a new human being.
4. Hmong animists believe in creation. Though the general belief is that God (*Yawmsaub*) is the Creator, Hmong animists are still confused about who really was the creator. The Showing the Way chants give too many names as the creators and recorded too many conflicting accounts of creation.
5. Hmong animism teaches that the universe exists spontaneously in both seen and unseen worlds. The unseen world is the spirit world that Hmong called "*Dlaabteb*," which translates into English as "Demon World." The following are the different names for the spirit world: *Dlaabteb* (demon world); *Ntuj qhua teb nkig, ntuj txag teb tsaus,* (parched sky dried land, frozen sky darkness land); or most often used is *ntuj txag teb tsaus* (frozen sky darkness land); *tub tuagteb* (land of the dead). They are similar to Hades and Hell.
6. The truth can only be found in the Scripture. The Scripture is the true Word of God and it was inspired

Preface

by the Holy Spirit to be written to reveal the who is the Creator. Only the Holy Scripture c the way for the fallen human race to return to their Creator. Hmong Christians believe that Jesus Christ is the Son of God who came down in the human flesh to save human beings and to give eternal life to those who believe in Him.

Hmong have practiced animism for thousands of years and those who practice it believe that it should remain the only religion of the Hmong. Though Hmong animism is deeply rooted in the lives of the Hmong animists, the substances fundamental to Hmong animism are only myths. They see Christianity as a threat to Hmong animism and persecute those who convert to Christianity. Despite persecution and ostracism, the number of Hmong converting to Christianity is increasing. Many converted to Christianity as a last resort to be delivered from the oppression of the household demons and ancestors that they had been worshipping; but others turned to Christ because they realized that all that Hmong animism can offer are a lot of false hopes and empty promises. This book, *Hmong Animism: A Christian Perspective* is written to offer a comparative study on Hmong animism and Christianity. It counters those beliefs that Hmong animists hold dear to their hearts and postulates that Hmong animists are the most demonic-oppressed people.

The main emphasis of this book is to expose Hmong animism. However, it cannot be fully appreciated without a short history of the Hmong. The history of the Hmong is a synoptic account of over 5,000 years of history. There is no history written about the Hmong prior to them already living in China. However, the history of the Hmong living in China dates back to 3,000 BC. Hmong probably developed animism while living in China because all references in the Showing the Way Chants and shamanism are contain within the period Hmong had already settled in China. Therefore, it is important to know the history of the Hmong in order to understand why they believe and practice animism.

CHAPTER 1

A SHORT HISTORY OF THE HMONG

Hmong are a group of people who are recorded to have been living in China since 3,000 BC. However, since little is known about the Hmong, a short history about who they are and their origin is in order. The Hmong are known in China, Thailand, Laos, and Vietnam as "Miao." However, the name "Miao" encompasses four different ethnic minority groups of people in China, Hmong being one of the groups. The name "Miao" was assigned to these four ethnic groups by the Chinese and for that reason the world also knows them by that name. But the Hmong outside of China, especially the Hmong of the United States, Canada, Argentina, Germany, France, and Australia who originated from Laos, dislike being called "Miao." The name "Miao" is used here for historical reference only.

Among the four groups of Miao are the Hmong; Guo-ne, who are known by the Chinese as Black Miao or Heh Miao; Ahmao, who are known by the Chinese as the Flowery Miao;

and the Guo-Xiong.¹ It is not clear whether all four Miao groups came from the same ancestral root, but history indicates that they shared the same oppression by the Chinese for thousands of years. William Geddes states that all Miao people have similar legends about being the descendants of one common ancestor Chih-you (*Txiv-yawg*).² They also have similar legends such as the universal flood that non-Miao peoples including the Chinese do not have.

ORIGINS OF HMONG

The origin of the Hmong people remains a mystery, but according to Chinese history and Hmong legends, Hmong had already been living in the basin of the Yellow River of today's Honan Province in China as early as 3,000 BC. No one knows where the Hmong originated from, but many historians agree that their origin is not from China. Until recently, Hmong did not have written language (Hmong legends say that Hmong writing was lost as a result of centuries of war between the Hmong and Chinese). Therefore, history was passed down orally from generation to generation. However, Hmong oral history does not mention where they came from other than to say that Hmong originally came to China from the north where there was light for six months and darkness

---

[1] Steven X. Her, "Contextualizing the Gospel for Miao Animists" (PhD. diss., Western Seminary, 1999), 11-13. Dr. Steven X. Her spent about two years conducting his research in China. He was a Christian and Missionary Alliance (C&MA) missionary to the Hmong in China for eight years. He was elected the District Superintendent of the Hmong District of the C&MA in 2011-2014.

[2] William R. Geddes, *Migrants of the Mountains: The Cultural Ecology of the Blue Miao (Hmong Njua) of Thailand* (London: Oxford University Press, 1976), 3.

A Short History of the Hmong

for the other six months of the year.³ European Catholic missionaries first penetrated Hmong territories in China in the 17th century and found them to have many European physical characteristics. It was not uncommon to find many of them with red or blond hair and blue eyes. These were the Hmong who had never assimilated into the Chinese culture and did not have any history of intermarriage with Caucasians. They played many games that the European children played such as hide-and-seek, marbles, and spinning tops. They did not eat with chopsticks like the Chinese, but with spoons.⁴

Two Western scholars have written about the origin of the Hmong and where they might have come from. F. M. Savina was a French Catholic missionary who was sent to Laos and Vietnam in the early 1900s by the Society for Foreign Mission from Paris. During his mission work among the Hmong in Laos and Vietnam, Savina saw many Hmong with blond hair and blue eyes. He also learned from Hmong stories and legends that through centuries of wars with the Chinese, Hmong men were exterminated and so Hmong women married Chinese. Though most of the Hmong now have black hair and brown eyes with light skin, naturally they continued to have a few people with blond hair and blue eyes. These led many anthropologists who studied the Hmong in Laos and Thailand to "classify them as the most Caucasian population of Southeast Asia."⁵ These Caucasian physical characteristics, features of European cultures, and Hmong stories and legends led Savina to theorize that Hmong were of Caucasian origin, a Caucasian group of people that may have shared the "Turanian"⁶ ancestors, who

---

³ Keith Quincy, *Hmong History of A People* (Spokane: Eastern Washington University Press, 1988, 1995), 25.
⁴ Ibid., 17.
⁵ Ibid., 18.
⁶ Ibid., 26.

lived in the Iranian plateau between the Tigris and Euphrates rivers about 5,000 BC. They may have been forced to move from there by the "Aryan invaders." The Hmong may have slowly moved from the Iranian plateau to Siberia, Mongolia, Manchuria, and finally settled in the basin of the Yellow River around 3,000 BC.[7]

Another Western writer on Hmong history who suggested that Hmong could be Caucasians is Keith Quincy. Quincy agrees with Savina that because of the abundant Caucasian physical characteristics among the Hmong today, there's no doubt that they were originally Caucasians. He does not necessarily agree with Savina that Hmong were originally from the plateau of the Tigris and Euphrates rivers in Iran. He believes that they migrated to Siberia about 5,000 BC at the time when the glacial ice was receding due to the rise in temperature. The consequent opening of northern Europe, Eurasia, and Siberia allowed the Europeans to move north. The Hmong may have been one of those European groups. He based this assumption on the many legends that indicate that Hmong lived in the far northern land where days and nights are six months long prior to living in China. From there, they slowly moved south and ended up in the basin of the Yellow River sometime before 3,000 BC.[8]

---

[7] Ibid., 26.
[8] Ibid., 29.

Figure 1.1: Photo courtesy of Jerre Ekstrand. He took this photo several years ago during one of his trips to Laos. In this photo the hair color of the tallest girl is naturally blond. All are Hmong girls.

Figure 1.2: Photo of the Vang family. In this photo, both parents and the three older children have black hair, but the youngest child has blond hair.

Other writers who disagreed with these propositions of the origin of the Hmong are Williams R. Geddes, Gary Yia Lee, Christian Culas, Jean Michaud, and Nicholas Tapp. Pointing to the Chinese record of the first Hmong and Chinese conflict in the basin of the Yellow River about 2,700 BC, various accounts of conflicts between the Hmong and Chinese following this first major conflict, and of the various accounts of Hmong history written by various authors, Geddes believes that the Hmong may have always been in southern China. If they were not originally from there, he argues, they might have migrated from the south either from India, the Tonkin region of northern Vietnam, or Myanmar.[9] Gary Yia Lee argues, using Savina's words, that if "from times immemorial there exists in China a race of men whose origin no one knows," who called themselves Hmong, then they should have originated somewhere in China, not far from where they were first recorded by the Chinese.[10]

HISTORICAL CONFLICTS BETWEEN HMONG AND CHINESE

History indicates that Hmong fought many wars with the Chinese to resist assimilation as well as to repel oppression. Literatures recorded that the Chinese attempted to force assimilation of the Hmong starting as early as 2,356 BC.[11] If this is true, Hmong had lived in harmony with the Chinese for hundreds of years without any problem. The disharmony started about 2,700 BC during the Huan-Yuan Dynasty when a massive group of Han Chinese encroached on the lands of

---

[9] Geddes, 3-12.

[10] Gary Yia Lee, "Diaspora and the Predicament of Origins: Interrogating Hmong Postcolonial History and Identity," *Hmong Studies Journal* 8, 2007, 14.

[11] Quincy, 32-59.

the Hmong in the valley of the Yellow River. A war broke out between the Hmong and the Han Chinese, which the Hmong eventually lost. This marked the first migration of the Hmong out of the Yellow River to the east and south.[12] The policy of assimilation did not start until over three hundred years after the first war between Hmong and the Han Chinese. Why did they resist assimilation? What's so bad about assimilation into another culture? For today's rapid globalization of cultures, it seems hard for the modern person to understand the reason for resisting assimilation in the ancient times. For the modern person, assimilation may mean adapting to or accepting other cultures or languages, but for the ancient Hmong, assimilation meant totally abandoning their own culture, ethnicity, and language to completely immerse in another culture and language. The Chinese's main purpose of assimilation of the Hmong was not for them to become Chinese Hmong but for them to completely become Chinese and no longer be Hmong. It is not the same as being Americans without being Caucasians. The Chinese policy of assimilation in ancient times was to completely absorb the whole ethnicity of the Hmong so that even if they continued to exist, they would exist as Chinese and not Hmong. This was one of the reasons the ancient Hmong put up so much resistance to the Chinese effort to assimilate them. Instead of assimilating, they chose to sacrifice their lives to maintain their own identity as a distinct ethnic people.

Another problem with the assimilation policy was that it was a disguised policy of the Chinese emperors to forcibly seize the Hmong lands and then redistribute them to their own people. Again, the Hmong had to put up the resistance due to the unbearable pain and suffering in the name of assimilation of having their lands taken away. Time and time again throughout history, Hmong would rebel against

---

[12] Steven X. Her, 8.

Chinese authorities only when the oppression and maltreatment became unbearable. Historians agree that Hmong were first settled in the lowlands, such as the basin of the Yellow River, fertile lands where large communities were built, and goods were freely traded with other groups. Being a minority group and independent of the ruling majority, the Hmong were envied by the Chinese for the rich lands they occupied. The Chinese employed several methods of grabbing lands from the Hmong and redistributing them among the Chinese people. One of which the Chinese authority would systematically and in some case force relocation of their own people into Hmong lands and forcibly taking possession of their lands. Throughout the history of wars between Hmong and Chinese, this seems to be the case until as recently as two centuries ago. Each time the Chinese ruler implemented the policy of assimilation, Hmong were oppressed and mistreated, followed by lands being forcibly taken and given to the Chinese people. Then Hmong rebelled and more stringent policies were forced upon them. Many times, the policies of the Chinese rulers were to set up different criminal codes or to totally exterminate the Hmong. Due to being minority and lacking advanced weapons, each time there was a war between Hmong and the Chinese, Hmong ended up losing and had to retreat further away from the Chinese. Eventually, in order to live in peace by themselves, the Hmong retreated to the high mountains. Currently, Hmong occupy the worst of the worst lands of China, not by freewill but by choice of survival in the face of thousands of years of Chinese oppression and maltreatment through the disguised policy of assimilation.[13]

---

[13] Quincy, 32-59.

HMONG IN VIETNAM AND LAOS

Some writers attribute the Hmong migration to Northern Vietnam, Myanmar, Laos, and Thailand as part of their continued search for new virgin lands to live. History has it that a small group of Kweichow Hmong moved southward into northern Vietnam in the late 1740s for the first time due to the Chinese military campaign against them. They started to cross over to Vietnam in large numbers as the Chinese, under the Manchu emperor Shih Tsung, continued their military campaign against them. From Vietnam, Hmong further moved into Laos, Myanmar, and Thailand. According to history, Hmong appeared in northern Laos about 1818 and they continued to migrate to Vietnam and Laos until late 1870s.[14]

The Hmong who crossed over to Vietnam and then into Laos to escape the onslaught of the Chinese military in China in search for peace, tranquility, and independence were able to find them in their newfound land, but it did not last long. Soon after they settled in Laos, they were marginalized by the Lao and the Khmu peoples. Although the Hmong's settlement in northern Laos, specifically in Xieng Khouang and Nong Het, did not trouble the lowland Laotians much, they were unwelcomed by the Khmu people who had lived in the areas for centuries. At the turn of the 20th century, armed feuds broke out between Hmong and the Khmu over who should have the right and authority to rule over the high plateau of Xieng Khouang. The Khmu, armed only with crossbows and sabers, were no match for the Hmong who had the firepower of flintlock rifles. The Khmu were defeated and many were forced to move out of the areas, but

---

[14] Ibid., 58-64.

those who remained accepted the Hmong as their neighbors, and peace was restored.[15]

In 1893, not long after Hmong settled in Xieng Khouang, Laos became a French colony. In 1896, the French and Lao authorities passed a new tax system that required Hmong to pay taxes at higher rates than the lowland Lao and other ethnic minority groups. The Hmong Kiatongs or chieftains considered it unfair and refused to collect taxes from their people. The French colonial authority and Lao government sent soldiers to Xieng Khouang to intimidate the Hmong, but Hmong leaders organized a resistance force and attacked the soldiers. When the news of attack reached the French authorities, they ordered an immediate cease-fire. The soldiers retreated and the Hmong who wanted peace stopped further attack.[16] The Lao governor who fomented the situation was removed from his position by the French colonial authorities. The French authorities met directly with the Hmong leaders to negotiate peace and leaders were chosen. Authority was granted to these newly created leaders from the French authorities. As part of the peace negotiation, taxes were lowered, the Hmong were willing to pay, and the Hmong leaders were authorized to collect taxes from Hmong instead of having Laotian authorities collect the taxes. As a result, Hmong were able to live in peace for about 20 years.[17]

The Hmong continued to be marginalized and oppressed by the Lao and French authorities. The Lao officials who lost

---

[15] Dao Yang, *Hmong at the Turning Point* (Minneapolis: WorldBridge Associates, Ltd, 1993), 36. Hereafter will be called Yang Dao as he is always been known. He's the first Hmong of Laos ever to attain a Doctorate Degree in the Western World. He received his doctorate degree in economics and social development at the Sorbonne in France in 1972.

[16] Ibid.

[17] Paul Hillmer, *A people's History of the Hmong* (St. Paul: The Minnesota Historical Society Press, 2010), 40.

tax revenue because they no longer were allowed to collect taxes from Hmong appealed to the French authorities and they re-instated Lao officials as tax collectors once again. The Hmong leaders appealed to the French colonial administration, but the French authorities not only ignored the Hmong's appeals, they doubled the taxes and expanded taxes on the Hmong in 1916. The 1916 taxes were not applied equally. The Hmong and other minority groups had to pay heavier taxes than the lowland Lao people. The Hmong were forced to pay many different kinds of taxes: "two annual per capita taxes, as well as a semi-annual tax."[18] The Hmong had to pay taxes not only on income, but on livestock, fields, and provide two weeks of free human labors that they called "corvee," for government projects. The taxes that the Hmong had to pay were based on the number of family members in a household, including widows and minors. The French authorities not only increased taxes on the Hmong in Laos, the same method of taxing was also used on the Hmong in Vietnam. Many poor Hmong families who did not earn enough income had to sell their children in order to have enough money to pay their taxes. The resentment of this maltreatment boiled over into armed revolt once again in 1918, both in Vietnam and in Laos. They were led by a well-known Hmong leader in Vietnam by the name of Pa Chay Vue and another Hmong leader in Laos by the name of Shong Zer Lo. The insurrection was known as the "Madman's War." Not every Hmong sided with the rebel leaders. Those who benefited from the French administration sided with the French to fight against the rebels. This was the first time the Hmong who fled from Chinese oppression were divided in their struggles against oppressors, but it would not be the last time. This insurrection lasted for three years and cost thousands of lives. The rebels lost their fight, not from the superior firepower

---

[18] Quincy, 123.

of the French military, but because of the disloyalty by one of the Hmong leaders. Kiatong Lo Bliayao, who sided with the French authority, wanted to be treated favorably by the French administration, revealed the weakness of the flintlock firing power of the Hmong rebels to the French military. The Hmong rebels who were initially very successful in the fight against the French soldiers eventually lost the fight because their flintlock rifles could not fire in the rain. Since the French military knew the secret, they started to engage the Hmong rebels only when it was raining and the Hmong rebels were decimated. Pa Chay Vue was eventually assassinated by two non-Hmong hired by the French authorities. Once again, the local Laotian chiefs who were responsible for tax collection were blamed for this unfair treatment of the Hmong. After this insurrection, the French authority in Indochina decided to grant special administrative status to the Hmong and taxes were lowered again.

The Hmong were able to live peacefully until World War II when the Japanese invaded Laos. The Hmong, this time, sided with the French to fight against the Japanese invaders. The Hmong who 20 years ago were decimated by the French now came to their aid. They hid French soldiers in their houses, at their farms far away from the villages, and in the thick of the woods nearby their farms and villages, so that the Japanese soldiers would not find them.[19]

Following World War II was the Vietnam War. For the Hmong in Vietnam, they were all in North Vietnam, so they sided with the Vietnamese Communists fighting against France and later against United States. But the Hmong in Laos split. The majority of them sided with French colonial administration and the Royal Lao Government and later with the Americans, but a sizable number of Hmong took side with the Communist Pathet Lao who revolted against the Royal

---

[19] Yang, 38.

Lao Government. They were led by Prince Souphanouvong, who was the half-brother of Prince Phetsarath Ratanavongsa, the Vice-King of Laos, Prince Souvanna Phouma, the Prime Minister, and nephew of the Lao King Sisavang Vong. He was supported militarily by the Vietminh. The Vietnam War marked the first time in Hmong history that Hmong fought against Hmong in a major war.[20]

HMONG WAR

The rift among the Hmong was nothing more than the inter-clan feuds between the father-in-law of the Lo and the son-in-law of the Ly families. These two families were Kiatong Lo Bliayao who was the father-in-law and Ly Xia Foung who was the son-in-law. According to history, Xia Foung Ly married Bliayao Lo's daughter May. He soon became the personal secretary of Kiatong Lo Bliayao and rose to prominence. However, some years later, Xia Foung Ly took a second wife and the relationship between the father-in-law and the son-in-law became strained. The already strained relationship between the two men completely broke after the suicide of May, the daughter of Lo Bliayao, the first wife of Xia Foung Ly. In 1922, shortly after May's death, Xia Foung Ly was fired from his position as the personal secretary of Kiatong Lo Bliayao. Though the rift between the two families happened long ago, it culminated in the split of the Hmong into two opposing camps during the Vietnam War. After the death of Lo Bliayao in 1935, his son Song Tou Lo was appointed to replace him as the Tasseng of the district that Lo Bliayao used to govern, but Song Tou Lo quickly fell from grace as he was an incompetent local official for the French. He was not able to collect taxes, but he used whatever amount of taxes he was able to collect to

---

[20] Hillmer, 68.

pay for his own personal and gambling debts. At the same time, Xia Foung Ly became a favorite of the French colonial administration because he was able to make up for the lost taxes that Song Tou Lo was not able to collect. To show gratitude to Xia Foung Ly, the French authorities dismissed Song Tou Lo from his position and gave it to Xia Foung Ly. Now the son-in-law of Kiatong Lo Bliayao was firmly in control of his late father-in-law's position. Song Tou Lo's younger brother Faydang Lo lodged a complaint with the Royal Lao Government in Luang Prabang. Prince Phetsarath, the Vice-King of Laos, promised Faydang Lo that he would be appointed the next Tasseng when Xia Foung Ly passed away as he was already well into his old age and had frail health. In fact, in 1939, nine months later Xia Foung Ly died, but the French colonial administration did no honor the promise Prince Phetsarath made to Faydang Lo. Instead the French appointed Touby Lyfoung, one of Xia Foung Ly's sons to replace him. This infuriated Faydang Lo to the point which he, his brothers, and the Lo clan decided to take side with the Communists. They spent the rest of their lives fighting against French colonialism, the Royal Lao Government, and the Americans during the Vietnam War until Laos fell to Communism in 1975.[21] Faydang Lo and several men of the Lo clan were prominent members of the Lao Communist Party when Pathet Lao took over Laos in 1975. Meanwhile Touby Lyfoung became the first Hmong to serve in the Royal Lao Government as the Minister of Justice, Minister of Social Welfare, and Minister of Health. However, he was misled by his archenemy that he would be treated fairly so he remained in Laos and even chastised those who tried to escape Laos to Thailand. But that was only a deceptive snare of his archenemy. His mistake of believing that he would be fine staying in Laos gave his archenemy the opportunity

---

[21] Quincy, 140.

to wage the ultimate revenge on him. He was arrested by the communists and sent to the Re-Education Camp. Touby Lyfoung died in the Communist Pathet Lao's Re-Education Camp a few years later. Vang Pao became the first Hmong General to serve the Royal Lao Government as well as the CIA operation that led Hmong soldiers to fight against Hmong and Vietnamese Communists. Thus this war was officially known as the Vietnam War or the CIA Secret War in Laos, it was known unofficially as the Lao Revolutionary War and was also called the Hmong War because this was the first major war in which Hmong served on both sides of the conflict fighting against each other since they fled Chinese oppression in the mid-1800s. It was also rightly called the Hmong War because since 1961, General Vang Pao and his Hmong soldiers were the main defenders of Laos against Communist Laotians, Hmong, and Vietnamese.[22] When Laos was overtaken by Communist Pathet Lao, General Vang Pao led the Hmong out of Laos to Thailand and then to other western countries. The majority of the Hmong who fled the Communist Pathet Lao resettled in the United States, but some also chose to resettle in France including French Guyana, Canada, Australia, Argentina, and Germany.

HMONG CONTINUE TO EXIST DESPITE OPPRESSION AND PERSECUTION

The Hmong have not had a country of their own for thousands of years, but they continued to be able to maintain their own identity while other groups of people either completely assimilated or disappeared altogether from the record.[23] For thousands of years, this was the goal of the Chinese

---

[22] Ibid., 189.

[23] Ya Po Cha, *An Introduction to Hmong Culture* (Jefferson, NC and London: McFarland & Company Inc., Publishers 2010), 7-21.

authorities who tried to implement the assimilation policy on the Hmong. However, the Hmong continued to exist as a unique group of people even though they numbered less than four millions worldwide if one counted only those who speak the Hmong languages or more than 11 millions if one included all groups that China officially classified as Miao. The Hmong endured oppression and persecution wherever they lived and had many times been designated for extermination. They had also been forcibly separated by the Great Wall; in particular, the southern portion of the Great Wall was built to separate the Hmong from the Chinese people.[24] Despite all this, Hmong continue to exist today.

---

[24] Ibid., 11; Quincy, 31.

CHAPTER 2

INTRODUCTION TO HMONG ANIMISM

My interest in writing about Hmong animism was influenced by the following reasons: First, as a young animist myself, I had seen much demonic oppression in my family before we converted to Christianity. My father had two wives. My mother was the first wife and she had a total of 11 children. All died except three of us. Some died of natural illness, one died of medication overdose, but the cause of death of at least two of my siblings were the result of demonic oppression. The death of my sister Pla happened as described here. The year was probably in 1970 and she was about three years old. One day she went with my mother to a town about three kilometers from our village. While in the town, she tripped on a small rock and fell, and then she cried for a long time, so my mother rebuked her for crying too long. She stopped crying, but before my mother noticed, she had vanished. My mother spent several hours looking for her, but she was nowhere to be found. My mother was tired and worried, so she decided to come home to inform the family about the situation and have all of us going back to look for her. But when she arrived home, my sister was already home. I remember having asked my sister the following question when she came home alone: "Why did you come home without mother? And she said "because mother made me mad." My mother said to my sister, Pla, "Why did you come home without me? I was so worried about you and had been looking everywhere for you." A week later, my sister got sick and my parents asked a shaman to conduct a diagnostic ritual. The shaman told my parents the following words: "They, meaning the demons, had already captured her spirit during her fall. Therefore, nothing can be done to help her – neither medicine nor healing shamanic ritual could help." Two weeks later, she died. On the thirteenth day following her death, my parents and relatives went to her grave to call her spirit back to visit the home in order to conduct the ritual of *xw plig*. My mother came home very angry and scared. She shared that while at the grave, she was wailing by the side of her grave and remained there by herself after everyone else had left. Then she heard some loud tapping noise coming from inside the grave. While she was at the head of the grave, the tapping was heard coming from the foot area, but when she moved over to the foot area, the tapping was coming from the head, so she got scared and stopped wailing. Ever since then, my mother rarely talked about this daughter of hers until the day she died. My stepmother had two children, a son and daughter. My stepmother probably also died in the year of 1970 or early 1971, just several months after the death of my sister Pla, but in the town of Ban San, during the peak of the Vietnam War. Hmong animists believe that after death, they can come back as demons to cause death or trouble to their living children. My stepmother had said that if she died, she would come back to get her two children. Less than two years after her death, my half-sister died. My mother described her death this way: One day, my half-sister, Mee, complained that she had a headache. A neighbor happened to perform a shamanic ritual and slaughter a pig the same day she fell ill. In a few minutes after the slaughtered of the pig, my half-sister was eating a mouthful of blood and she died shortly after. After her funeral, my parents had to call for a shaman to perform a protective shamanic ritual for my half-brother and give him a new name. My parents believed that her death was caused by her mother. The shaman also said that without giving him a new name, he too would die. The death of my youngest sister, Yer, was rather mysterious. The year was 1975 and it was shortly before Laos fell to Communism. One day, my father made a quick decision to want to convert to Christianity and asked me and my half-brother to quickly go to the town to get our Christian relatives and the pastor to come over to pray for us. However, it was already late in the afternoon, so we were unable to make the trip that afternoon because the distance from our village to the town was more than five kilometers away. My baby sister died that night. She was not sick as far as I knew. My parents were very angry at the household demons and the ancestors that were supposed to protect the family. They did not perform the *xw plig* and the release of the spirit (*tso plig*) rituals as required by Hmong animism for Yer. We converted to Christianity a few days after her funeral.

    Secondly, every written material about Hmong animism talks almost exclusively about the good deeds and blessings Hmong animists receive from the demons they worship. The world deserves to know the whole truth about Hmong animism and the consequences of worshipping the demons, ancestors, and Satan. This book will expose the undeniable truth about Hmong animism. However, when the truth is exposed, it hurts. The truth is that instead of receiving blessings, protection, and good fortunes, their rewards are spiritual and physical tortures, demon-possessed, and tragic deaths for worshipping them. The human toll, psychological toll, and spiritual toll of being tortured by the very demons they worship are very high. Many Hmong animists are so traumatized and constantly live in fear of the demons. Even so they continue to worship them.

And thirdly, as I prepare myself for the work of the Lord, I believe that it is important to know what Hmong animism is all about, so that with the will of the Lord, I can steer many of them toward the loving God.

FOCUS STATEMENT

This book investigates Hmong animism. The purpose of this study is to identify the core values of beliefs in Hmong animism, to systematically analyze its contradictions of beliefs and practices, and to challenge Hmong animists to seriously search for the truth in their beliefs because in Hmong animism there is no truth but only myths. This book reveals the false promise of hope to the believers and practitioners of Hmong animism. In order to establish a solid argument against the contradiction of beliefs and practices in Hmong animism, the focus areas of this book will include the following:

1. To systematically analyze the core values of Hmong animism, using the writings of many different researchers worldwide and oral history including interviews and media recordings.
2. To explain point-by-point the contradiction of Hmong animism.
3. To compare and contrast the worldview of Hmong animism to the biblical worldview.
4. To explain Hmong animism from the Christian perspective.

CORE VALUES OF HMONG ANIMISM

Hmong animism has its origin going back thousands of years and until recently it was the only religion of the Hmong people. In Hmong animism, there are several core values that Hmong animists strongly believe in. They are: 1) the belief that there is an almighty and good deity called *Yawmsaub*[25] (God), but he has nothing to do with human affairs; 2) the belief that there is a wicked deity called *Ntxwgnyoog* (Satan) who causes sickness and death to human beings, but Hmong animists worship him;[26] 3) the belief that the human body dies, but the spirit does not die and it reincarnates; 4) the belief in shamanism. Hmong animists believe that spiritual cause underlies every illness. They believe that shamans can heal illness; 5) the belief that there are household demons residing everywhere in the house; and 6) the belief that there are wild demons in every river, mountain, rock, tree, and so on.

CONTRADICTIONS OF BELIEFS AND PRACTICES

There is much literature written about Hmong animism – its beliefs and practices. Some of them were written by Hmong scholars and many were written by non-Hmong anthropologists or ethnographers. But all of them only write about why Hmong animists believe what they believe and how they practice what they believe. This book examines

---

[25] Ibid., 99.

[26] Timothy T. Vang, "Coming A Full Circle: Historical Analysis of the Hmong Church Growth 1950-1998" (Ph.D. diss., Fuller Theological Seminary, 1998), 91. Dr. Timothy T. Vang is the current senior pastor at Hmong American Alliance Church. He was the District Superintendent of Hmong District of the Christian & Missionary Alliance for nine years.

Hmong animism, but the main focus of this study will concentrate on the contradictions of beliefs and practices. The purpose of this book is to fill the void – the contradictions in the belief system that until now no writer has attempted to answer. This book will examine: (1) the core values of Hmong animism as the sources of contradiction among beliefs and practices; (2) Hmong animism as Satanism; (3) Hmong animism as a distorted cosmological view; and (4) to discuss Hmong animism from Christian perspective.

In attempt to answer the question why Hmong animism is full of contradictions, I will examine three general areas of Hmong animism to draw conclusions about the issue of conflicting beliefs and practices. They are: (1) shamanism; (2) funerary rites; and (3) the worship of household demons which includes the family ancestors and the adopted demons, prominent Hmong figures that have passed away, wild demons, and the most hated but also the most depended on for giving life, who is Satan (*Ntxwgnyoog*). The objective of this book is to encourage Hmong animists to search beyond their beliefs in order to know the truth about who is the true God who should be worshipped. It will encourage them to step outside of the box, which is their religion and even to take on the role of an outsider to look into their belief system, in order to see the contradictions of the belief system and the false promise of hope that Hmong animism offers them.

COSMOLOGY OF HMONG ANIMISM

Hmong animism comprises (1) shamanism; (2) funerary rites; and (3) the worship of household demons including family ancestors and prominent Hmong figures that have passed away, natural objects such as rocks, rivers, mountains, trees and the like and wild demons. These three components make up the whole foundation of beliefs of Hmong animism. Out of these beliefs come the distorted views of cosmology of Hmong animism. The cosmology of Hmong animism can be divided into two opposing parts. First, is the cosmology of the Showing the way chant and the second part is the Hmong shamanism. The cosmology of the Showing the Way chant derives from the first three values and the cosmology of the shamanism comes from the last three values of the Hmong animism.

CHRISTIAN PERSPECTIVE ON HMONG ANIMISM

This book offers Christian perspective on Hmong animism. It expounds that *Yawmsaub* is the God in the Bible. He is the Creator God and Jesus is the Lord and Savior of the world. God (*Yawmsaub*) created heaven and earth, mankind and everything in the universe, but Satan (*Ntxwgnyoog*), the rebellious angel of God, deceived the first two humans to sin against God and turned their given authority to rule the world over to Satan. It argues that Satan uses Hmong animism to enslave the Hmong animists and steer them away from God. But those who accept Jesus Christ as their Lord and Savior have been set free from the bondage of the Satan and the demons.

This book will involve the use of the Scripture to present the Christian perspective on Hmong animism.[27] The Scripture will point out the false belief system of Hmong animism. It will reveal that many rituals that Hmong animism practices may have been borrowed from the Scripture. However, instead of using them to worship the Creator God, they use them to worship Satan and his demons. It will reveal that Hmong animists refuse to believe and worship God the

---

[27] All Scripture quotations are taken from the New International Version unless otherwise noted.

Creator, but they believe and worship everything that God created as well as things that created by human hand.[28]

The Scripture will reveal the false hope of the reincarnation of the spirit and the false belief in the blessings from the spirits of the dead, divine trees, and cast metal statues. The Scripture will also point out that Hmong animism worships the main enemy of God, Satan (*Ntxwgnyoog*) in the Bible. While believing that Satan (*Ntxwgnyoog*) causes sickness and death, Hmong animists also worship him as life-grantor. The Scripture will affirm their belief that Satan is the one that causes sickness and death to human beings, but God is love and He sent Jesus Christ to die on the cross to give human beings eternal life. The Scripture will also point out that without accepting Jesus Christ as Lord and Savior, the spirit that Hmong animists believe will reincarnate in an endless cycle will instead face eternal judgment. This book will offer those who are believers and practitioners of Hmong animism the light to see the true God. It will be enlightenment for them to see the true eternity of the spirit, and will empower them to break free from the bondage of Satan who binds them and blinds them from seeing the true God. This book will also discuss how the first Hmong Christian family came to believe in Jesus Christ and why that has been the trend of Hmong conversion to Christianity even today.

---

[28] Exodus 20:4-6 "You shall not make for yourself an idol in the form of anything in heaven above or on the earth beneath or in the waters below. You shall not bow down to them or worship them; for I, the Lord your God, am a jealous God, punishing the children for the sin of the fathers to the third and fourth generation of those who hate me, but showing love to a thousand [generations] of those who love me and keep my commandments."

PERSECUTION OF HMONG CHRISTIANS

This book will also look at the persecution of Hmong Christians. As Christians throughout the world and throughout history have been persecuted for no apparent reason other than the name of Jesus Christ, Hmong Christians also face persecution for the same reason. Hmong Christians are not only being persecuted by various intolerant authoritarian governments, but also by the hands of their own non-Christian kinsmen.

Hmong animists accuse Hmong Christians as traitors, turning their backs on their own religion and being brain-washed to accept a white-man's religion. They believe that animism should be the only religion of the Hmong because it is the religion that has been passed down from generation to generation for thousands of year. However, from the Hmong Christian's perspective, Hmong animism is Satanism and demonolatry, a religion of confusion both in beliefs and in practices. Hmong Christians are not being brain-washed to accept a white-man's religion, but they have found the true God, the God who created them, and the God who liberates them from the bondage of Satan and the demons.

TERMINOLOGY

The following terms and definitions are provided to aid the readers to understand the terms and names use in Hmong animism.

- *Qeej* pronounce "kheng," a reed pipe that is played during a Hmong animist's funeral service. It could also be used as musical instrument during cultural events. The *qeej* is the symbol of the Hmong religion of animism the same way the cross is the symbol of Christianity.

Hmong Animism

- *Nruag* pronounce "jua" is a drum played with the *qeej* during the Hmong animist's funeral service.
- *Yawmsaub* (pronounced "Yershao," interchangeably called "Shao") is the good, benevolent, and virtuous deity who is considered to be the highest spiritual being. Hmong Christians believe *Yawmsaub* is the Creator God in the Bible. Most Hmong animists also believe that *Yawmsaub* is the creator God. He is a good and benevolent God, but He rarely has anything to do with human affairs. Some groups of Hmong believe that *Yawmsaub* is the one who grants permission for the spirit of the dead to reincarnate.
- *Ntxwgnyoog* ("Juenyong") is the wicked deity who is considered to be the second highest spiritual being. Hmong Christians believe that *Ntxwgnyoog* is Satan in the Bible. Hmong animists believe that *Ntxwgnyoog* is the deity that causes sickness and death to humanity. Hmong animists believe and worship *Ntxwgnyoog* as the grantor of permission to the spirit of the dead to reincarnate.
- *Nyuj Vaab Tuam Teem* (Nyiu Vang Toua Teng) is Satan's personal secretary. Hmong animists believe that *Nyuj Vaab Tuam Teem* is the one that issues the new permit for the spirits of the dead to be reincarnated. The name of this deity has three different spellings – *Nyuj "Vaab" Tuam Teem; Nyuj "Vaaj" Tuam Teem, and Nyuj "Vaag" Tuam Teem*.
- *Dlaab* or *Dab*, depending on which dialect one speaks, are the lowest level spiritual beings. Hmong animists translated *dlaab* into English as "spirits," i.e., the spirits of the ancestors, or wild spirits. A more accurate translation of the word *dlaab* or *dab* is "demon." They can be good or bad or both. They are the spiritual beings that Hmong animists worship the most. They are called for help, for protection,

Introduction to Hmong Animism

for giving wisdom, and sometimes to harm or kill another person. Hmong animists have a proverb that says, "Living is human, dying is demon." They believe that the minute a person dies, the spirit of that person becomes a demon. This is the reason why Hmong animists are fearful of the dead. This is contradiction to spiritual reincarnation.

- *Dlaab nyeg* are the tamed demons. They are the demons that ancestors adopted as their household demons. They are usually referred to as the "household spirits" in most of the writings about Hmong animism. But they are called "household demons" in this book to conform to the accuracy of translation of the Hmong term "dlaab vaaj dlaab tsev."
- *Dlaab qus* are wild demons. They are the wild demons that govern rivers, mountains, forests, and so on.
- *Ntsujplig* or *plig* ("ju-plee") is "spirit." This is the spirit of a living person. Hmong rarely call demons *plig* or "spirits" although most of the literature translates *plig* that way. When Hmong call demons as spirits is when they refer to them as spiritual beings.
- *Ntsuj* ("ju") is "soul." Some Hmong animists believe that ntsuj ("soul") and *ntsujplig* ("spirit") are one and the same. Others believe that *ntsuj* are minor spirits and *ntsujplig* are major spirits.
- *Vaajtswv* or *Vajtswv*, depending on which dialect one speaks, is the proper name for Lord in Hmong. The word *Vaajtswv* was coined by Hmong Christians after they became Christians. The words *Vaajtswv* means "Lord" and *Yawmsaub* means "God," but they are used interchangeably to mean "God." The name *Vaajtswv Yawmsaub* is the proper name for Lord God in Hmong.

- Hmong animism is the religion of Hmong animists. It is Satanism, ancestral worship, and demonolatry. The majority of the Hmong are animists.
- *Dlaabteb* (demon world); *Ntuj qhua teb nkig, ntuj txag teb tsaus,* (parched sky dried land, frozen sky darkness land); *tub tuagteb* (land of the dead); or *ntuj txag teb tsaus* (world of darkness) are the names referred to the spirit world where the spirits of the dead, demons, and Satan reside. They are similar to Hades and Hell.
- *Zaaj Qhuabke* or *Zaaj Tawkev* is translated into English as the "Showing the Way" chant. The "Showing the Way" chant is the most valued chant in Hmong animism. The chant tells the accounts of creation, the universal flood, the origins of sickness and death, and life after death. The chant is usually sung at the beginning of the funeral and the purpose of chanting is to guide the spirit of the dead to the demon world, the world of the dead, or the world of darkness where the spirit of the dead is reunited with the deceased's ancestors. It also guides the spirit of the dead to Satan to ask for another letter of provision for a new life of reincarnation. The chant is never allowed under any circumstance to be sung at home without a dead person for fear that it might cause someone's spirit to travel to the world of the dead and that person may die.

CHAPTER 3

COSMOLOGY OF HMONG ANIMISM ACCORDING TO THE SHOWING THE WAY CHANT

The Showing the Way chant is one of the core foundations of beliefs of Hmong animism which formed the first part of the cosmology. It teaches that human spirit is immaterial and immortal. The spirit lives forever in an unending cyclical journey - born to die and die to be reborn. It teaches that each person required three major spirits and several minor spirits in order for the person to function normally. It perceives the physical life to be a separate entity from the spiritual life, but both are interdependent of each other in order to make the person a complete human being. With such belief, it is a bitter-sweet of hope for the Hmong animists because they believe that the spirit will reincarnate, but the physical life only lives once and then dies. Believing that the spirit that indwells in the body is a reincarnated one, it is foreign to the body, and it will abandon the body and move on when the body dies.

Hmong animism teaches that the universe exists spontaneously in seen and unseen worlds. The seen world, or in other words, the world of light (*yaajceeb*) is the physical world where life flourishes; not only human beings but all other living things live in the seen world. Hmong animists believe that demons can live in both the seen and unseen worlds, but human eyes cannot see them even though they live among us. The unseen world (*yeebceeb*) is the demon world where the spirits of the dead, their ancestors, demons, and Satan reside and Satan is the ruler of that world.[29] The unseen world has several names attached to it. They are called: "demon world" (*dlaabteb*), the "parched sky dried land, frozen sky darkness land" or simply the "world of darkness" (*ntuj qhua teb nkig, ntuj txag teb tsaus*), and the "land of the dead" (*tub tuagteb*). It is believed that those reside in the unseen world face a lot of hardship and they depend on the living family members to provide for their continue survival as spirits. This is the reason why Hmong animists are obligated to feed their dead. Though knowing that this unseen world is, as Vincent Her states, "a harsh, desolate place, lacking and devoid of life,"[30] this is the place Hmong animists send all of their dead to and that's where those still alive will also go when the time comes for them to depart this earthly life. From this cosmological view, Hmong animism formed its first half of the belief system according to the following core values – the belief that *Yawmsaub* is the good God, the belief that Satan (*Ntxwgnyoog*) is the evil deity, and the belief that spirit does not die – presented in this chapter and in the next two chapters below.

---

[29] Timothy T. Vang, 99.

[30] Vincent K. Her, "Hmong Mortuary Practices: Self, Place and Meaning in Urban America" (PhD diss., University of Wisconsin – Milwaukee, 2005), 100.

THE BELIEF THAT *YAWMSAUB* IS THE GOOD GOD

The unbeliever knows God without confessing it. Perhaps the foundational epistemological insight that is most significant for the practice of Christian apologetics, yet is most often ignored, is that all men already knew God – long before the apologist engages them in conversation – and cannot avoid having such knowledge. . .Thus, all men know that God exists, that He is almighty and all-knowing, that His holy character forbids theft and murder, that we will all be judged by Him, etc.[31]

Hmong animists know very well the existence of a good God called *Yawmsaub*. However, Hmong animists believe that God (*Yawmsaub*) exists in both genders: Grandfather God (*Yawmsaub*) and Grandmother God (*Pujsaub*) and they are working in coordination in the affairs of mankind. They believe that when people are in great distress and call on him, he will appear at that moment to help. Hmong animists characterize him as the good God; he is virtuous, benevolent, and everything that is good comes from him. He is almighty, could calm extreme winds and prevent natural disasters. He could create life, and he is the creator of heaven and earth and the savior of human race. *Yawmsaub* is the good God and he will punish the wrongdoers. When they are alone and thinking about doing something bad, illegal, or otherwise improper, they often think to themselves that even though no one sees them committing the offense, "heaven sees" (*ntuj pum*), referring to God (*Yawmsaub*) as heaven, and that heaven will punish (*ntuj yuav tsau txim*) if they commit the wrongdoing.

---

[31] Greg L. Bahnsen, *Van Til's Apologetic: Readings and Analysis* (Phillipsburg: P&R Publishing Co., 1998), 179-180.

Hmong Animism

But Hmong animists are still confused about who this God (*Yawmsaub*) really is. Below are some descriptions and concepts about what and who God (*Yawmsaub*) really is from different writers:

> Sau Ntuj (heaven) is located above and Yawm Saub presides over it. Although Hmong Americans acknowledge his presence, Yawm Saub is only a peripheral figure to their practices. Rarely do they appeal to him for help. In zaaj qhuabkev (Showing the Way chant), he is depicted as someone who grants destinies to souls. A destiny is envisioned as a letter, appropriately called "ntawv noj ntawv haus," or letter of provision. A soul must obtain this "letter" before it can return to earth. In this context, Yawm Saub is imagined as a grantor (source) of life; the letter he offers is essential to the soul, as well as its movements and continuity. (Added emphases are the author's).
>
> Vincent K. Her[32]

> The creator and ruler of the world is Hua Tai (*Hua Tais Ntuj*). Unlike the Christian God, Hua Tai has little interest in the affairs of man. Indeed they bore him. He lost interest in mankind, in all their bickering and feckless ways, almost as soon as he created them. One of his lieutenants though had compassion for man. He is Yer Shau (Yawm Saub). As the Hmong portray him, Yer Shau is not only God's personal representative to mankind, he

---

[32] Vincent K. Her, 99.

is also half man, half God. He is godlike in the sense that he sees and knows all, but he is like a man in that he has material substance and lives in a house. And as a man he is more like the Hmong than any other race of men. He tends a garden and raises pigs. He is an earthy fellow who likes to eat and drink and have long discussions with friends. Also like the Hmong, he is polygamous.

Keith Quincy[33]

There is also a benevolent Hmong deity, saub or Yawm Saub, but he is what is called a deus otiosus or an absentee god, somewhat similar to the idea of the ancient Greeks and Romans. That is, he is a deity who was around to help people at the dawn of time but is now generally absent. He may be called on in times of need and sometimes reappears at points of crisis in the course of history. He was responsible for finding seeds at the dawn of time and causing the first hen to lay eggs, and he advised the couple who survived the flood what to do to re-create humanity. What he is not is a Creator, for, like the Chinese, the Hmong have felt no need to explain the origins of the earth in personal terms. But the origins of life itself and many other things are explained in the song that is sung by a ritual expert (who is not necessarily a shaman) when somebody dies, the Qhuab Ke or song

---

[33] Quincy, 88.

of "Opening the Way," a prime example of Hmong oral literature.

Lee and Tapp[34]

At the beginning, there was a virtuous being named Shao (Saub). He was a man, but he possessed great powers. He held the power to create life according to shaman (puj saub siv yis tsim noob neej). In wedding rites, Shao is said to have had the power to stabilize the extreme turbulence in the world when it was first created. He knew everything, and he could foretell the future. He was a savior of the human race.

Ya Po Cha[35]

The different concepts of God (*Yawmsaub*) can be summarized as follows: Vincent K. Her says that God (*Yawmsaub*) is just a peripheral figure in Hmong animism. Hmong animists rarely ask God (*Yawmsaub*) for help and He is not an important figure to be worshipped. But God (*Yawmsaub*) is believed to be the one who grants permits for the spirits of the dead to reincarnate.[36] Her is contradicting himself by claiming that while God (*Yawmsaub*) is not an important figure in their worship and rarely do they ask him for help, he, at the same time, states that God (*Yawmsaub*) is the grantor of new life for the spirits of the dead to reincarnate. Even if Hmong animists are the only people in the world who needed new letter of provision to reincarnate, there are more than 11

---

[34] Gary Yia Lee and Nicholas Tapp, *Culture and Customs of the Hmong* (Santa Barbara: Greenwood, 2010), 31. The words "Opening the Way" are just another term used in the place of "Showing the Way."

[35] Ya Po Cha, 133.

[36] Vincent K. Her, 99.

million of Hmong/Miao in the world which most of them are animists and they are dying every day. If God (*Yawmsaub*) has to issue new permits, the letter of provision, for every spirit of the dead of Hmong animists that reaches his office, God (*Yawmsaub*) is very much involved in the affairs of the Hmong animists. The question is, if God (*Yawmsaub*) is not important in their religious practice and if He is not being worshipped, why should He grant new letter of provision to the spirits of the dead of Hmong animists to reincarnate back on the earth knowing that after granting the permits to them, He no longer is considered important in their lives? Keith Quincy states that Hmong animists believe that *Yawmsaub* is one of God's lieutenants. He is God's representative to mankind, but he is half man and half God. Hmong animists called God "Hua Tai," but he is not the same God in the Bible. Actually, Hmong do not believe that there's another deity call God or Hua Tais who is superior to *Yawmsaub*. The two highest deities that Hmong acknowledge to have existed are *Yawmsaub* and *Ntxwgnyoog*. However, the problem is that Hmong animists do not believe that *Yawmsaub* is the Creator God in the Bible. The Hmong word "Hua Tai" (*Huabtais - White Hmong or Fuabtais - Green Hmong*) means "King," but it never implies God. The word "*ntuj*" (pronounce "du") means heavens, heaven, or sky. Hmong Christians use the term "*Huabtais Ntuj or Fuabtais Ntuj*" to ascribe God as the "Heavenly King," but Hmong animists never use this term as they do not believe that *Yawmsaub* is the Heavenly King or the Most High and Almighty God. As stated earlier, Quincy describes that *Yawmsaub* is half-man, half-God, but he looks and behaves more like the Hmong because he tends garden, raises pigs, and practices polygamy. If this is what his Hmong informants described *Yawmsaub*, it truly reveals how erroneous Hmong animists know about *Yawmsaub*. Even the highly educated Hmong animists still confuse who *Yawmsaub* really is or if they know, they refuse to acknowledge him as who he really is because they do not want to glorify him as God. Gary Yia Lee and Nicholas Tapp state that *Yawmsaub* is a benevolent god. He could be called for help and he will appear to help in time of great needs. He provided plant seeds to mankind at the beginning of time, caused the first chicken to lay eggs, and advised the brother and sister who survived the universal flood on how to re-create humanity, but otherwise he is "an absentee god."[37] While acknowledging God's involvement in human affairs at the beginning of time and in time of great needs, Lee and Tapp contradict themselves by claiming that *Yawmsaub* rarely has anything to do with human affairs. He is either too remote to be involved or is not interested in human life.[38] And Ya Po Cha states that *Yawmsaub* is a virtuous god. He possessed a great deal of power. He created life, stabilized extreme natural occurrences, and he was the savior of mankind, but he was a man. Some Hmong animists even believe that God (*Yawmsaub*) is the older brother of Satan (*Ntxwgnyoog*)[39] only that *Yawmsaub* is gentle, kind, and virtuous, but *Ntxwgnyoog* is vicious and evil. Though Hmong animists refuse to acknowledge and worship *Yawmsaub* as the Most High God, they often call on him for help when they are in great trouble. Timothy T. Vang states that in such time, they often promise God (*Yawmsaub*) in their vow that they would sacrifice a big animal like a cow or a water buffalo in return if God (*Yawmsaub*) answers their prayer.[40] However, as always when Hmong animists sacrifice animal in propitiation, they give thanks to the demons and Satan (*Ntxwgnyoog*) instead of God (*Yawmsaub*).

---

[37] Lee and Tapp, 31.
[38] Quincy, 88.
[39] Timothy T. Vang, 105.
[40] Ibid., 103.

All versions of the Showing the Way chants attribute the good character to God (*Yawmsaub*) and evil character to Satan (*Ntxwgnyoog*). The Showing the Way chants say that long ago or at the beginning of the human race, whenever they were hopeless, they went to seek advice from God (*Yawmsaub*). For example, the Showing the Way chants say that knowing that the universal flood was coming, Jau Ong (*Nraug Oo*) and Gao Ah (*Nkauj Ab*) went to ask God (*Yawmsaub*) about what to do and God (*Yawmsaub*) advised them to build a wooden drum for themselves and they survived the universal flood by riding in the wooden drum. After the flood, the two of them went back to ask God (*Yawmsaub*) about what to do to re-create humanity. God (*Yawmsaub*) advised them to marry each other, even though they were brother and sister, in order to re-populate the earth because the people of the whole world had perished. From there on mankind from generation after generation continued to seek advice and help from God (*Yawmsaub*). But the Showing the Way chants blame Satan (Ntxwgnyoog) for every evil thing that has ever occurred in the world. The 17th stanza of the Showing the Way chant by Yang Chong Chee says:

> Long ago the world was without sickness, the earth was without death. Because Satan (*Ntxwgnyoog*) had a cruel heart, Satan (*Ntxwgnyoog*) unleashed sickness and death down to the world...[41] Translation is the author's.

Satan (*Ntxwgnyoog*) is portrayed as the Evil One in all of the versions of the Showing the Way chants. Satan

---

[41] Yves Bertrais and Va Thai Yang, "*Kab Ke Pam Tuag: Txheej Txheem*" (Funeral Rites and procedures), (Guyane, France: Association Communaute Hmong, 1985), 42.

(*Ntxwgnyoog*) is accused of unleashing rain on the earth that caused the universal flood that led to the extinction of human race.[42]

Hmong as a whole understand that *Yawmsaub* is the highest deity, above and beyond all other spiritual beings. Unlike the Hmong animists who are unsure who this *Yawmsaub* is, Hmong Christians believe that *Yawmsaub* is the Almighty, all knowing, the omnipresent, and the Creator God in the Bible. But Hmong animists have serious problem with it. Though they believe that *Yawmsaub* is the virtuous and benevolent god, everything that is good comes from him, and he is the grantor and creator of life, the creator of heaven and earth, the answer for all human troubles, and the savior of human race, they continue to deny that *Yawmsaub* is the Most High God and refuse to worship Him. The problem with Hmong animists is not because they don't know who this *Yawmsaub* is, but just that they don't want to acknowledge that *Yawmsaub* is the Most High God. If they do, they have to glorify Him as the Most High God, the Creator God of the universe. With that in mind, they have to reduce God (*Yawmsaub*) to a mere man and "an absentee god" who is just a peripheral figure in their religious belief and practice. The following are the different names and titles Hmong Christians use in reference to God (*Yawmsaub*): 1) "*Vaajtswv Yawmsaub tug tsim ntuj tsim teb*" – "Lord God who created heaven and earth;" 2) "*Fuabtais Ntuj* or *Huabtais Ntuj*" – "Heavenly King;" 3) "*Vaajtswv*" – "Lord" of the universe; 4) "*Yawmsaub*" – "God:" and 5) *Vaaj Leejtxiv* – Heavenly Father. The name "*Vaajtswv*" is used interchangeably as God or Lord. The name "*Vaajtswv*" means that God created everything and He is Lord of His creation. Hmong animists never use these terms to glorify God (*Yawmsaub*). When they use them, they only use them to mock and ridicule God.

---

[42] Ibid, 28-29.

CREATION

The assumption ever since the ancient Greeks has been that the material world is eternal. Christians have denied this on the basis of biblical revelation, but secular science always assumed the universe's eternality. Christians just had to say, well, even though the universe appears static, nevertheless it did have a beginning when God created it. So the discovery in the twentieth century that the universe is not an unchanging, eternal entity was a complete shock to secular minds.[43]

The fine-tuning of the physical laws and constants of the universe and the precise configuration of its initial conditions, dating back to the very origin of the universe itself, suggest the need for a cause that is intelligent. Theism affirms the existence of an entity that's not only transcendent but intelligent as well – namely, God.[44]

New evidence which could potentially have refuted the [design] hypothesis has only ended up confirming it. Once again, we find the evidence of science pointing in the direction of a Creator.[45]

Buddhism is one of the world religions that completely deny the existence of a Creator God and creation by stating

---

[43] Lee Strobel, *The Case for a Creator: A Journalist Investigates Scientific Evidence That Points Toward God* (Grand Rapids: Zondervan), 124.

[44] Ibid., 98.

[45] Ibid., 192.

that creation is not a concern of its religion.[46] Buddhism does not even try to entertain the notion of creation. It claims that such knowledge is only "wasting valuable time," unnecessarily discomfort the minds of millions of people, and it is not important for living spiritual "holy life."[47] Hmong animism, on the other hand, boldly claims that it believes in creation. The source of knowledge in creation in Hmong animism are the Showing the Way chants. But the Showing the Way chants instead of helping Hmong animists to understand clearly how the universe was created and who created it, they are the sources of confusion about creation. The notion that God (*Yawmsaub*) is the Creator is very much aligned with the biblical teaching and that is the general consensus among the Hmong. But the Showing the Way chants also teach that heaven and earth were created by men and frog, which throw the Hmong animists into confusion. The confusion is further aggravated by the teaching that the universe was created long after the universal flood. Below are presentations of the various accounts of creation that are contained in different versions of the Showing the Way chants. They contradict one another in several ways such as when creation was taking place, who were the creators, and by whom mankind was created. In some versions, there are more than one stanza containing creation and each stanza records creation differently with different creators. There are two different creators in almost every version of the Showing the Way chants. In each of the Showing the Way chants, the creators were either men and God (*Yawmsaub*) or men and the frog. In Yang Chong Chee's version, the creators were Chi Tu (*Ci Tuj*) and Tu Blu (*Tuj Nplug*) and God (*Yawmsaub*) – men

---

[46] Damien Keown, *Buddhism: A Very Short Introduction* (Oxford: Oxford University Press, 2013), 5.

[47] Walpola Sri Rahula, *What the Buddha Taught* (New York: Grove Press), 13-14.

and God (*Yawmsaub*). Yang Chong Jai's version, the creators were *Qas Tuj* and *Tuj Lug* and the lady frog – men and frog. [48] Also in Kenneth White's version, the creators were the frog and Krang Tu (*Qaav Tuj*) and Krang To (*Qaav Taug*) – frog and men. Vincent K. Her's version has only mankind as creators. The Hmongism's version completely excludes the creator. All versions that contain universal flood place the creation of heaven and earth several generations after the flood and long after the creation of mankind, and each recorded the survivors of the flood with different names. Those versions that do not have the event of the universal flood tend to suggest that Gao Ah (*Nkauj Ab*) and Jau Ong (*Nraug Oo*) were the first two human beings created by the lady frog on earth. In Yang Chong Chee's version, Gao Ah (*Nkauj Ab*) and Jau Ong (*Nraug Oo*) were recorded as the first two human beings on earth as well as the brother and sister that survived the universal flood.[49]

The Showing the Way chants indicate that there were heaven and earth and the earth was full of people prior to the universal flood. But then after the universal flood, the Showing the Way chants say that heaven and earth were not firm. Heaven shook like the chicken droppings and the earth was not solid and it shook like duck poops. Yang Chong Chee's version of the Showing the Way chant, Stanza 12 says that after they survived the universal flood in a wooden drum, Gao Ah (*Nkauj Ab*) and Jau Ong (*Nraug Oo*) said to each other, "All people on earth have perished, so who will repopulate the earth?"[50] They went to ask God (*Yawmsaub*) for advice and Grandmother God (*Pujsaub*) and Grandfather God (*Yawmsaub*) said to them that the whole world was destroyed and no one was left, except the two of them. Even

---

[48] Bertrais., 66.
[49] Ibid., 12, 28-27.
[50] Ibid., 29.

though they were brother and sister, they had to marry each other and repopulate the world. They followed the instructions of Grandfather God (*Yawmsaub*) and Grandmother God (*Pujsaub*) and they had their first son, but he was deformed, without mouth, eyes, arm, or legs. He looked like a pumpkin, so they went back to tell God (*Yawmsaub*) about their deformed son. God (*Yawmsaub*) told them to chop their deformed son into pieces and throw the pieces in different directions. They did it and the pieces transformed overnight into people, forming the different clans of the Hmong tribe. They had another son and a daughter. The son they named Shing Lee Qong (*Txiv Seev Lis Qoos*) and the daughter they named Pu Tong Mua Gao Jao (*Puj Toog Muam Nkauj Ncaus*). When the brother and sister grew up, they married each other. Full of knowledge and wisdom, they wanted to rule heaven and earth. They went to ask God (*Yawmsaub*) about how to create heaven and earth. Though they followed God's (*Yawmsaub's*) instruction, they were not able to create heaven and earth and they remained shaking and unstable. Shing Lee Qong (*Txiv Seev Lis Qoos*) and Pu Tong Mua Gao Jao (*Puj Toog Muam Nkauj Ncaus*) gave birth to a son who they named Jau Moua (*Nraug Muas*) and a daughter who they named Gao Nyiu (*Nkauj Nyw*). Jau Moua and Gao Nyiu grew up and they wanted to rule heaven and earth. They attempted to create heaven and earth after seeking advice from God (*Yawmsaub and Pujsaub*), but they were not able to create them. Heaven and earth remained shaking and unstable. Jau Moua and Gao Nyiu married each other and had a son and named him Chi Tu (*Ci Tuj*) and a daughter they named her Tu Blu (*Tuj Nplug*). When Chi Tu and Tu Blu grew up, they sought advice from God (*Yawmsaub*) on how to create heaven and earth. After receiving advice from God

(*Yawmsaub and Pujsaub*), they were able to create heaven and earth.[51] Stanza 12 says:

> It seemed Chi Tu grew up full of wisdom, he wanted to rule heaven. Tu Blu grew up full of knowledge, she wanted to rule the earth. Chi Tu went to ask for advice from Grandmother God (*Pujsaub*); Tu Blu went to ask for advice from Grandfather God (*Yawmsaub*). Grandmother God (*Pujsaub*) said, "Chi Tu, if you are going to rule heaven, you have to use a hammer to hit to the front of you." Grandfather God (*Yawmsaub*) said, "Tu Blu, if you are going to rule the earth, you have to use a hammer to hit to the back of you. Heaven will be as firm as a rock and the earth will be as firm as the rocky mountain."
>
> Upon their return, Chi Tu made a hammer and hit to the front of him; heaven became firm. Tu Blu made a hammer and hit to the back of her, the earth became still. Chi Tu and Tu Blu asked who would measure heaven to find out how high it is and measure the earth to find out how wide it is. Chi Tu and Tu Blu said that the leaf frog could measure heaven and earth. The leaf frog said to Chi Tu and Tu Blu, "My hands and legs are too small, I could not measure heaven and earth. . ."[52]
> Translation is the author's.

According to this account, heaven and earth were not created until the fourth generation after the universal flood.

---

[51] Ibid., 31-35.
[52] Ibid., 34.

Though it seemed more like re-creating the heaven and earth after the universal flood, but the Showing the Way chant and Hmong animists claim that this was the original creation and how the universe came to being. Though stanza 12 clearly states that heaven and earth were created by men, the chant contradicts itself in stanza 13 by stating that heaven and earth and mankind were created by God (*Yawmsaub and Pujsaub*), specifically by Grandmother God (*Pujsaub*). The stanza 13 says:

> In the beginning, it's Grandmother God (*Pujsaub*) who created humankind to live, created humankind in the world, created heaven and earth, created 30 female suns and 30 male moons. The female suns ruled 30 days, the male moons ruled 30 nights. It was said who would have the knowledge? It was heard that the peacock had a huge copper crossbow. He used the copper crossbow to shoot the female sun and 29 of them were shot down. He used the copper crossbow to shoot the male moons and 29 of them were shot down. Only one female sun and one male moon left. The female sun hid herself under the edge of the earth, so the earth was darkened for seven eras. The male moon hid himself under the edge of the mountain, so the earth was darkened for seven years.
> Tu Blu (*Tuj Nplug*) and Chi Tu (*Ci Tuj*) said, "The world has to ask for advice from Grandmother God (*Pujsaub*) and Grandfather God (*Yawmsaub*)." Grandmother God (*Pujsaub*) advised Tu Blu and Chi Tu that if you want the female sun and the male moon to come up, upon your return to the earth,

you have to request the rooster to crow so that they would come up. Upon their return from seeking the advice from Grandmother and Grandfather God, Tu Blu and Chi Tu had the rooster crow three times and the female sun came up from the edge of the world. The rooster crowed three times and the male moon came up from the edge of earth.[53] Translation is the author's.

In this stanza, the two people (*Chi Tu and Tu Blu*) that the previous stanza claimed to be the creators of heaven and earth were no longer being portrayed as such. They were desperate because they had shot down 29 suns and 29 moons that God (*Yawmsaub*) had created. The remaining sun and moon were so afraid to come up, so they hid themselves, leaving the earth in darkness for a long time. They did not know how to entice the sun and the moon to come up from their hiding, so they had to seek advice from God (*Yawmsaub*). The sun and moon came up from their hiding only after they followed the instructions God (*Yawmsaub and Pujsaub*) gave to them.

In the beginning of Stanza 3 of Yang Chong Jai's version, it says that heaven and earth were created by *Qas Tuj* and *Tuj Lug*, twin sons of Gao Ah (*Nkauj Ab*) and Jau Ong (*Nraug Oo*), but toward the end of the stanza, it says that heaven and earth and mankind were all created by the lady frog. Stanza 3 says:

> ...*Qas Tuj* and *Tuj Lug* asked their mother, Gao Ah, and father, Jau Ong (*Nkauj Ab* and *Nraug Oo*), who created mankind on the earth? Gao Ah and Jau Ong replied, mankind on earth was created by the lady frog. *Qas*

---

[53] Ibid., 38-39.

Tug and *Tuj Lug* were unsettled, they went to ask the lady frog, if mankind on the earth was created by you, then do you see how high the sky is and do you know how wide the earth is? The lady frog replied it was true that I created mankind on the earth. *Qas Tuj* and *Tuj Lug* continued to press on the lady frog, so you were able to create mankind on the earth, do you know how high the heaven is and do you see how wide the earth is? The lady frog thought why *Qas Tug* and *Tuj Lug* came to ask her. The lady frog thought to herself that she did not want the people on earth to die. The lady frog had to lie to *Qas Tug* and *Tuj Lug*, "as frog I neither know how wide the sky is nor see how wide the earth is. I leaped for three days, covering three vast areas, but it was only as large as the footprint of a cow. I, the frog, have short legs and hands, leaped for three days, covering three vast plains, but it only as large as the footprint of a mouse. It seems heaven is as narrow as the hand palm; the earth is as narrow as the sole of a foot. It seems it is neither enough for mankind to live nor enough for the demons to gather."

Qas Tuj and *Tuj Lug* were unhappy they asked the eagle to fly over to measure the world. You go to measure heaven to find out if it is possible to see how high heaven is. You go to measure the earth to find out if it is possible to know how wide earth is. The eagle flew over for three days, covering three vast areas and only saw the back of the sun and moon from a far distance. The eagle turned around to return, exposing its tail feathers to the burning sun and the sun scorched its tail feathers to curve like a cow's rib. The eagle flew over for three nights, covering three vast plains, but the eagle only saw the sun and moon from a far distance. The eagle turned around to return, exposing its tail to the burning sun and the sun scorched its tail feathers to curve like a mouse's rib. The eagle arrived back from heaven. *Qas Tuj* and *Tuj Lug* hastily go to ask the eagle, "we sent you to measure heaven and earth, did you see how high heaven was and did you know how wide earth was?" The eagle replied, "*Qas Tuj* and *Tuj Lug*, you sent me, the eagle, to measure heaven and earth. I flew for the three days, covering three vast areas, but I only saw the sun and moon from a very far distance. As I turned around to return, I exposed my tail to the burning sun and the sun scorched my tail feathers to curve like a cow's rib. You sent me, the eagle, to measure earth. I flew for three days, covering three vast plains, but I only saw the sun and moon from a very far distance. As I turned around to return, I exposed my tail to the burning sun and the sun scorched my tail feathers to curve like the mouse's rib. Heaven is eight times the height of the sky and earth is eight times the width of the earth. It will be enough for mankind to live and demons to gather."

Qas Tuj was angry he picked up a cowherd's stick upon his return. *Tuj Lug* was mad he picked up a horse stick upon his return. *Qas Tug* hit the lady frog three times with the cowherd's stick, the lady frog cried out echoing to the sky and died face down in the cow's footprint. Hitting the lady frog three times with the horse stick, the lady frog cried out echoing to the air and died face down in the horse's footprint. The lady frog flew up and landed on Satan's (*Ntxwgnyoog's*) tip of the sky; landed on Satan's (*Ntxwgnyoog's*) rocky top. Satan (*Ntxwgnyoog*) asked the herdsman, "Go out to find out who was it that landed on our tip of the sky that caused it to shake so violently, who was it that landed on our rocky top that caused it to rattle so tremendously?" Satan's (*Ntxwgnyoog's*) herdsman went out and saw that it was the lady frog. The herdsman yelled back at Satan (*Ntxwgnyoog*) that it was the lady frog that landed on the tip of the sky; it was the lady frog that landed on the top of the rock.

Satan (*Ntxwgnyoog*) went out to see and it was really the lady frog. Satan (*Ntxwgnyoog*) raised his voice to ask, "Lady frog, mankind on the earth was created by you and you would not let them die, why you came?"

The lady frog replied, Satan (*Ntxwgnyoog*), it was because heaven was created, so Gao Ah (*Nkauj Ab*) was created to stay and the earth was created, so Jau Ong (*Nraug Oo*) was created to live. Gao Ah lived for seven eras, but she did not have any son. Jau Ong lived for seven years, but he did not have any offspring. Therefore, Gao Ah went to ask Grandmother God (*Pujsaub*) and Jau Ong went to ask Grandfather God (*Yawmsaub*). Gao Ah asked why she did not have any son and Jau Ong asked why he did not have any offspring. Grandmother God (*Pujsaub*) said to Gao Ah, you will return to live forever and never die, you will reside by the edge of the village, lying down on the shining bed then you will have offspring. Grandfather God (*Yawmsaub*) said, Jau Ong, you will return to live forever and never die, residing on the edge of the village, lying on a luxurious bed then you will have a child.

Gao Ah and Jau Ong said others knew how to give birth, they gave birth from within, Gao Ah and Jau Ong did not know how to give birth, so they gave birth by their shins. Others knew how to give birth, they gave birth from inside of their bodies, but Gao Ah and Jau Ong did not know how to give birth, so they gave birth by their fingertips. It seemed, Gao Ah's son was the older son and Jau Ong's son was the younger son. Gao Ah and Jau Ong complained that others knew how to name their children, but Gao Ah and Jau Ong did not, so Gao Ah named her son who was the older son as *Qas Tuj* and Jau Ong named his son who was the younger son as *Tuj Lug*.

Qas Tuj grew up with full of knowledge he picked up the cowherd's stick to hit the sky. *Tuj Lug* grew up with full of wisdom he picked up the horse's stick to hit the earth. *Qas Tuj* and *Tuj Lug* went on hitting the sky without returning, hitting the earth without coming back. Gao Ah and Jau Ong had the bamboo rat dig holes, gnawing through rocks and rocky mountains, tracking down *Qas Tuj* and *Tuj Lug*, and requiring them to return.

Gao Ah and Jau Ong had the rat dig holes, gnawing through rocks and rocky mountains, tracking down *Qas Tug* and *Tuj Lug*, and making them coming back.

Upon their return, *Qas Tuj* and *Tuj Lug* inquired Gao Ah and Jau Ong about who created mankind on the earth. Gao Ah and Jau Ong quickly answered that mankind on the earth was created by me, the lady frog.

It seemed, *Qas Tuj* and *Tuj Lug* were unsettled, and they thought that they had to come to ask me, the lady frog. They said, it was told that mankind on the earth were created by you, if so, did you see how high heaven was and did I know how wide earth was? I, the lady frog, replied to *Qas Tuj* and *Tuj Lug* that it was true that mankind on the earth was created by me. Then *Qas Tuj* and *Tuj Lug* forcefully inquired, since mankind on the earth were created by you, therefore, did you see how high heaven was and did you know how wide earth was? I thought why *Qas Tuj* and *Tuj Lug* had to ask me? I did not want the people on earth to die, so I lied to *Qas Tuj* and *Tuj Lug* by saying, "as for me the lady frog, I did not know how wide heaven was and I did not see how wide earth was. I leaped for three days, covering three vast areas, but it was only as large as the footprint of a cow. I, the frog, have short legs and hands, leaped for three nights, covering three vast plains, but it was only as large as the footprint of a mouse. It seemed heaven was as narrow as the hand palm and earth was as narrow as my foot sole. It seemed it was neither enough for mankind to live nor enough for the demons to gather.

Qas Tuj and *Tuj Lug* were unhappy; upon their return they asked the eagle to fly over to measure heaven. "You go to measure the sky to find out if it is possible to see how high heaven is. You go to measure the earth to find out if it is possible to know how wide earth is." The eagle flew over for three days, covering three vast areas and only saw the back of the sun and moon from a far distance. The eagle turned around to return, exposing its tail to the burning sun and the sun scorched its tail feathers to curve like a cow's rib. The eagle flew over for three nights, covering three vast plains, but the eagle only saw the sun and moon from a far distance. The eagle turned around to return, exposing the tail to the burning sun and the sun scorched its tail feathers to curve like a mouse's rib. The eagle arrived back from heaven. *Qas Tuj* and *Tuj Lug* hastily go ask the eagle, "we sent you to measure heaven and earth, did you see how high heaven was and did you know how wide earth was?" The eagle replied, *Qas Tuj* and *Tuj Lug*, "you sent me, the eagle, to measure heaven and earth. I flew for the three days, covering three vast areas, but I only saw the sun and moon from a very far distance. As I turned around to return, I exposed my tail to the burning sun and the sun scorched my tail feathers to curve like a cow's rib. You sent me, the eagle, to measure earth. I flew for three nights, covering three vast plains, but I only saw the sun and moon from a very far distance. As I turned around to return, I exposed my tail to the burning sun and the sun scorched my tail feathers to curve like the mouse's rib. Heaven is eight times the height of the sky and earth is eight times the width of the earth. It will be enough for mankind to live and for the demons to gather.

Qas Tuj was angry he picked up a cowherd's stick upon his return. *Tuj Lug* was mad he picked up a horse stick upon his return. *Qas Tug* hit me, the lady frog, three times with the cowherd's stick, I the lady frog, cried out echoing to the sky and died face down in the cow's footprint. Hitting me, the lady frog, three times with the horse stick, I, the lady frog, cried out echoing to the air and died face down in the horse footprint. Therefore, I, the lady frog flew over to land on your tip of the sky, causing it to violently vibrate; I flew over to land on your rocky tip, causing it to tremble.

Satan (*Ntxwgnyoog*) hastily asked, you, the lady frog, when you lived on earth, mankind was created by you, so now that you have come, what did you curse the world? The lady frog replied to Satan (*Ntxwgnyoog*), now that I, the lady frog, have come, I cursed the world that I was the one who created the earth and mankind. I did not want the world to die, so while I, the lady frog, lived on earth, flesh was like flesh of woods, bones were like bones of rocks, sickness could recover quickly, dead rose again. Now that I, the lady frog, have come, the world's flesh is like flesh of bee's wax, bones are like bones of hemp straws. The flesh of bee's wax will melt in the burning sun and the bones of hemp straws will crack in the soaking rain. Therefore, when the old dies, he will follow my lead and when the young dies, he will follow my path.[54] (Translation is the author's.)

In this Showing the Way chant, the lady frog who claimed to be the creator of heaven and earth and mankind was portrayed as being lazy and a liar who failed to fulfill its duty of measuring heaven and earth as demanded by *Qas Tuj* and *Tuj Lug*, the two human beings who also claimed to be the creators of heaven and earth. The lady frog was eventually murdered by *Qas Tuj* and *Tuj Lug*, the two sons of the first two human beings that the lady frog created. It is so preposterous that these creators, who had the ability to create heaven and earth were unable to know how big the heaven and earth were. And it is absurd to believe that the frog and eagle could understand human language to meet the demands of the creators.

Stanza 5 of Vincent K. Her's version of the Showing the Way chant states that before the universal flood, "people lived everywhere, occupied every corner of the earth," then one day "*Puj Dlaab*," which he translated as the "Lady Spirit" (correct translation is Lady Demon), tipped heaven and earth causing the universal flood.[55] Though it was clearly stated that all humans were wiped out, when God (*Yawmsaub*) told the two survivors of the flood to go search for their mates, Gao Doua (*Nkauj Nruag*) was still able to find a young man, a "son of a dignitary who has a foul mouth" in the south and Noushee Qong also found a crippled girl in the far north.[56]

---

[54] Bertrais, 61-68.
[55] Vincent K. Her, 189.
[56] Ibid., 190-191.

While all people were wiped out, somehow these two individuals were able to ride out the violent flood that killed the whole world and survived. They refused to marry these two individuals, so Gao Doua and Noushee Qong went back to complain to God (*Yawmsaub*) about not able to find any suitable mates. God (*Yawmsaub*) put them into a test, which each of them had to carry a large stone up the hill and roll them down the opposite hillsides and if they came together "side by side" or on top of each other at the bottom of the valley, then would they be allowed to marry each other. In Yang Chong Chee's version, it was God (*Yawmsaub*) who told them that they had to marry each other in order to repopulate the earth. The test of rolling the stones down the hillsides was only to assure them that they had to marry each other. But in Her's version, God (*Yawmsaub*) reluctantly allowed them to marry each other only after the stones came together at the bottom of the valley. This is different from other versions. Similar to other versions of the Showing the Way chants, Her's version also states that they had their first son who was deformed. They went back to ask God (*Yawmsaub*) what to do with their deformed son and God (*Yawmsaub*) told them to cut him in pieces and hang them on different tree branches. They did according to God's (*Yawmsaub's*) advice and these pieces of flesh became human beings forming the different clans of people. In Her's version, Gao Ah (*Nkauj Ab*) and Chao Au (*Nraug Au*), who were the parents of the creators of heaven and earth, were the descendants of the deformed son of Gao Doua and Noushee Qong, but other versions of the Showing the Way chants contradict this claim. Yang Chong Chee's version says that Gao Ah (*Nkauj Ab*) and Jau Ong (*Nraug Oo*) had another son whom they named him Shing Lee Qong (*Txiv Seev Lis Qoos*) and another daughter that they named her Pu Tong Mua Gao Jao (*Puj Toog Muam Nkauj Ncaus*). The creators of heaven and earth who were Chi Tu (*Cis Tuj*) and Tu Blu (*Tuj Nplug*) were descendants of

Shing Lee Qong (*Txiv Seev Lis Qoos*) and Pu Tong Mua Gao Jao (*Puj Toog Muam Nkauj Ncaus*), not from the deformed child. In Her's version, heaven and earth were created in the third generation after the universal flood, but in Yang Chong Chee's version, heaven and earth were created in the fourth generation. In Her's version, the brother and sister who survived the universal flood were not Jau Ong (*Nraug Oo*) and Gao Ab (*Nkauj Ab*), but they were Noushee Qong (*Nuj Sis Qoob*) and Gao Doua (*Nkauj Nruag*). Jau Ong and Gao Ah who were the brother and sister who survived the universal flood in the Yang Chong Chee's version became the son and daughter of Noushee Qong (*Nuj Sis Qoob*) and Gao Doua (*Nkauj Nruag*) in Her's version. However, in Her's version, Jau Ong was named Chao Au. Gao Ah (*Nkauj Ab*) and Chao Au (*Nraug Au*) were the parents of Tou Chi Tu (*Tub Cis Tuj*) and Tou Chi Blu (*Tuj Cis Nplug*) who created heaven and earth. Gao Ah (*Nkauj Ab*) and Jau Ong (*Nraug Oo*) were portrayed as the first two human beings on earth whom were created by the lady frog in Yang Chong Jai's and Kenneth White's versions of the Showing the Way chants, but in Yang Chong Chee's version, they were recorded as the first two human beings on earth as well as the two sole survivors of the universal flood. In Yang Chong Chee's version, Chi Tu (*Cis Tuj*) was a man and Tu Blu (*Tuj Nplug*) was a woman, but they were brother and sister. However, in Her's version, Tou Chi Tu (*Tub Cis Tuj*) and Tou Chi Blu (*Tuj Cis Nplug*), similar names, were both men and they were twin brothers.[57] Stanza 6 says:

> . . .Upon returning, Gao Ah and Chao Au would name the older son, *Tub Cis Tuj*, and the younger, *Tuj Cis Nplug*. As *Tub Cis Tuj* grew up, he blossomed with knowledge. One

---

[57] Ibid., 191 – 194; Bertrais, 34.

day, picking up a hammer made of stone, he struck the ground in front of him three times. With that, he created an earth that is as spacious as it is huge. When *Tuj Cis Nplug* matured into a young man, he possesses all kinds of wisdom. Seizing a hammer made of metal, he swung it three times to the back of him. In that instant, he made a universe that is so infinitely cosmic...[58]

Kenneth White's version of the Showing the Way chant states that the frog and Krang Tu (*Qaav Tuj*) and Krang To (*Qaav Taug*) all claimed to be the creators of heaven and earth. Therefore, they challenged each other to measure heaven and earth. Krang Tu (*Qaav Tuj*) and Krang To (*Qaav Taug*) first challenged the frog to measure heaven and earth to find out how high and wide heaven and earth were if the frog was the creator. After the frog return from measuring heaven and earth, the frog then challenged Krang Tu (*Qaav Tuj*) and Krang To (*Qaav Taug*) to go measure heaven and earth if they were the creators of heaven and earth. Krang Tu (*Qaav Tuj*) and Krang To (*Qaav Taug*) weren't able to measure heaven and earth, so they cried out to the eagle for help. The words "*Qaav*" means frog and "*Tuj* and *Taug*" mean poisonous or venomous in Hmong. *Qaav Tuj* and *Qaaj Taug* mean "poisonous frog" in Hmong. However, in this version, Krang Tu (*Qaav Tuj*) and Krang To (*Qaav Taug*) were said to be the sons of Gao Ah (*Nkauj Ab*) and Jau Ong (*Nraug Oo*) as well.[59]

It is good that Hmong have accounts of creation. Many groups of people on earth do not even have the slightest idea

---

[58] Ibid., 189-194.

[59] Kenneth White, *Kr'ua Ke* (*Showing the way*): *A Hmong Initiation of The Dead,* (Bangkok: Pandora, 1983), 14, 47.

that the universe has its beginning in creation, including people who believe in Buddhism. It is undoubtedly that those who do not believe in creation believe that the universe is static and eternal. Hmong believe in creation, which means that the universe has a beginning, but only that Hmong animists, including the Hmong animist intellectuals, believe that heaven and earth were created by men as well as mankind and heaven and earth were also created by frog, and the universe was created long after the universal flood. The Showing the Way chants are not worth believing. They are too misleading. They do not have the slightest clue of how the universe was created and who created it. The Showing the Way chants are supposed to provide a clear understanding of creation and the Creator, but they only aggravate the confusion. As a result, Hmong animists are more confused about creation than those who are without any account of creation. And they are more unresolved than other groups of people about who created heaven and earth – whether the creators were men, God (*Yawmsaub*), or the lady frog. They are confused because the things that they worship as their gods are not the true God and the Showing the Way chants that they believe to be the guiding light for their spirits are not the word of the Creator. Therefore, they cannot explain the origin of the universe according to the truth. This leads Lee and Tapp to argue that "the Hmong have felt no need to explain the origins of the earth in personal term."[60] But that is not true. The creation accounts in the Showing the Way chants tell us that Hmong animists are very interested in knowing how the universe came to existence. But the embarrassment is that the Showing the Way chants give wrong account on creation and the Creator.

Though Hmong animists refused to acknowledge that God (*Yawmsaub*) is the Creator, scientific discoveries in the

---

[60] Lee and Tapp, 31.

past several decades have demanded scientists to admit that only the Bible could explain the beginning of the universe and the Creator whose intelligence is so amazing that He created the earth and set it so precisely at the right place where the "basic structure of the universe is balanced on a razor's edge for life to exist. The coincidences are too fantastic to attribute this to mere chance or to claim that it needs no explanation."[61] These scientific discoveries alone are enough to demand Hmong animist intellectuals to explain why they rather believe creation as taught by the Showing the Way chants. Many scientists confessed that their faith in God the Creator (*Yawmsaub tug tsim ntuj tsim teb*) became stronger and many more have admitted that they became Christians as a result of their scientific findings.[62] But Hmong animists continue to believe that heaven and earth were created by men as well as mankind and the universe were created by a frog, one of the least living creatures God (*Yawmsaub*) had created. Not only do they believe that men and frog created heaven and earth, but Hmong animists even believe that it was possible that heaven and earth were created long after the universal flood. The placement of creation long after the universal flood embarrassingly exposes the absolute fallacy of the Showing the Way chants. To avoid such embarrassment, Hmongism (a group of Hmong animists who banded together to revise the Showing the Way chant called their organization "Hmongism") completely eliminates the universal flood and the name of the creator of heaven and earth from its revised version of the Showing the Way chant. It only says "long ago, in the beginning when heaven and earth were created." [63] By eliminating the

---

[61] Strobel, 159-160.
[62] Ibid., 84-85, 109, 151, 182.
[63] Hmongism, "Zaj Taw Kev (Showing the Way chant)," http://www.hmongism.org (accessed September 18, 2013).

creator from the Showing the Way chant does not eliminate the confusion about who created heaven and earth. It only provides better evidence that Hmong animists truly do not know the Creator of heaven and earth. Scientific discoveries in the past five decades concluded that the universe has a beginning and that the cause of the beginning of the universe points toward an intelligent and a transcendent designer who is God (*Yawmsaub*). Without God (*Yawmsaub*) as the First Cause, it is impossible for the universe to come to existence. There is no question based on these scientific discoveries that God (*Yawmsaub*) is the Creator, but Hmong animists simply cannot admit so because they do not want to glorify Him as God. Therefore, even though Hmong animists generally believe that God (*Yawmsaub*) is the Creator of heaven and earth, they rather give credit to some fictional human characters and one of the lowest creatures God ever created, the frog, as the creators of heaven and earth and say what Lee and Tapp said of God, "What he is not is a Creator,"[64] in order to avoid giving God (*Yawmsaub*) the glory. But when people look at the natural things, they should see God's fingerprint on all of them. It's time for Hmong animists to understand and accept the fact that mankind and the frog could not have created heaven and earth and discredit the Showing the Way chants as nothing but false teaching of faith. The "fine-tuning"[65] of the universe points toward an intelligent and a transcendent God, not men or frog. So true are the words of the Apostle Paul in Romans 1:18-23:

> The wrath of God is being revealed from heaven against all the godlessness and wickedness of people, who suppress the truth by their wickedness, since what may be known

---

[64] Lee and Tapp, 31.
[65] Strobel, 192.

about God is plain to them, because God has made it plain to them. For since the creation of the world God's invisible qualities-his eternal power and divine nature-have been clearly seen, being understood from what has been made, so that people are without excuse. For although they knew God, they neither glorified him as God nor gave thanks to him, but their thinking became futile and their foolish hearts were darkened. Though they claim to be wise, they became fools and exchanged the glory of the immortal God for images made to look like a mortal human being and birds and animals and reptiles.

THE REAL CREATOR

When thinking about the Creator of heaven and earth, mankind and everything in the universe, one is to think about a being that is omnipotent, omnipresent, omniscient, nothing else and no other being is greater than this being. He must have existed prior to the creation of heaven and earth and he must be infinite. Christian philosophers believe that this "Greatest Conceivable Being"[66] is God (*Yawmsaub*). God (*Yawmsaub*) is the "First Cause." Without the "First Cause," nothing that exists would have come to existence. The universe did not only come to existence by God's initial act of creation, but it continues to depend on Him to sustain its existence,[67] Jeremiah 10:11-16.

---

[66] Steven T. Davis, *Reason & Religion: God, Reason, & Theistic Proofs* (Grand Rapids: WM B. Eerdmans Publishing Company, 1997), 17.

[67] Ibid., 63.

[11] "Tell them this: 'These gods, who did not make the heavens and the earth, will perish from the earth and from under the heavens.'"
[12] But God made the earth by his power;
he founded the world by his wisdom
and stretched out the heavens by his understanding.
[13] When he thunders, the waters in the heavens roar;
he makes clouds rise from the ends of the earth.
He sends lightning with the rain
and brings out the wind from his storehouses.

[14] Everyone is senseless and without knowledge;
every goldsmith is shamed by his idols.
The images he makes are a fraud;
they have no breath in them.
[15] They are worthless, the objects of mockery;
when their judgment comes, they will perish.
[16] He who is the Portion of Jacob is not like these,
for he is the Maker of all things,
including Israel, the people of his inheritance—
the LORD Almighty is his name.

The above description of the Creator of heaven and earth definitely discredited the claims made by the Showing the Way chants about who were the creators of heaven and earth. It issues a direct challenge to the Hmong animist intellectuals to reconsider their beliefs and refine their cosmological views on creation. The fastest growing scientists are those rejecting the Evolution Theory that claims that life started out billions of years ago by itself. Even the agnostic astronomer Robert Jastrow had to admit that the sudden appearance of man at a "definite moment in time, in a flash of light and energy" is astronomically similar to the creation account in

Genesis.[68] At the current time, the atheists who claim that the universe is infinite, have to really believe that the world has no beginning because now all scientific discoveries have affirmed the biblical claims that the universe has a beginning. All scientists who studied the origin of the universe, both Christians and non-Christians agree that the existence of the universe involves an intelligent designer and the evidence points toward God (*Yawmsaub*) as the Creator, the "Master Designer."[69] Patrick Glynn, a former atheist, states:

> The anthropic principle raised fundamental questions not only about the modern interpretation of Copernicanism, but ultimately about Darwinism as well. It certainly showed that Darwin's theory of "natural selection" could no longer be taken as an exhaustive explanation for the phenomenon of life. The notion that the whole process could be reduced to the workings of a single, simple "blind" mechanism was fundamentally flawed... Indeed, what twentieth-century cosmology had come up with was something of a scientific embarrassment: a universe with a definite beginning, expressly designed for life. Ironically, the picture of the universe bequeathed to us by the most advanced twentieth-century science is closer in spirit to the vision presented in the Book of Genesis than anything offered by science since Copernicus.[70]

---

[68] Strobel, 132.
[69] Ibid., 132-133, 148, 155.
[70] Patrick Glynn, *The Evidence: The Reconciliation of Faith and Reason in a Post secular World* (Rocklin: Prima Publishing), 26.

Strobel states that most of the brilliant scientists and "virtually all the cosmologists"[71] who have the best credential in academia, who have studied the origin of the universe, have affirmed that the universe was created by a transcendent Creator God (*Yawmsaub*). It's believed that some if not most of Hmong animists who have advanced degrees have come across some of these scientific discoveries, but they rather believe that heaven and earth were created by men and frog according to the teaching of the Showing the Way chants. How can anyone believe that the frog, one of the least living things, could have created heaven and earth and human beings? If Hmong animists really believe that the frog was the creator of heaven and earth and mankind, why don't they call the frog divine and worship it as God? If the frog was able to create heaven and earth and mankind, why did it have to argue with those human creators and lied to them that the world was very small – as small as its hand palm and the sole of its foot?[72] Does this sound like someone who has the ability to create heaven and earth? Does the frog meet the test as the "Greatest Conceivable Being?" Does it all knowing, all powerful, and does it exist infinitely? A frog with this much ability should still live, but where is it today? What are the rational explanations let alone scientific proof that the frog was the creator of heaven and earth and mankind? Where is the evidence to prove that a frog, one of the lowest creatures God ever created, was the creator of heaven and earth and mankind? If it was the creator, why was it being murdered for being lazy and a liar? As stated above, Patrick Glynn was formerly an atheist, but he converted to Christianity after his scientific discovery proved the existence of the Creator God. If Hmong animists cannot truly believe that the frog could create heaven and earth and

---

[71] Strobel, 349.
[72] Bertrais, 66-68.

mankind, what makes them continue to believe the Showing the Way chants? Or can they believe that heaven and earth were created by mankind according to Yang Chong Chee's (*Yaj Txoos Txhim's*)[73] and Vincent Kou Her's[74] versions of the Showing the Way chants? They were not just any humans, but these two versions of the Showing the Way chants seemed to suggest that these men who were credited as the creators were Hmong. If men were able to create heaven and earth, shouldn't they also be able to know how high and wide heaven and earth were? How can anyone possibly provide a rational and scientific explanation that creation could take place long after the universal flood as claimed by the Showing the Way chants? How can anyone believe what the Showing the Way chants teach about creation? Again, do these men meet the test of the "Greatest Conceivable Being," a Spiritual Being or a Supreme Being that exists infinitely? Were these men omniscient, omnipresent, omnipotent, and exist infinitely? Where are Chi Tu (*Ci Tuj*) and Tu Blu (*Tuj Nplug*), Tou Chi Tu (*Tub Cis Tuj*) and Tou Chi Blu (*Tuj Chi Nplug*), *Qas Tuj* and *Tuj Lug*, Krang Tu (*Qaav Tuj*) and Krang To (*Qaav Taug*), and Chi Tu (*Ci Tuj*) and Tu Chi (*Tuj Ci*), the individuals named in the Showing the Way chants as the creators, today? Mankind definitely could not have created heaven and earth. Until recently, Hmong were one of the least educated people. Therefore, anything is believable to them. But it is embarrassing for the Hmong animist intellectuals to continue to believe in such false teaching. The Showing the Way chants are nothing but myths and only in myths that a dead frog still could talk and curse. This is also the reason why Hmong animists believe that a dead person can bless the living. It is one thing for the non-Hmong researchers to study about Hmong beliefs,

---

[73] Ibid., 34.
[74] Vincent K. Her., 219.

but it is quite primitive for the Hmong animists, particularly the Hmong animist intellectuals to continue to believe that the Showing the Way chants teach the truth about creation. Hmong animists are challenged to rethink about how the universe came to existence. They should refute the teaching of the Showing the Way chants and search for the truth in the Bible. As Strobel says, "Science tells you how the heavens go, and the Bible tells you how to go to heaven."[75] The Showing the Way chants can only tell Hmong animists how to go to hell. That is what the Showing the Way chants are all about. They cannot be trusted for the teaching of how heaven and earth, mankind, and everything in the universe were created.

There is a better way to explain the origin of the creation, which science has already proved it to be true. The whole Christian Bible talks about this "Greatest Conceivable Being" who is omnipresent, omnipotent, and omniscient. He is the "First Cause" of all things in the universe. He is God (*Yawmsaub*) who lived before heaven and earth were created. He is living now and He will live forever in the future. The Bible tells us how heaven and earth and everything in the universe were created by this Greatest Conceivable Being. Without the Bible, no creation account, whether be it the Evolution Theory, Big Bang Theory, or the Showing the Way chants, could provide a plausible explanation about creation. The Evolution Theory and many other scientific theories that men ever created were created to counter the claims of creation taught by the Bible, but they eventually were either discredited by new scientific discoveries or forced to affirm the biblical account of creation.[76] The accounts of creation in the Showing the Way chants are no different. They were definitely created to counter the creation account in the

---

[75] Strobel, 90.
[76] Ibid., 192.

Bible, but they should be considered shams to teach creation. Strobel reported of Allen Sandage's statement:

> The Big Bang, he told the rapt audience, was a supernatural event that cannot be explained within the realm of physics as we know it. Science had taken us to the First Event, but it can't take us further to the First Cause. The sudden emergence of matter, space, time, and energy pointed to the need for some kind of transcendence.[77]

The biblical account of creation starts as stated in the first and second chapters of the Book of Genesis:

> Genesis 1: 1 In the beginning God created the heavens and the earth. ² Now the earth was formless and empty, darkness was over the surface of the deep, and the Spirit of God was hovering over the waters.
> ³ And God said, "Let there be light," and there was light. ⁴ God saw that the light was good, and he separated the light from the darkness. ⁵ God called the light "day," and the darkness he called "night." And there was evening, and there was morning—the first day.
> ⁶ And God said, "Let there be a vault between the waters to separate water from water." ⁷ So God made the vault and separated the water under the vault from the water above it. And it was so. ⁸ God called the vault "sky." And there was evening, and there was morning—the second day.

---

[77] Ibid., 84.

⁹ And God said, "Let the water under the sky be gathered to one place, and let dry ground appear." And it was so. ¹⁰ God called the dry ground "land," and the gathered waters he called "seas." And God saw that it was good. ¹¹ Then God said, "Let the land produce vegetation: seed-bearing plants and trees on the land that bear fruit with seed in it, according to their various kinds." And it was so. ¹² The land produced vegetation: plants bearing seed according to their kinds and trees bearing fruit with seed in it according to their kinds. And God saw that it was good. ¹³ And there was evening, and there was morning—the third day.

¹⁴ And God said, "Let there be lights in the vault of the sky to separate the day from the night, and let them serve as signs to mark sacred times, and days and years, ¹⁵ and let them be lights in the vault of the sky to give light on the earth." And it was so. ¹⁶ God made two great lights—the greater light to govern the day and the lesser light to govern the night. He also made the stars. ¹⁷ God set them in the vault of the sky to give light on the earth, ¹⁸ to govern the day and the night, and to separate light from darkness. And God saw that it was good. ¹⁹ And there was evening, and there was morning—the fourth day. ²⁰ And God said, "Let the water teem with living creatures, and let birds fly above the earth across the vault of the sky." ²¹ So God created the great creatures of the sea and every living thing with which the water teems and that moves about in it, according to their

kinds, and every winged bird according to its kind. And God saw that it was good. ²² God blessed them and said, "Be fruitful and increase in number and fill the water in the seas, and let the birds increase on the earth." ²³ And there was evening, and there was morning—the fifth day.

²⁴ And God said, "Let the land produce living creatures according to their kinds: the livestock, the creatures that move along the ground, and the wild animals, each according to its kind." And it was so. ²⁵ God made the wild animals according to their kinds, the livestock according to their kinds, and all the creatures that move along the ground according to their kinds. And God saw that it was good.

²⁶ Then God said, "Let us make mankind in our image, in our likeness, so that they may rule over the fish in the sea and the birds in the sky, over the livestock and all the wild animals, and over all the creatures that move along the ground."

²⁷ So God created mankind in his own image, in the image of God he created them;
male and female he created them.

²⁸ God blessed them and said to them, "Be fruitful and increase in number; fill the earth and subdue it. Rule over the fish in the sea and the birds in the sky and over every living creature that moves on the ground."

²⁹ Then God said, "I give you every seed-bearing plant on the face of the whole earth and every tree that has fruit with seed in it. They will be yours for food. ³⁰ And to all the

> beasts of the earth and all the birds in the sky and all the creatures that move along the ground—everything that has the breath of life in it—I give every green plant for food." And it was so. ³¹ God saw all that he had made, and it was very good. And there was evening, and there was morning—the sixth day.

Unlike the Showing the Way chants that contained conflicting and unreliable mythical stories about creation, the Bible clearly proclaims that God (*Yawmsaub*) is the Creator of the universe. Unlike the claim made by Hmong animists that God (*Yawmsaub*) is "an absentee god," the Bible says that God (*Yawmsaub*) continues to sustain the universe; otherwise the world would no longer exist.⁷⁸ Furthermore, unlike the Showing the Way chants that named one of the lowest creatures, the frog, and men as the creators, but after they had created them, they did not know how big the universe was. God (*Yawmsaub*) knew exactly how big the universe was and He purposely left traces of his creation work to be discovered by science. The Bible further proclaims that God created all things for his own glory, Colossians 1:15-17:

> The Son is the image of the invisible God, the firstborn over all creation. ¹⁶ For in him all things were created: things in heaven and on earth, visible and invisible, whether thrones or powers or rulers or authorities; all things have been created through him and for him. ¹⁷ He is before all things, and in him all things hold together.

---

[78] Davis, 63.

Now, it is important to know who you rather believe as the creator of the universe and which teaching you rather believe to teach the truth about creation. If you are willing to accept that God (*Yawmsaub*) is the Creator and believe that the biblical account of creation is true, don't hesitate to invite Him into your life. Once you accept Him as your God, He will teach "you into all the truth"[79] about the Creator and creation. He will be your Father, and His truth will teach you how to go to heaven. However, if you rather believe that the Showing the Way chants are the truth, be warned because the Showing the Way chants can only teach you how to go to hell (*ntuj txag teb tsaus, ntuj tshaav teb nqhuab*) and your Father is Satan (*Ntxwgnyoog*).

---

[79] John 16:13.

CHAPTER 4

THE BELIEF THAT SATAN (*NTXWNGYOOG*) IS THE EVIL DEITY

Ntxwg Nyug (author's note: this is a misspelling: Nyug should be Nyoog instead) is an entirely indigenous Hmong spirit, who inhabits a mountain grotto above 12 ascending mountains in the Otherworld and keeps a herd of heavenly cattle who graze beneath it and whose souls are the souls of living mortals he has captured and made his own. It was when Ntxwg Nyug was observed to be killing people as fast as they were born that Siv Yis arose to challenge him with the arts of healing. And so the struggle continues today between the forces of death and the forces of healing.[80]

                     Gary Yia Lee and Nicholas Tapp

---

[80] Lee and Tapp, 31.

Hmong animists believe that Satan (*Ntxwgnyoog*) is the second highest and most powerful spiritual being besides God (*Yawmsaub*). Though Hmong animists' knowledge of Satan (*Ntxwgnyoog*) is mainly based on legends and myths, they have a fairly accurate knowledge of who Satan is; except that some believe that Satan (*Ntxwgnyoog*) is an "indigenous Hmong spirit" only known by the Hmong while others believe that Satan (*Ntxwgnyoog*) is a universal wicked deity. Hmong animists believe that everything that is bad comes from Satan (*Ntxwgnyoog*). Cha says "He is the originator of all evil forces in both the natural and supernatural worlds."[81] Vincent K. Her says that Satan (*Ntxwgnyoog*) is the lord of the demon world (*dlaabteb*) and he is associated with death. The demon world (*dlaabteb*) over which Satan (*Ntxwgnyoog*) is lord is "a harsh, desolate place, lacking and devoid of life."[82] The spirits that reside in the demon world (*dlaabteb*) often suffer from hunger and depend on the living for subsistence through the regular invitation of the spirits of the dead to join the living at the various festivities.[83] Knowing that the demon world (*dlaabteb*) or the world of darkness is harsh and the spirits of the dead constantly suffer hunger, Hmong animists continue to send their dead there. Her believes that God (*Yawmsaub*) is the grantor of life for the deceased spirits to reborn.[84] His claim is considered an untraditional belief of Hmong animism, as most versions of the Showing the Way chants claim that Satan (*Ntxwgnyoog*) is the grantor of new life for the spirit of the dead to be reborn.

As recently as August 2012, a new breed of Hmong animism called Hmongism was established. The purpose of Hmongism is not to create a new religion of Hmong

---

[81] Ya Po Cha, 136.
[82] Vincent K. Her, 100
[83] Ibid,. 100.
[84] Ibid., 99.

animism, but it is to streamline Hmong animism to eliminate some of the contradictions and to shorten the funeral service by cutting down many rituals that have too many repetitions. However, what is interesting about Hmongism is that the proponents now proclaim that Satan (*Ntxwgnyoog*) is not as bad a deity as Hmong ancestors have always portrayed him to be. The Bylaws of Temple of Hmongism, Article II: Statement of Faith, section 9 states, "We believe that, while we are still researching for more information, *Ntxwg Nyoog* is not as bad a figure as our ancestors have made Him to be, and we believe that *Ntxwg Nyoog* might be the Hmong word for God." While proclaiming that Satan (*Ntxwgnyoog*) is God, they continued to accuse *Ntxwgnyoog* of unleashing sickness and death on mankind. While believing that *Ntxwgnyoog* is not as bad as their ancestors have portrayed him to be, they now prefer to guide their dead to God's Kingdom of Heaven instead of sending the dead to the demon world (*dlaabteb*) or, in other words, the parched sky dried land, frozen sky darkness land (*ntuj qhua teb nkig, ntuj txag teb tsaus*) where Satan (*Ntxwgnyoog*) is lord and ruler, as Hmong animists always have done. In their revised version of the Showing the Way chant, they avoid using the traditional terms "*dlaabteb (demon world), ntuj qhua teb nkig, ntuj txag teb tsaus* (parched sky dried land, frozen sky darkness land), or the world of darkness. Instead they guide the dead to the Kingdom of Heaven (*Ntuj Ceebtsheej*) to reside with the Heavenly Ruler (*Tswv Ntuj*).[85] The term *Ntuj Ceebtsheej* (Du Jengcheng) was used primarily by Hmong Christians to refer to the Kingdom of Heaven. This term is rarely used by Hmong animists either during their normal conversation or at funeral service. Whenever they use this term, they use it only to mock Christianity, Hmong Christians, and God.

---

[85] Hmongism, "The Bylaws of Temple of Hmongism," http://www.hmongism.org (accessed September 18, 2013).

Hmong Animism

Hmong Christians believe that the Kingdom of Heaven (*Ntuj Ceebtsheej*) is created by God (*Yawmsaub*) exclusively for people who believe in Jesus Christ as their Lord and Savior and believe that God (*Yawmsaub*) is the Creator of all things. However, now Hmong animists who completely deny Jesus Christ and God the Creator also want to send their dead to God's Kingdom of Heaven.[86] This new idea of Hmong animism shows a stark contrast to its traditional belief. They continue to believe that Satan (*Ntxwgnyoog*) is the grantor of life and guide the one spirit that will be reborn to *Ntxwgnyoog*, but the spirit that is to remain with its ancestors is guided to God's Kingdom of Heaven (*Ntuj Ceebtsheej*) far away from the world of darkness where Satan (*Ntxwgnyoog*) is the lord and ruler and where its ancestors are.

The claim that the word *Ntxwgnyoog* "might be the Hmong word for God" warrants further scrutiny. Hmong animists have always differentiated *Ntxwgnyoog* from *Yawmsaub*. They always associated *Ntxwgnyoog* with evilness and *Yawmsaub* with goodness.[87] Hmong Christians always understand that *Ntxwgnyoog* is Satan and *Yawmsaub* is God. There is no dispute that *Ntxwgnyoog* is the evil deity that the Bible called Satan and *Yawmsaub* is the good God who created the universe as the Bible claims. It is very clear from the discussions above that Hmong animists believe that *Ntxwgnyoog* is the Evil One and all evils originated from him.[88] To say that Satan (*Ntxwgnyoog*) is the Hmong word for God is blasphemy of God's (*Yawmsaub's*) holy name. It is a direct insult tantamount to character assassination of His goodness and holiness. The claim that Satan (*Ntxwgnyoog*) is not as bad as Hmong ancestors have always portrayed him to be does not change the view that Satan (*Ntxwgnyoog*)

---

[86] Ibid., "Zaj Taw Kev (Showing the Way chant)."
[87] Vincent K. Her, 100.
[88] Ya Po Cha, 136; Lee and Tapp, 31.

is the Evil One. This claim will only invite criticism from informed people that Hmong animists don't really know who *Ntxwgnyoog* (Satan) is even though they have worship him for thousands of years. Stanza 3 of the revised version of the Showing the Way of the Hmongism says:

> Now (name of the deceased), long ago, in the beginning when heaven and earth were created, mankind did not know how wide or narrow the world was, mankind asked the frog to measure the world to find out how wide or narrow heaven was and how wide or narrow the earth was. Upon returning from measuring heaven and earth, the frog said heaven was as narrow as a rocky cave, the earth was as narrow as the tree hole, and it was neither enough for mankind to live nor for demons to gather. Unhappy, mankind asked the black eagle to measure heaven and earth. Upon returning, the black eagle said heaven and earth were so big and wide, neither would mankind overpopulate it nor would demons be able to fill it. Mankind was angry and struck at the frog three times, and the frog died face down. Therefore, Satan (*Ntxwgnyoog*) unleashed sickness and death down to the earth. As a result, Tong Chai Sheeyee (*Tooj Nchai Sivyig* – another name for *Sivyig the first shaman*) was not able to cure the sickness nor able to raise the dead. Translation is the author's.

By claiming that Satan (*Ntxwgnyoog*) is not as bad as he is portrayed by the ancestors is in direct contradiction of their own belief that Satan (*Ntxwgnyoog*) is the Evil One who unleashed sickness and death to mankind as stated in their revised version of the Showing the Way chant.[89]

SATAN (*NTXWGNYOOG*) THE ORIGINATOR OF ALL EVILS

The central theme that constitutes the origin of all evils is the sickness and death that Satan caused to affect mankind. The *Sivyig* myths and the Showing the Way chants provide conflicting accounts about the original sickness and death, but both agree that Satan (*Ntxwgnyoog*) perpetrated them on mankind. From this catastrophic event, the whole world changed and humankind has since been plagued with all kinds of evil things in addition to sickness and death. Though Hmong animists rarely explicitly attribute human conflicts and hardships to Satan, they implicitly acknowledge that this catastrophic event triggered all kinds of negative consequences to human beings. If they believe that all evil things come from Satan, then every imaginable bad thing – war, murder, disagreement, famine, natural disaster, just to name a few – that mankind faces in the world is attributable to Satan.[90] In the Showing the Way chant, Satan (*Ntxwgnyoog*) is seen as the wicked deity because he unleashed sickness and death and all other human hardships on mankind. In shamanism, Satan (*Ntxwgnyoog*) is portrayed as the "Savage One" that not only unleashed sickness and death upon mankind, but he was believed to capture the human spirits, keep them as his cattle, and kill and eat them.[91]

---

[89] Hmongism, "Zaj Taw Kev (Showing the Way chant)."

[90] Vincent K. Her, 198.

[91] Jacques Lemoine, "Commentary: The (H)mong Shaman's Power of Healing: Sharing the Esoteric Knowledge of a Great Mong Shaman," *Hmong Studies Journal* 12 (2011), 27.

LIFE BEGINS AND ENDS WITH SATAN (*NTXWGNYOOG*)

Satan (*Ntxwgnyoog*) is everything for the Hmong animists. He is the Evil One that unleashed sickness and death to mankind, unleashed rain that caused the universal flood that destroyed the whole earth, and eats human spirits that he captured and raised as his cattle in his heavenly ranch. But on the other hand, life begins and ends with him. There is nothing more telling of this belief than the Showing the Way chant and shamanism. The Showing the Way chant teaches that the human spirit could not die. It is immaterial and immortal and could live with or without the human body. But each time the human body that the spirit resides in dies, the spirit has to return to Satan (*Ntxwgnyoog*) to ask for a new life permit and only when it obtains one, would it be allowed return to earth to reborn. Therefore, they believe that the human body is new, but the human spirit is old and recycling time after time in an endless reincarnation process.[92]

On the other hand, shamanism teaches that human spirit has substance and is mortal. The spirit does not resemble the human image, but it is believed to have the body form of a chicken, goat, horse, reindeer, bull, or other kinds of animals and insects. If one of these spirits is captured by the demons, shaman could barter for the return of the spirit by sacrificing an animal to appease the demons that keep the spirit captive. In this case, the animal is sacrificed and the spirit of the animal is given to the demons as a substitute for the human spirit. But if the spirit is being captured by Satan (*Ntxwgnyoog*), Hmong animists believe that Satan is keeping it as his cattle to be slaughtered and consumed by him.[93] According to Lee and Tapp, the "heavenly cattle" of

---

[92] Bertrais, 44-45.
[93] Lemoine, 27.

Satan (*Ntxwgnyoog*) are the spirits of the living people that he captured.[94] While the spirits are being kept captive, the bodies experience sickness or other health problems, but they are still alive. When Satan slaughters and consumes the spirit, death is certain for the person whose spirit is being killed and consumed by Satan. The teaching of shamanism that Satan eats human spirits implies that human spirits have flesh or spiritual flesh. Without flesh, there's nothing for Satan (*Ntxwgnyoog*) to eat. This contradicts the teaching of the Showing the Way chant that says spirit is immaterial. The belief that Satan (*Ntxwgnyoog*) eats human spirits also contradicts the Showing the Way chant that teaches that when a person dies, his spirit has to be guided to Satan to request a new permit from him (*Ntxwgnyoog*) to be reborn. The question is if Satan (*Ntxwgnyoog*) keeps a herd of heavenly cattle that are the spirits of the living human beings to be killed and consumed, what then is the rationale for guiding the spirit of the deceased directly to Satan? What is the rationale for believing that Satan (*Ntxwgnyoog*) will grant the spirit a new permit to be reborn? If he loves eating human spirits, wouldn't he rather keep all of the spirits that reached him as his livestock to be killed and consumed? Again, if Satan eats human spirits then what is left of a spirit after being consumed by Satan to be reborn? According to human experience, anything that is consumed is gone and it could never be recovered again. What then is the belief that even when a spirit is being completely eaten, the same spirit is still alive to be reborn? What kind of religion is Hmong animism that on the one hand teaches that Satan (*Ntxwgnyoog*) is the "Savage One"[95] who unleashed sickness and death to humankind, but on the other hand, he is the one who is

---

[94] Lee and Tapp, 31.
[95] Quincy, 91.

The Belief that Satan (Ntxwngyoog) is the Evil Deity

sought out to grant a permit to be reborn?[96] Again, while believing that Satan kills human spirits and eats them, why do they still send all of the spirits of their loved ones to this spirit eater Satan (*Ntxwgnyoog*)? Furthermore, what kind of a belief system is this in which on the one hand *Ntxwgnyoog* is believed to be a spirit eater, but on the other hand, he is believed to be a life grantor? For these reasons, it can be argued that Hmong animism is a religion of contradictory. Confusion is Hmong animism. And for Hmong animism, life begins and ends with Satan (*Ntxwgnyoog*) who is believed to be the spirit eater as well as life grantor.

---

[96] All of the "Showing the Way" chants teach that Satan (*Ntxwgnyoog*) is the grantor of a new life for the spirit of the dead to be reborn, except Vincent Kou Her's version of the chant. It is not improbable that he might have changed the content from *Ntxwgnyoog* to *Yawmsaub* in his version.

CHAPTER 5

THE BELIEF IN THE REINCARNATION OF THE SPIRIT

Most writers prefer to use the word "Soul" when referring to the immortal and immaterial part of the person that makes a human a complete being. The Webster New World College Dictionary defines "soul" as follows: 1) an entity which is regarded as being the immortal or spiritual part of the person and, though having no physical or material reality, is credited with the functions of thinking and willing, and hence determining all behavior; 2) the moral or emotional nature of a human being. It also defines "spirit" as follows: 1) a. the life principle, esp. in human beings, originally regarded as inherent in the breath or as infused by a deity; b. soul; 2) the thinking, motivating, feeling part of a person, often as distinguished from the body; mind; intelligence; 3) life, will, consciousness, thought, etc.., regarded as separate from matter. Based on the definitions above, the "soul" and "spirit" are essentially one and the same. This is probably the reason why most writers used both words interchangeably and most writers who write about Hmong animism prefer to use the word "soul" rather than "spirit" in reference to the immortal or spiritual part of a human.

How do Hmong animists define "soul" and "spirit?" Not many writers about Hmong animism have attempted to define how Hmong animists believe about the soul and the spirit. Ya Po Cha defined the soul and spirit as follows: "A soul (*plig*) is the spirit that lives in the body to keep the body alive. It is like an invisible body double that resides in the body. As a spirit, it is immortal." He goes on to say that Hmong animists believe that each person has "three main souls called plee (*plig*) and many lesser souls called ju (*ntsuj*.)" Other writers define the lesser souls as shadows.[97] These are typical Hmong animists' beliefs about the soul and spirit. Both are essentially one and the same. Though Hmong animists believe that each person has multiple spiritual beings, such beliefs do not necessary constitute the tripartite nature of human beings taught by Christianity. Hmong animists believe that the physical person comprises the mind, emotion, and will and the spirit comprises the other half of the body, making Hmong animism a bipartite nature of a person.

Figure 5.1: Represents the bipartite nature of a person Hmong animists believe comprise a human being.

How do Hmong Christians define "soul" and "spirit"? Taken from one of my pastor's sermons, Dr. Timothy T. Vang, Senior Pastor at Hmong American Alliance Church,

---

[97] Ya Po Cha, 148.

he defines the soul as ju (*ntsuj*) and spirit as plee (*plig*). The soul or *ju* is the emotion, feeling, thinking, and mind of the person. The spirit is the immortal and immaterial part of the human being that imparted by God. He believes in the tripartite nature of a person that reflects the trinity of God the Father, the Son, and the Holy Spirit.[98]

How do Bible scholars define "soul" and "spirit?" Joseph Bohac defines these two entities as follows: "The Spirit is generally considered as that part of man that came from God as he breathed into the nostrils of His creation as recorded in Genesis 2:7." "The soul of man is that which is comprised of the **mind** (intellect), the **emotions** (feelings), and the **will** (volition.)"[99] Jessie Penn-Lewis goes further to say that the soul is the "meeting place, the point of union between body and spirit." The body is the seat of the soul whereas the soul is the "vessel of the spirit."[100] The soul relates to the external world of sense through the body and the body connects to the spiritual world through the soul.

Figure 5.2: Represents the tripartite nature of a person as the Scripture describes it.

---

[98] Timothy T. Vang, Sermon at Hmong American Alliance Church, June 23, 2013.

[99] Joseph Bohac, Ph.D. *Human Development: A Christian* Perspective (Ramona: Vision Publishing, 1993), 18.

[100] Jessie Penn-Lewis, *Soul & Spirit: How to Find Freedom from the Tyranny of the Soul* (New Kensington: Whitaker House, 1997), 7-17.

Based on these definitions, I prefer to use the word "spirit" when referring to the animating, immortal, or immaterial part of a person. However, from time to time the word "soul" may be used to refer to the immortal spirit as well if direct quote is necessary.

NEWBORN AND THE SPIRIT

The two most important events in the life of a Hmong animist are the birth and death of the person. These are the occasions when the spirit of the person matters the most. The former is when the spirit makes the person a full human and the latter is when the spirit that makes the person a full human departs. The first occasion is when the newborn brings happiness and joy to the family. The second occasion is when the family members and loved ones mourn over the departure of the person. They will also become fearful of the body because they believe that as soon as someone is dead, the spirit of the person becomes a demon.

Hmong animists believe that a baby is born without a spirit. From the point of conception to three days after birth, the infant is not a complete human being because the infant is without a spirit. At this stage, the body and the spirit are two entirely separate entities and a person becomes whole only when the two entities join together during the spirit calling ritual (*huplig*). Traditionally, Hmong animists do not give a name to their newborn until the spirit calling ceremony. The spirit calling ritual is not only to call in the spirit of the infant; it is also a naming occasion. If the newborn dies before the spirit calling ritual, the child dies without a name because no name has been given. Not only does the child die without a name, but the infant may not even be entitled to a proper funeral service or a burial because the child is not fully human. For some families that often have stillborn babies or infant deaths, they would dig a hole and bury the dead child head down. This is done to despise the reincarnated spirit of the infant and hope that the next child would not die too soon or would not have the same reincarnate spirit. Hmong animists believe that a newborn is without spirit prior to the spirit calling ritual, but if there are frequent stillborn babies or infant deaths, they believe such mishaps are caused either by family curse or by the spirit of the infant who does not accept the biological parents or both. This belief contradicts the claim that an infant does not have spirit until the spirit calling ceremony.

Hmong animists believe that the spirit that lives in the person is foreign to the body. They could only be joined together as one by the spirit calling ritual. Therefore, on the third day after birth, the parents of the newborn have to prepare a spirit calling ceremony (*huplig*) that an elder of the family or a shaman is summoned to conduct. The purpose of the spirit calling ritual is to search for the spirit of the newborn.[101] They believe that the spirit of the newborn is wandering about and cannot find its way to join the body. According to Patricia Symonds, Hmong animists believe that the spirit that is to be called to inhabit the newborn is the spirit of one of the family's ancestors. The spirit calling ritual is the occasion when the spirit of one of their ancestors is called from the world of darkness to come to the world of light to re-unite with a human body.[102] In this case, it is believed that the spirit of one of the ancestors is reincarnated as one of its descendants. A small table is set up inside the threshold of the main door and on the table are a bowl of uncooked rice, two boiled eggs, two boiled chickens, a bottle of wine, and three burning joss sticks. The man stands behind the table inside the front door to perform the spirit calling ritual. The nature of the ritual depends on how articulate the

---

[101] Symonds, 83-91.
[102] Ibid,. 84.

elder or shaman is. Some shamans or elders are very thorough in the search for the spirit of the newborn. He searches for the spirit in every possible place, but others may not be that thorough and only search for the spirit in a few possible places where the spirit of the newborn might be wandering about. The spirit calling has to be very cordial and purposeful in order to entice the spirit to come. The search for the spirit leads the elder or shaman to call the spirit from the edges of the mountains, the river banks, the forests, or even from as far away as the sky above and beyond. The elder or shaman uses the rice, eggs, chickens, wine, and the fragrance of the incense sticks that are burning to entice and lead the spirit to come to indwell the body of the newborn. The spirit that unites with the newborn, does not just to become a part of the body, it becomes the newborn, to be a family member in the loving parents' household, to be a brother or a sister to the older siblings. Besides being a part of the household, the spirit of the newborn has to be dedicated to the household demons, to be accepted by them, in order for them to protect the newborn. Otherwise, the newborn will be considered an unwanted intruder and will meet with a lot of undesirable consequences. According to Patricia Symonds, Hmong animists in Thailand believe that spirit changes sexes at the next reincarnation. The spirit of the female will reincarnate as a male in the family line to maintain the patrilineal of the clan, and the spirit of the male will reincarnate as a female in the next life and be married off to a different clan.[103] However, Hmong animists in the United States do not necessarily believe these claims.

---

[103] Ibid., 21.

CONFLICTING NUMER OF SPIRITS

Hmong animists do not agree on the number of spirits a person has. Most Hmong animists believe that a person has at least three major spirits and several minor spirits. Some believe that there are 12 and still others even believe that a person has up to 32 spirits. In general, Hmong animists believe that a person has three spirits, but regardless of how many spirits a person has, the most important one is the one that the elder or shaman calls in on the third day after birth. It is quite confusing how Hmong animists believe how these spirits come to join the body because on the one hand, they believe that a newborn is without any spirit until the spirit calling ritual, but on the other hand, they believe that two of the three major spirits have already inhabited the newborn at birth. In her book, "Calling in the Soul," Symonds states that Hmong animists believe that the first of the three spirits inhabits the fetus when its bones start to grow in the mother's womb. The second spirit suddenly arrives at the newborn by the force of the wind when the infant takes its first breath immediately following birth. It's only the third spirit that requires the spirit calling ritual. According to Symonds, Hmong animists believe that this third spirit is the spirit of the ancestor that has been residing in the world of darkness. When the pregnant woman begins her labor, the spirit somehow notices that it is time to be reborn. This spirit then obtains the permit to be reborn from Satan's (*Ntxwgnyoog's*) personal secretary, *Nyuj Vaab Tuam Teem* (Nyiu Vang Toua Teng), and waits patiently at the gate of the ancestral village for the moment to be united with the newborn. When the elder or shaman conducts the spirit calling ritual that calls for the spirit, it immediately comes out of the world of darkness to indwell the body of the infant.[104] This explanation of

---

[104] Ibid, 94.

The Belief in the Reincarnation of the Spirit

how a spirit comes to join the body is in direct conflict with the teaching of the Showing the Way chant. According to the Showing the Way chant, the spirit that is to be reincarnated is neither the one that stays at the grave nor the one that is guided to the world of darkness to stay with the ancestors. It rather is the one that is guided to get a new letter of provision, a permit of a new life, to be reborn from Satan (*Ntxwgnyoog*) during the funeral. Therefore, to say that the reincarnate spirit is coming from the world of darkness contradicts the popular belief that this spirit will stay there forever with its ancestors. And according to the Showing the Way chant, the spirit that will be reincarnated does not wait until the time of reborn to obtain the new letter of provision from Satan, but it has already obtained it during the 13 days of journey to meet Nyiu Vang Toua Teng (*Nyuj Vaab Tuam Teem*) at Satan's palace. The explanation also contradicts the belief that this "to be reincarnate spirit" becomes a wandering spirit after the performance of the release of the spirit ritual (*tso plig*). Therefore, the spirit calling chanter has to search for it in the depth of the forest, at the river banks, on the mountain sides, and in the sky above and beyond in order to find it and bring it home to unite with the body of the newborn.

Hmong animists believe that the newborn is without a spirit and is an incomplete human. Therefore, the spirit calling ritual is necessary to install the spirit. But as stated above, they also believe that by the first breath immediately following birth a newborn already has two spirits indwelling the body. If this is what they truly believe, then the stillborn or the infant that dies before the spirit calling ritual is not without a spirit. In fact, it already has two spirits. Therefore, not providing a proper funeral service or a burial is inhumane.

Jacques Lemoine states that his informant, a Hmong shaman Tchue Yao Xiong (*Tsuj Yob Xyooj*), reported that a person has 12 spirits, no more, no less. The following are the 12 spirits Lemoine describes: 1) the "projecting shadow" soul; 2) the "running bull" soul; 3) the "reindeer" soul; 4) the "cicada" soul; 5) the "chicken" soul; 6) the "returning" soul; 7) the "breath" soul; 8) the "source of cucumbers and pumpkins" soul; 9) the "life expectancy" soul; 10) the "sun and moon" soul; 11) the "bamboo" soul; and 12) the "life demanding" soul.[105] Some of these are major spirits and others are minor spirits. Patricia Symonds likened the sun and moon soul to the first spirit that will stay with the body at the grave, the breath soul as the wandering spirit that will return to remain forever in the world of darkness upon death, and the returning soul as the reincarnated spirit.[106] However, Ya Po Cha states that his father, who also is a shaman, insisted that a person has 32 spirits. Cha describes that each body part has its own spirit in order to keep the body in balance of health. Though many, there are only three major spirits and the rest are minor spirits and "they become lost when the host body perishes."[107] The Showing the Way chant makes no mention of the minor spirits, but it states that in addition to the three spirits, a person also has seven shadows and they die with the body.[108]

In the Hmong language, there are words that can be split and still have the same meaning and there are other words that when split have totally different meanings. For example, the word *kwvtij* (*ku-tee*) means "relatives," but when the word is split into two words then the word *kwv* means younger brother or someone who is younger than you are and not necessarily related. The word *tij* becomes a title of respect for a person who is older than you and also not necessarily related. If the word *laug* (*lau*) is added to the word *tij* to form another word *tijlaug* (*tee-lau*) then it means "older

---

[105] Lemoine, 7, 21.
[106] Symonds, 21.
[107] Ya Po Cha, 148 -149.
[108] Bertrais, 49.

brother." In Hmong, the complete word for spirit is "*ntsujplig*" ("ju-plee"), but the word "*ntsujplig*" could be split into two words "*ntsuj*" (ju) and "*plig*" (plee) and each could stand by itself. By splitting the word, the word *plig* continues to have the same meaning as the spirit, but the word *ntsuj* means soul. However, most Hmong are unable to distinguish between the individual essences of spirit and soul, so they mostly use the word "soul" in the place of "spirit." For example, Cha explains, "A human being, though, has three main souls called plee (*plig*) and many lesser souls called ju (*ntsuj*)."[109] He believes that the ju are lesser spiritual beings and they disappear or become nothing when the person dies, but the *plig* are major spirits that never die. The Showing the Way chant splits the word *ntsujplig* into two separate words, but only to augment the impact and the meaning of the word, and the two words still carry the same meaning of "spirit." For example, stanza 19 Yang Chong Chee's version of the Showing the Way Chant says *ib tug neeg peb (3) tug ntsuj peb (3) tug plig* (one person three souls (*ju*) three spirits (*plig*)), but the stanza immediately before says "one person three souls (ju)" and leaves the three spirits (*plig*) out, but it still has the same meaning as three spirits (*plig*) or three souls (ju), which Cha describes as the main spirits.[110] The word "*ntsuj*" by itself should be understood as "soul" and the word "*plig*" by itself should be understood as "spirit." However, due to the belief in the bipartite nature of a human being, Hmong animists understand that the soul and spirit are one and the same and the body is the other half of the person. Grammatically, the word "*ntsuj*" could also be used as a prefix for other words such as *dluab, xyw*. The word "*dluab*" has two meanings: 1) shadow; 2) picture. The word "*xyw*" means a ghost-like image, but it is believed to be a

---

[109] Ya Po Cha, 148.
[110] Bertrais, 44-45.

spiritual being. When the word "*ntsuj*" is prefixed with the word "*plig*" (*ntsujplig*), it makes a more complete word for "spirit." When the word "*ntsuj*" is combined with the word "*dluab*" (*ntsujdluab*), it means a "shadowy spiritual being." The *ntsujdluab* or shadow here is thought to be a spiritual being that has a property or essence similar to the spirit, but Hmong animists believe that the *ntsujdluab* is a minor spiritual being. Hmong also have another spiritual being called "*xyw*" (xu). Hmong imagine the xu (*xyw*) to have a ghost-like body form. However, when expanding the word *xyw*, to "*ntsujmaag fuabxyw*" (ju-maa fua-xu), the term implies a breath-like spiritual being. It is like the breath of life which has no bodily substance. When the person stops breathing, the person dies and the spirit flies away. All of these spiritual beings are believed to be personal spirits. Hmong animists believe that a person has to have all of these spiritual beings. This is the reason why Hmong animists contend that a person has up to 32 spirits.

Again, while Hmong animists believe that a person has many spirits, they cannot agree on how many spirits a person actually has. Some believe that every part of the body has its own spirit. For examples, the arm has its own spirit as well as the fingers, the head, the foot, and so on. They also cannot agree on the names of these spirits. Some believe that the *ntsuj* is a separate spiritual being and it is lower than the *plig* while others believe that the *ntsuj* and the *plig* are one and the same. When the elder or shaman performs the spirit calling ritual, he does use the plural form to indicate that he is calling several spirits for the newborn. In fact, he calls twelve of them. But in life and in general speaking, Hmong never say to a person "your spirits" or in Hmong "*koj cov plig*," they always refer to "your spirit" or "*koj tug plig*," which is singular. When the elder or shaman calls for the spirit of the newborn, he usually uses plural form to imply that he is calling many spirits, but he never calls them by

The Belief in the Reincarnation of the Spirit

their individual names. Hmong do use hyperbole to imply overemphasis and the plural form of words are usually used for that purpose, but it does not necessarily mean that the subject referred to is more than one. For example, Hmong sometimes use the word "*peb*" or "we" instead of "*kuv*" or "I" to exaggerate position, power and authority, or presence. Patricia Symonds records the actual chant of the spirit calling rites as follows:

> Today is a good day to receive,
> tonight is a good night to call,
> I call this child Qig – his twelve reindeer souls
> Which may have stood wavering on the mountains
> and on the sides of the mountains
> To get up. Come, get up.
> There are chickens and eggs
> on the doorstep to guide the hands,
> And there are eggs on the doorstep to guide the feet.
> I call Qig to get up and to return
> to have a mother and father,
> To have a place to live and to sleep,
> To be a brother to the hearth pole,
> Get up and return.[111]

If a person has 12 different spirits as Lemoine reports, shouldn't the performer of the spirit calling ritual call each and every one of them by their names? Would it make more sense if each of the twelve spirits is different from one another? Why does a newborn need twelve reindeer souls or twelve of the same spirits (*12 tug nyuj cab nyuj kaus*)? This may only be a statement of hyperbole. The elder or shaman does not actually call for twelve of the same spirits for the newborn. But if this is what they actually believe, it

---

[111] Symonds, 85.

is contrary to the teaching of the Showing the Way chant. In the last two versions of the Showing the Way chant discussed below, both mention that a person has three spirits and seven shadows. Why at the beginning of a person's life, the newborn needs twelve of the same spirits or even 32 of them, but during the course of life, these 12 of the same spirits changed names, and at the end of the person's life, the Showing the Way chant tells the deceased that he only has three spirits and seven shadows?[112] These conflicting accounts contribute to the confusion about how many spirits a person actually has.

ANCESTRAL SPIRIT OR WILD SPIRIT

Who really is the spirit of the newborn? Is it a spirit of an ancestor or a wild spirit? Though Hmong animists believe that the spirit of the newborn is a spirit of one of their own ancestors, the elder or shaman, who performs the spirit calling ritual, makes no explicit call for the spirit of the ancestor to come to indwell the child. Ya Po Cha says, "The main cross beam (*nqaaj nthaab*) that runs horizontally across and through the middle of the house is where all the ancestors (*dlaab nam dlaab txiv*) dwell."[113] Lee and Tapp believe that the living family connects to the ancestors through the center pole, implying that the spirits of the ancestors live in the center pole.[114] Patricia V. Symonds and Anne Fadiman also say that the spirits of the ancestors reside inside the house, but they are in the corner pillars instead of the cross beam or the center pole.[115] On the other hand, wild spirits are

---

[112] Bertrais, 44; Symonds, 264.
[113] Ya Po Cha, 138.
[114] Lee and Tapp, 37.
[115] Symonds, 12; Anne Fadiman, *The Spirit Catches You And You Fall Down: A Hmong Child, Her American Doctors, and the Collision of Two Cultures* (New York: Farrar, Straus and Giroux, 1997), 282.

The Belief in the Reincarnation of the Spirit

everywhere else beyond the doors and walls of the house. Patricia V. Symonds says that Hmong animists believe that "wild spirits live in the fields and the forest, in trees and rivers and rocks."[116] If Hmong animists truly believe that the spirit of the newborn is a reincarnated spirit of one of their own ancestors, the search for the newborn's spirit should not have gone beyond the inside walls of the family's house. When the calling for the spirit of the newborn reaches the edges of the mountains, the river banks, the depths of the forests and the sky above and beyond, the search could not be considered a call for the reincarnated spirit of the ancestor. It seems that the elder or shaman is calling for some wild spirit to become the spirit of the newborn. Otherwise, the elder or shaman would not chant, "I called this child Qig – his twelve reindeer souls, which may have stood wavering on the mountains and on the sides of the mountains."[117]

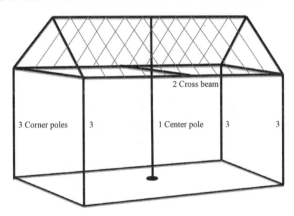

Figure 5.3: The ancestral spirits are believed to reside inside the house, but Hmong animists cannot agree on where the actual aboding place of the ancestors is. The three areas suggested as the aboding places of the ancestors are identified by the numeric numbers above: 1) Gary Yia Lee and Nicholas Tapp believe that ancestral spirits reside in the center pole;

---

[116] Symonds, 18
[117] Ibid., 85.

2) while Ya Po Cha says they are in the cross beam; and 3) Anne Fadiman and Patricia Symonds state that they reside in the four corner poles.

The belief that the spirit of the newborn is the spirit of one of their ancestors also contradicts the Showing the Way chant. In his Doctoral Dissertation, Vincent Kou Her writes the last stanza of the Showing the Way chant as follows:

> In good spirits, you have finally arrived
> in the Upper Realm of Yawm Saub.
> You will now seek a new letter,
> a document to begin fresh life on earth.

If Yawm Saub presents you the life of a chicken, you should refuse, stating: As a chicken on earth, the fear of having my throat slit is constant and assured.
I would rather not be one.

As he assigns you the life of a pig, strongly reject it: As a pig, death by the blade is certain. I cannot accept that.

When he offers you the life of a dog, clearly state: On earth, a dog faces frequent beatings. I do not want such a fate.

As soon as he hands you a document to live as a bull, you should tell him: As a bull, how could I tolerate the harsh work on the field, pulling the plow that rips open the earth?

If he makes you a horse, quickly decline it: A horse is an animal people would ride. I must refuse that offer.

Finally, he will then inquire: What is it that you want to be?

You will reply:

The Belief in the Reincarnation of the Spirit

> I want to be a "npauj kaab quas ntxi," or moth.
> On rainy days, I could just hang leisurely
> on the underside of a house beam.
> When the sun rises, I can fly away,
> drifting freely with the wind.
> Just like that, I can return to see
> my children as they toil the land.
>
> I want a document to be a beautifully colored moth.
> When it rains, I could just rest,
> clinging to the underside of a thatch leave.
> As the sun reappears, I can take flight,
> soaring through the air.
> Like so, I would be on my way to visit my children, to see them work, trying to satisfy the needs of this earthly realm.

He explains that the reason there is a strong desire to be a moth is that a moth can transform from one kind of insect to another, symbolizing "a life without suffering." If this is true, many Hmong animists who died would have been re-animated as moths in their next life. Surely a moth could undergo metamorphosis, but to claim that "moth faces no death" is completely inaccurate. In fact, a moth lives only a short life and then dies. With regards to reincarnate back to the family line, he explains that the desire to return to earth to be with one's children is not necessarily through reincarnation as a new person in the family line, but it could be reconnected spiritually.[118] These explanations are in conflict with the popular belief that all spirits of the dead are destined for reincarnation as humans.

Another version of the Showing the Way chants states as follows:

---

[118] Vincent K. Her, 125.

> You lived this life, you were poor, did not live to an old age; you should remember to get your letter of provision, the mandate for a new life. To get the letter of provision to be a dog, you are afraid to be beaten; to be a pig, you are afraid to be killed; to be a bull, you are afraid having to carry heavy load; to get a letter of provision to be a horse, you are afraid to be ridden; to be an insect or a bird, you are afraid they will shoot you or kill you. You should remember in your mind, recognize in your heart that you will search for it at the center, that's where the letter of provision for leadership is. You arrive at *Nyuj Vaab Tuam Teem* (Nyiu Vang Toua Teng). You should search deep in the depth of the sea because that's where the letter for lordship is.[119] (Translation is the author's)

In this version of the Showing the Way chant, the spirit of the deceased is to look for the letter of provision for leadership and lordship, but nothing is said about returning to the family line.

A third version of the Showing the Way chant was collected by Patricia V. Symonds from the Hmong animists in Thailand. She states the following: #159.

> Now *Txawj Nkiag* (Cher Gia, the title of the chanter of the Showing the Way chant) has taken you to exchange for a new letter of provision from *Nyuj Vaab Tuam Teem* (Nyiu Vang Toua Teng) at his palace. Therefore, *Txawj Nkiag* is taking you back to earth.

---

[119] Bertrais, 45.

Remember in your heart that *Txawj Nkiag* will send you to be reborn as a leader and lord for the Chinese so that your life will be more prosperous.[120] (Translation is the author's)

Again, this version of the Showing the Way chant does not mention anything about reincarnate back to the family line after getting the letter of provision for a new life from Satan. Instead, the chant tells the deceased's spirit to reincarnate in another ethnic; the very people that had persecuted and attempted to exterminate the Hmong for over several thousands of years. To claim that the spirit of the newborn is a spirit of one of the family's ancestors is inconsistent and contradictory to the teachings of the Showing the Way chant.

Furthermore, when Hmong animists perform the release of the spirit ritual (*tso plig*) so that the spirit is free to be reincarnated, they never ask the spirit of their dead to reincarnate back to the family line either.[121]

By all accounts, it seems the spirit that the elder or shaman is calling for the newborn is not an ancestral spirit, but it is a wild spirit coming from the forest or the sky above

BORN WITH OR WITHOUT SPIRIT

If it is true that humans are born without a spirit then the spirit calling ritual is necessary in order to impart the spirit in the body. If this is true, then almost all of the people living on earth today are without personal spirits because probably only the Hmong animists perform spirit calling ritual. But while Hmong animists believe that their infants are born without spirit, they don't necessary believe that the same principle is applicable for every other group of people.

---

[120] Symonds, 262
[121] Lee and Tapp, 34.

They believe that spirit calling ritual is by and for the Hmong animists only. But then they are contradicting themselves because they do not believe that other groups of people have to have some kind of spirit calling ritual for their newborns. By this, they agree with those who believe that the spirit is imparted in the fetus at the moment of conception, or with those who believe that human beings do not have spirits, thereby making the spirit calling ritual effectively irrelevant and unnecessary. This is a distorted cosmological view that has no universal truth.

Another point of contradiction is the belief that the first three days following birth is the most vulnerable period for the infant because the newborn is without the protective third spirit.[122] Hmong shamanism teaches that demons or malevolent spirits could only capture the spirit of the person, not the physical body. The body dies as a result of the spirit being killed by demons (*dlaab*) or Satan (*Ntxwgnyoog*). If the child is without spirit during this period, the infant should be free from such danger because there is nothing in the infant for the demons or malevolent spirits to capture.[123] Concern about the danger of being captured by evil demons should only start after and not before the impartation of the spirit by the spirit calling ritual.

IMPRACTICALITY OF THE SPIRIT CALLING RITUAL

The social and health systems in the United States make it impractical to conduct the spirit calling ritual as prescribed. In the United States, no baby is delivered at home, all are delivered at the hospital, and some infants and mothers are required to stay at the hospital longer for various health

---

[122] Symonds, 83.
[123] Lemoine, 27.

reasons, so it is practically and religiously impossible to meet the rigid requirement of the spirit calling ritual exactly three days following birth. Some might say that adaptation to the social and cultural environments is necessary. But that would indicate that the belief that the spirit calling ritual is required becomes unnecessary.

HMONG ANIMISM'S REJECTION OF GOD

It is true that each ethnic group has its own religion and culture peculiar to themselves. Hmong animism is peculiar to the Hmong animists. Though Hmong have practiced animism for thousands of years, this does not mean that what they believe and practice is both good and right. What Apostle Paul says is very true; Romans 1:20: "For since the creation of the world God's invisible qualities – his eternal power and divine nature – have been clearly seen, being understood from what has been made, so that people are without excuse." As natural theologians such as R. C. Sproul, John Gerstner, and Arthur Lindsley have argued, "Paganism is established upon the basis of a thorough going rejection of the knowledge of God the Father," Hmong animism rejects God because it accepts Satan as its Supreme Being – life begins and ends with him. The refusal to acknowledge and give glory to *Yawmsaub* as the God in the Bible is not because they don't know Him (*Yawmsaub*), but simply because they just don't "like the God who is"[124] because they are the chosen ones of Satan (*Ntxwgnyoog*). Hmong animists know that *Yawmsaub* is the Creator of heaven and earth, but they just don't want to glorify Him as the Creator God. Therefore,

---

[124] Arthur Lindsley, John Gerstner, and R. C. Sproul, *Classical Apologetics: A Rational Defense of the Christian Faith and a Critique of Presuppositional Apologetic* (Grand Rapids: Zondervan Publishing House, 1984), 39.

they have to replace Him with some fictitious human characters and the frog as the creators. As Romans 1: 21 says, "For although they knew God, they neither glorified him as God nor gave thanks to him, but their thinking became futile and their foolish hearts were darkened." Hmong animists know that *Yawmsaub* is the good God and *Ntxwgnyoog* is the wicked spiritual being, but they choose to shun God (*Yawmsaub*) and worship Satan (*Ntxwgnyoog*). Hmong animists believe that every physical illness is the result of one's spiritual condition and that is true because they are being oppressed by the demons. Even so, they continue to live in darkness under the oppressive authority of Satan. Hmong animists claim that what they believe and practice is the right thing for the Hmong, but the truth is because they refuse to acknowledge God, worship God, and give glory to God who created them, so God gave them away to Satan. Satan becomes their god as Hmongism says, "*Ntxwgnyoog* might be the Hmong (animists') word for God." This is exactly what the Apostle Paul said in Romans 1:22-23: "Although they claimed to be wise, they became fools and exchanged the glory of the immortal God for images made to look like a mortal human being and birds and animals and reptiles." Hmong animists exchanged God for Satan and so believe that the name of Satan (*Ntxwgnyoog*) is the Hmong word for God. This might be true for Hmong animists, but not for Hmong Christians. Hmong Christians do not exchange the name of Satan (*Ntxwgnyoog*) for God (*Yawmsaub*). Though Hmong animists never make any image for the purpose of worship, but they do worship images made by other religions, particularly Buddhist images. They erect altars and hang fetishes in their houses for household demons and the spirits of their ancestors, hoping that these demons and ancestors would protect them. But as Patricia V. Symonds says, "The ancestors and household spirits, who are the tame spirits, must be treated with honor and respect. They must be

The Belief in the Reincarnation of the Spirit

cared for, or the result can be bad crops, illness, or even death in the household."[125] They worship trees, rocks, mountains, rivers, and so many more. They believe that a tree or a rock has the power to protect, bless, and has eyes to watch over a village.[126] For Hmong animists, the chicken they raise in the chicken coop is their guide. They do not make any major decision without first consult with a sacrifice chicken. Ya Po Cha put it this way:

> A chicken is certainly a guiding light for Hmong. Hmong people believe that a chicken knows everything. Be it personal well-being, impending death, or safe travel, a chicken can foretell the future quite reliably. How it works is very simple, but the chicken has to be young, for older chickens have feet that are too rigid. A chicken the size of a pigeon is ideal. Before the chicken is slaughtered, a lit stick of incense is swirled over the chicken's head. At the same time, the chicken is told what the problem is and what kind of answer is being sought. Then the chicken is slaughtered, dressed and boiled with head and feet intact. As the chicken is cooked, the feet are kept from touching any part of the pot that it is being boiled in. When the chicken is half-cooked, it is taken out to be read. The feet, the tongue, skull and thigh bones are the

---

[125] Symonds, 18.
[126] Ya Po Cha, 144; Nicholas Tapp, Jean Michaud, Christian Culas, and Gary Yia Lee, *Hmong/Miao in Asia* (Chiang Mai: Silkworm Books, 2004), 340-341.

commonly read parts of a chicken. These parts of a chicken hold clues for things to come.[127]

For the Hmong animists, chicken is their guide and the pig they raise in the pig pen, the cow, or water buffalo they raise in the barn or purchased from the slaughter house is their savior. These animals are not only raised for food or to sell for cash, but the most important reason for raising them is to become their saviors when the animals are sacrificed to appease the demons or Satan. The two groups of people considered most important leaders of Hmong animism are the shamans and the people who perform at funeral. Historically, almost all Hmong shamans have no formal education. Even in the United States, most of them have very low education, some with high school education, and very few have higher education. Though many shamans may be highly respected as they play important roles in the Hmong animistic society, not all shamans are highly regarded. Historically, the majority of shamans are the poorest among the poor.[128] Many of them became opium addicts after becoming shamans, as opium is usually served as appreciation for performing the ritual. No shaman has the power of healing. There is no guarantee that the sick will be cured after the shamanic healing ritual. Similarly, the people who lead the animistic funeral rituals are very traditional, mostly with little formal education, and many are alcoholics. When it comes to the teaching of Hmong animism, the most educated are completely relying on the least educated who know very little about universal cosmological views. The most educated blindly accept what the least educated taught them as the truth without any question. The futile about Hmong animism is the blind acceptance that chicken feet,

---

[127] Ya Po Cha, 158-159.
[128] Fadiman, 281.

tongue, and the front skull of the chicken head have divine power,[129] and that animals when sacrificed, can save human life. Hmong animists believe that God (*Yawmsaub*) lives in the highest heaven above and He is above and beyond the power of Satan. Hmong animists often appeal to Him when they are in need of help, but when they are in peace, prosperity, and in good health, they not only forget God, but they deny, mock, and insult Him. We see how futile people's thinking has become when they refuse to acknowledge God and worship Him. For the Hmong animists, not only do they worship God's creation, they worship God's archrival Satan (*Ntxwgnyoog*) who they know has done nothing good for humanity, but caused sickness and death, and also eat human spirits. The spirit calling ritual is not just to call in the spirit for the newborn, it is the time to dedicate the newborn to the household demons to be accepted and protected as part of the family. The main point of the dedication is for the household demons to protect the newborn from malevolent spirits, but who are the malevolent spirits and who are the household demons? Aren't they one and the same? Jesus says in Matthew 12:25-26 that demons, whether tamed or wild, good or bad, are one and the same and they do not fight among themselves. Hmong animists are blinded to this because they do not know the truth. They believe that by dedicating the newborn to the household demons, the infant will be protected from malicious spirits, but in actuality, both the household demons and the wild demons are in cohort to work against the family. Hmong animists believe that sometimes their household demons would barter the spirit of a family member to wild demons for a ransom. This in fact is true and it surely tells the truth that the household demons and the wild demons are one and the same.

---

[129] Ya Po Cha, 158-160.

The spirit calling ritual is the deception of the devil to enslave Hmong animists. All human beings are born with the personal spirit that God imparted at conception. This is in accordance with Genesis 2:7 "Then the Lord God (*Vaajtswv Yawmsaub*) formed a man from the dust of the ground and breathed into his nostrils the breath of life, and the man became a living being." Hmong animists deny God and so they also deny the spirit that God (*Yawmsaub*) already imparted in them. They are Satan's (*Ntxwgnyoog's*) children because the spirits that indwell them come from the demons. When Hmong animists conduct the spirit calling ritual, Satan (*Ntxwgnyoog*) imparts a devil's spirit in the body of the infant, replacing the original spirit God imparted at the conception. This spirit of the devil will make sure that the newborn grows up blind to the knowledge of the true God, but is full of wisdom and knowledge of Satan (*Ntxwgnyoog*) and the demons. This is the reason that Hmong animists are fond of all other religions but Christianity. This is also the reason that until a Hmong animist accepts Jesus Christ as Lord and Savior through conversion and allows God to remove the foreign spirit, which is the spirit of the devil, from the person and restores the original spirit God imparted in the person, no Hmong animist would ever understand, accept, or even acknowledge the existence of the true God.

SCRIPTURAL PERSPECTIVE ON SPIRITUAL IMPARTATION

What does the Holy Scripture say concerning the time when the spirit inhabits the human body? There are many passages in the Scripture that clearly imply when the unborn is fully human and when God imparts the spirit to the fetus. Genesis 2:7 states that when God created the first man, He breathed the breath of life into his nostrils and he became a living being. Bible scholars believe that the breath of life that God breathed into Adam's nostrils was the spirit God imparted to Adam.[130] Christians believe that God continued to create human in the mothers' wombs the same way He created Adam and Eve.[131] Psalm 139:13-16 reveals how God creates human in the mother's womb.

> [13] "For you created my inmost being;
> you knit me together in my mother's womb.
> [14] I praise you because I am fearfully
> and wonderfully made;
> your works are wonderful,
> I know that full well.
> [15] My frame was not hidden from you
> when I was made in the secret place,
> when I was woven together in the depths of the earth.
> [16] Your eyes saw my unformed body;

With Scriptural passages such as this, Christians believe that a developing fetus is fully human and God imparts the spirit to the body at the moment of conception. Each person has only one spirit. The spirit that lives in the body is an intimate part of the person's complete being from the time of conception and it will only depart the body when the person dies. The Scripture says that a person only dies once and after that awaits eternal judgment (Hebrew 9:27). Contrary to the popular belief in reincarnation in Hmong animism, this passage is clear that the spirit does not reincarnate, but awaits eternal judgment after the death of the body. Christians do not believe in the salvation of the reincarnation of the spirit, but only the salvation that the Lord Jesus

---

[130] Bohac, 17.

[131] Lewis B. Smedes, *Mere Morality: What God Expects from Ordinary People* (1983; repr., Grand Rapids: William B. Eerdmans Publishing Company, 2002), 107-108.

Christ has done for them on the cross. According to the "law of non-contradiction," human beings cannot have both the reincarnation of the spirit and the resurrection of the body. If both are true, there will be too many bodies for one spirit to raise from the dead at the second coming of the Lord Jesus Christ. This means that there will be a lot of bodies left in the graves because there are not enough spirits to raise them from the death. Reincarnation is contrary to the teaching of the Gospel of Jesus Christ the Lord of the universe. Therefore, if the Scripture is true then reincarnation of the spirit is false. I believe that the Scripture is the true Word of God and whatever the Scripture says is true. The doctrine of reincarnation is the word of the devil. It is the continue deception of the devil to the fallen human race, particularly the Hmong animists, to make sure that they cannot find their way back to the Lord, their Creator. The truth is there is no reincarnation of the spirit. The spirit that inhabits the body is not a reincarnated spirit. It is the original spirit that God imparted into the human bodies when He created them in the depth of the mothers' wombs. These Scriptural accounts provide solid foundation for Christians to believe that each person has only one spirit from the beginning of life to the end of life. The spirit that God imparts to the person never leaves the body until the moment the person dies. Christians also believe that the spirit is the agent or the part of the person that communicates with God because God is Spirit (John 4:24).

REINCARNATION AS SALVATION OF THE SPIRIT

Hmong animism has never been institutionalized like other religions. It does not require a place for corporate worship service like other religions. The Hmong animist's house is not just a house for the family; it is the place of

The Belief in the Reincarnation of the Spirit

worship. Unlike Christianity, Islam, or other religions that required compulsory service attendance by their followers, Hmong animism never requires such service. Growing up as an animist, one is not required to know anything about his beliefs. One just needs to know some basic rules in order to know how to participate in some functions of the various animistic rituals. It does not have any systematic written formulation of religious teaching, but it has been passed down from generation to generation orally. The most important doctrine fundamental to Hmong animism is the Showing the Way chant and the most important belief of Hmong animism is the reincarnation of the spirit. Other principles include the spirit calling ritual, shamanism, and the funerary rites. Historically, there was never a school to teach anyone about Hmong animism. They learn the core beliefs of animism by observation and participation in funeral rituals, shamanic rituals, weddings, and other animistic functions. However, the Hmong Cultural Center, Inc. was established in August 1992 for such a purpose. Hmong Cultural Center, Inc. in St. Paul, Minnesota could be the first ever non-profit organization established to teach, among other things, Hmong animism. In reality, culture and religion are always mixed. For example, the cultures of the Western World are always mixed with Christianity. Hmong culture is no different. It is very deeply rooted in the religion of Hmong animism. All aspects of Hmong animism can easily be hidden behind the veil of Hmong culture. Every animistic ritual Hmong animists perform inside the circle of Hmong world is religious, but it goes out to the outside world as Hmong culture. The veil of Hmong culture is so thick that outsiders are unable to poke their noses through to see that behind the veil of Hmong culture almost everything Hmong animists called Hmong culture actually is religious. Hmong Cultural Center, Inc. is the recipient of funding from various sources, including the funding from the Minnesota State Arts Board that allocated by the Minnesota State Legislature, to produce teaching materials, including the publication of two books – "Hmong Wedding Procedures" and "Hmong Funeral Procedures" which are the very cores of Hmong religion of animism – to teach Hmong animists and non-Hmong how to perform Hmong animistic funeral and wedding rituals.[132]

Hmong animistic cosmological view is found almost exclusively from the Showing the Way chant. It contains accounts of creation, origin of mankind, universal flood, origin of languages, birth, sickness and death,[133] and reincarnation. The last cosmological view or the belief in reincarnation is the focus in this discussion.

Stanza 18 of Yang Chong Chee's version of the Showing the Way chant talks about reincarnation. It starts:

> Now it seems that you are going to go, if the front door demon couple let you go, then you will be able to go meet your ancestors. You lived this life on earth, you did not live to an old age because Satan has a cruel heart and a wicked heart, you tended your farm by some path, you picked up Satan's sickness by your arm, you tended your farm by some way, and you picked up Satan's death by your hand. Now you have to die.
> You put on a fashionable outfit and go. One person has three spirits and seven shadows. One of the spirits will go to the ancestors. One of the spirits will go up to get the letter of provision for a new life to reincarnate back on the earth. When you wander

---

[132] Hmong Cultural Center, Inc., http://www.hmongcc.org (accessed May 28, 2013).

[133] Timothy T. Vang, 99.

The Belief in the Reincarnation of the Spirit

about to the plain, you will take Satan's silver ladder. When you wander to over there, you will take Satan's golden ladder.

You should remember in your mind, recognize in your heart, you shall remember to go get your letter of provision for a new life from *Nyuj Vaab Tuam Teem* (Nyiu Vang Toua Teng) and return to reborn on the earth, so that you will have a good life.

You will climb the ladder: one day you climb one step, two days you climb two steps, three days you climb three steps, four days you climb four steps, five days you climb five steps, six days you climb six steps, seven days you climb seven steps, eight days you climb eight steps, nine days you climb nine steps, ten days you climb ten steps, eleven days you climb eleven steps, twelve days you climb twelve steps, and thirteen days you climb thirteen steps. Then you have reached the first level of Satan's ladder.

Then you should remember in your mouth, recognize in your mind that you will climb the ladder: one day you climb one step, two days you climb two steps, three days you climb three steps, four days you climb four steps, five days you climb five steps, six days you climb six steps, seven days you climb seven steps, eight days you climb eight steps, nine days you climb nine steps, ten days you climb ten steps, eleven days you climb eleven steps, twelve days you climb twelve steps, and thirteen days you climb thirteen steps. Then you have reached the second level of Satan's ladder.

Then you shall remember in your mouth, recognize in your mind, remember in your heart, and stump it on your feet that you are going to get your letter of provision for a new life, the letter of birth to reborn back on the earth. Then you will still have to climb the ladder: one day you climb one step, two days you climb two steps, three days you climb three steps, four days you climb four steps, five days you climb five steps, six days you climb six steps, seven days you climb seven steps, eight days you climb eight steps, nine days you climb nine steps, ten days you climb ten steps, eleven days you climb eleven steps, twelve days you climb twelve steps, and thirteen days you climb thirteen steps. Then you have reached the third level of Satan's ladder, the *Nyuj Vaab Tuam Teem's* (Nyiu Vang Toua Teng's) place of obtaining the letter of provision for a new life.

You were poor and did not live to an old age in this life. You should remember to go get the letter of provision for a new life. To get the permit to be a dog, you are afraid to be beaten, to get a permit to be a pig, you are afraid to be killed, to get a permit to be a bull, you are afraid having to carry heavy load, to get a permit to be a horse, you are afraid to be ridden, to get a permit to be insect or bird, you are afraid they will shoot you or kill you. You should remember in your mind, recognize in your heart that you will search for it at the center, that's where the letter for leadership is. You arrive at *Nyuj Vaab Tuam Teem* (Nyiu Vang Toua Teng) and you should search deep in the depth of the sea because that's where the letter for lordship is.

After you've gotten your permit for a new life from *Nyuj Vaab Tuam Teem*, you will return to earth. *Txawj Nkiag* will lead you to reborn on earth. Now you have gotten your letter of provision for a new life, you should remember to climb down the ladder: one day you will climb down one step, two days you will climb down two steps, three days you will climb down three steps, four days you will climb down four steps, five days you will climb down five steps, six days you will climb down six steps, seven days you will climb down seven steps, eight days you will climb down eight steps, nine days you will climb down nine steps, ten days you will climb down ten steps, eleven days you will climb down eleven steps, twelve days you will climb down twelve steps, thirteen days you will climb down thirteen steps, and you have climbed down one level of Satan's ladder.

Then you should remember to climb down the ladder: one day you will climb down one step, two days you will climb down two steps, three days you will climb down three steps, four days you will climb down four steps, five days you will climb down five steps, six days you will climb down six steps, seven days you will climb down seven steps, eight days you will climb down eight steps, nine days you will climb down nine steps, ten days you will climb down ten steps, eleven days you will climb down eleven steps, twelve days you will climb down twelve steps, thirteen days you will climb down thirteen steps, and you have climbed down two levels of Satan's ladder.

Then you should remember in your mind, recognize in your heart that you should climb down the ladder: one day you will climb down one step, two days you will climb down two steps, three days you will climb down three steps, four days you will climb down four steps, five days you will climb down five steps, six days you will climb down six steps, seven days you will climb down seven steps, eight days you will climb down eight steps, nine days you will climb down nine steps, ten days you will climb down ten steps, eleven days you will climb down eleven steps, twelve days you will climb down twelve steps, thirteen days you will climb down thirteen steps, and you have arrived back on earth.

You should remember in your mind, recognize in your heart that *Txawj Nkiag* will now lead you to reborn.[134] (Translation is the author's)

This stanza states that a person has three spirits and seven shadows. Other stanzas also include the statement that the shadows die with the body, but the spirits cannot die. Therefore, one spirit will climb Satan's ladder up to Satan's palace to obtain a new mandate for a new life from Satan's personal secretary, *Nyuj Vaab Tuam Teem* (Nyiu Vang Toua Teng), and return to earth to reincarnate. A second spirit is to go to the world of darkness to find its ancestors and when

---

[134] Bertrais, 44-46.

The Belief in the Reincarnation of the Spirit

they are found, the spirit stays there forever with the ancestors. The third spirit is to remain with the body forever at the grave.[135] Stanza 18 is the most important stanza and it's the heart of Hmong animism's doctrine and hope because it contains reincarnation of the spirit. Hmong animism does not have an account of who created the spirits, how, and when they came to existence, but the Showing the Way chant teaches that spirits will not die and they will exist with or without the human bodies. The spirit becomes a wandering spirit until it re-animates in a new body. This spirit will repeat this same process again and again in an endless reincarnation cycle. However, only one of the three spirits is guaranteed a new life through reincarnation. The other two have to spend the rest of their spiritual lives in the grave and in the world of darkness, which means that every time a Hmong animist dies, two spirits are lost forever. Hmong animists fail to realize that if this is true, there would be fewer people born into the world now than a decade or a century ago because there are fewer spirits available to be reincarnated today. However, the opposite is true. There are more people born into the world now than a decade ago, not to mention a century ago. Therefore, the belief and explanation about reincarnation fail. The belief in the reincarnation of the spirit produces both false hope and fear of judgment for Hmong animists. The false hope is the belief that reincarnation is salvation. This gives false hope to the poor or the unfortunate, the oppressed, and the sickly that they may fare better in their next life. But at the same time they also believe that reincarnation is a judgment. Many, who have difficulties in life such as marriage problems, bad health, poverty, low social status, or other personal and social problems, believe that they are being cursed and punished for what they might have done in their previous lives. They also

---

[135] Timothy T. Vang, 119.

believe that the fortune of their next life depends very much on how they live their present life. This is the single most important moral principle that dictates their moral conducts and guides their moral decisions about how to lead their present lives. Many Hmong animists even talk about what they want to be in the next life, but they also believe that it is not a choice they can make. Though Hmong animists believe in reincarnation, no one talks about past life as no one knows who they were in their past lives. If someone says I was this person in my past life, even the Hmong animists who believe in reincarnation would say he is crazy.

The stanza above does not tell how long a spirit has to wander about before it can reincarnate again. Most Hmong animists believe that a deceased's spirit could be reincarnated as soon as it leaves the dead body. They even believe that a person's spirit has already sought reincarnation while the person is gravely ill.[136] For these reasons if there is a birth of a newborn occurring about the same time that someone dies, the parents of the newborn are fearful that the spirit of the deceased might have been re-animated in their newborn. However, according to this stanza of the Showing the Way chant, it seems that the spirit of the deceased has to climb up three levels of Satan's ladders with each level has thirteen steps and the spirit of the deceased has to spend thirteen days to climb up each thirteen steps, so it has to spend 39 days climbing up Satan's ladder in order to reach Satan's palace where it could obtain a new mandate for a new life from *Nyuj Vaab Tuam Teem* (Nyiu Vang Toua Teng). He then has to spend another 39 days coming down the ladder to earth after obtaining the new life mandate before it could find a new set of parents to reincarnate in a new body. In all it takes 78 days to climb up and come down Satan's ladder before the spirit could possibly reincarnate. During these first 78

---

[136] Lee and Tapp, 27.

The Belief in the Reincarnation of the Spirit

days, the spirit cannot wander about, but it has to strictly follow the directives of the Showing the Way chant. This is how one understands it from reading the text or by listening to it at the actual funeral performance. But this is not the way Hmong animists believe and practice. The thirteen days this stanza refers to is actually the first thirteen days after the person has died. The first thirteen days after the death of the person are very important for the Hmong animists as part of the continuation of the funeral service. Hmong animists believe that in thirteen days, not in 78 days, the spirit of the deceased has completed the journey to the realm of Satan (*Ntxwgnyoog*), has obtained the letter of provision for a new life from *Nyuj Vaab Tuam Teem* (Satan's personal secretary), and has arrived back on earth. Therefore, early in the morning of the thirteenth day after the death of the person, family and relatives would go back to the grave to invite the spirit of the dead (*xw plig*) back to visit its home. However, the rule that requires the conduct of the *xw plig* ritual on the 13th day after death has been repeatedly violated, especially in the United States, where funeral service never starts immediately after the death of the person. In most cases, funeral services would not be held until a month after the death of the person. Therefore, the 13th day *xw plig* ritual after death becomes the 13th day *xw plig* ritual after burial. The *xw plig* ritual is never held at the funeral home, as the purpose of the ritual is to bring the spirit back to visit its home. The word "*xw*" means dig out. Therefore, the term "*xw plig*" implies that the spirit is being buried with the body in the grave and it has to be freed from such captivity. In order to set the spirit free, the family has to go to the grave, some groups would drill a hole into the grave, to awaken the spirit and bring it back home for a visit. During the *xw plig* ritual, which lasts for a day, the spirit is represented by a winnowing tray that is covered with one of the dead's own shirt. The spirit is offered food, fruits, wine, and other things. When the feast is over, the family simply tells the spirit to return to the grave. The majority of the Hmong animists believe that this spirit will remain forever with the dead body at the grave. However, some group of Hmong animists believe that this spirit also reincarnates after the *xw plig* ritual. Patricia Symonds even goes further to say that after this ritual, the spirit is told that it no longer is a part of the family and should never come back to the house of the living members.[137] The Hmong animists in the United States do not disown this spirit. For some Hmong animists, this is the spirit that they worship and continue to invite to come back to the house of the living family members on special occasions to eat and drink with them and the family continues to bring food, drinks, and other things to it at the grave for years afterward. It is not unusual to see food, drinks, and other things on the graves of the Hmong animists.

Figure 5.4: This photo was taken during a funeral on August 18, 2013. This is a typical Hmong animist funeral. The photo shows the reed pipe (*qeej*/kheng) player and the drummer playing to entertain the guests. In

---

[137] Symonds, 148.

The Belief in the Reincarnation of the Spirit

the front left is spirit paper money dropping from the ceiling and also hanging on the wooden rack. In front of the casket are female family members. They sit close to the casket to guard the dead to prevent malevolent guests from planting metal objects in the casket or on the deceased's body. Hmong animists believe that metal object or any foreign object that remain in or on the deceased body will cause bad health to the person in the next life. At the funeral, her adopted son spoke to her saying "If it is true that there is reincarnation, I hope that you will reborn as a descendant of the family."

The final ritual the family has to conduct for the dead is the release of the spirit (*tso plig*) ritual so that it is free to reincarnate. Patricia Symonds translated the Hmong term *tso plig* to mean "freeing the soul."[138] In a way, it is. But the word *tso* (pronounced jo) actually means release. Though the spirit that is to be reincarnated is believed to have obtained the new provision for a new life from Satan's personal secretary *Nyuj Vaab Tuam Teem* during the first 13 days of death or after burial, Hmong animists continue to believe that the spirit still cannot reincarnate. They believe it is still being kept captive somewhere. Without this release of the spirit (*tso plig*) ritual, the spirit of the dead cannot reincarnate. Therefore, the *tso plig* is necessary to release the spirit from being held captive either in the grave or wherever it may be to be free to be reborn. But this is where the evidence of contradictions showed. On the one hand, they believe that the spirit is capable of and it's already well on its way to seek a rebirth without aid of the *tso plig* ritual when the person is terminally ill,[139] when it gets lost and cannot find its way back to reunite with the body, or when there's a new birth occurs about the same time the person dies. But on the other hand, they believe that the spirit cannot reincarnate without the *tso plig* ritual.

---

[138] Symonds, 149.
[139] Lee and Tapp, 28.

The *tso plig* ritual does not take place until at least six months, sometimes a year or more, after the death of the person. The spirit has to be awakened and led back to its house, somewhat similar to the *xw plig* ritual. But instead of going all the way to the grave, the family members and relatives would only go as far as the edge of the village. From there they would shoot an arrow from a crossbow into the woods. They believe that the arrow would awaken the spirit and with the aid of the reed pipe being playing, the spirit would follow the people home to participate in its *tso plig* ritual. What is irrational is that if the first spirit that was instructed to find a new set of parents to reborn had not already been reincarnated, this spirit would rather be roaming in the village or town in the midst of the people looking for a chance to be reborn. It would not stay in the forest. If the second spirit was sent to stay with its ancestors and warned to never come back, this spirit would be residing in the demon world (*dlaabteb*), not in the forest. And if the third spirit was told to remain forever with the dead body at the grave, it also could not have been roaming in the forest. Therefore, the spirit that follows them home has to be a wild and a pretender spirit as Hmong animists believe that wild demons live in the forest.

It is hard to conduct the *tso plig* ritual in the United States the same way it has been done. Therefore, sometimes they hold the *tso plig* ritual at a relative's farm, but mostly it is done at the funeral home. The crossbow is not a real one, but a very small crossbow to symbolize the real one. In this country, cemeteries are in the city surrounded by residential homes, so they either would stop at certain place to initiate the call of the deceased's spirit or they could just start the procession in the parking lot outside the funeral home. The body of the deceased is now represented by a winnowing tray covered by a shirt or jacket of the dead. The *tso plig* ritual is no longer an occasion of mourning because the purpose of the *tso plig* ritual is to release the spirit of the dead so that it is free to reincarnate.[140]

While believing that spirit reincarnates, they also believe that the same spirit becomes a demon the moment the person dies. Hmong animists have a saying: "living is human dying is demon (*nyob caj neeg tuag caj dlaab*)." What do they actually believe? The belief that a person has multiple spirits is logical with the concept that these personal spirits are foreign to the body and are imparted by demons during the spirit calling ritual, but it is antithetical to the belief that each person only has one spirit and it is imparted by God at the moment of conception. It also is antithetical to believe that while the body is alive all three spirits are working cooperatively to keep the body function normally. But when the body dies, only one gets the salvation of reincarnation and the other two are condemned to either stay with the body at the grave or sent to the land of darkness with the ancestors where, according to Vincent Kou Her, it is "a harsh, desolate place, lacking and devoid of life" that requires the continued support of the dead by the living members.[141] What have these two spirits done to deserve the eternal judgment? In life everything has name, but these different spirits that live in the body have no name. How does one determine which of these three spirits get to reincarnate and which of the other two get the ultimate condemnation? If one analyzes the Showing the Way chant carefully, the spirit that supposed to be reborn is the same one that is guided to the land of darkness to be with the ancestors and this same spirit also is believed to have stayed at the grave with the body. The Showing the Way chant also says that only the spirit that gets to wear the placenta (which the Showing the Way chant calls the "golden shirt" or *tsho tsuj tsho npuag*) gets to reincarnate.

---

[140] Symonds, 149-152.
[141] Vincent K. Her, 100.

However, the spirit that gets to wear the golden shirt also gets sent to the land of darkness to stay with the ancestors.[142] All three versions of the Showing the Way chants contained in the *Kab Ke Pam Tuag Cov Zaj* (Funerary rites and procedures) clearly state that the spirit that is guided to reincarnate also is the spirit that is being sent to meet the ancestors in the world of darkness.[143] Stanza 19 of Yang Chong Chee's version of the Showing the Way chant says:

> Now it seems that you have put on a fashionable outfit and are going to get your golden shirt (*tsho tsuj tsho npuag*) to wear. You have reincarnated once as a human being on earth in the village of. . . (Name the birth place of the deceased). You have to go get your golden shirt to wear in order to be able to reincarnate. One person has three spirits and seven shadows. You are leaving, your shadows die, but your spirits cannot die. One of the spirits will go get the golden shirt. You had lived. . . (Name the villages, cities, or towns that the deceased had lived). You had consumed a large portion of the forest, burned up a large number of fire woods, drank a large quantity of water. Now that you are leaving, the spiritual rulers of these places will block your way. You have to use the spirit money to pay for all the things that you had consumed and used, then the rulers of the places will let you go. Only then will you be able to be on your

---

[142] Bertrais, 44-46.
[143] Ibid., 46-47; 78;91-93.

way to meet your ancestors... (Translation is the author's).[144]

As discussed earlier, the doctrine of Hmong animism teaches that an infant is born without a spirit and that's why the spirit calling ritual is necessary. If the spirit is imparted in the body of the infant three days after birth, why is it necessary for the spirit that will be reincarnated to wear the placenta or the golden shirt? If the infant is born with a spirit, the spirit is born with the placenta then it makes sense that the spirit is necessary to have the golden shirt in order to be able to reincarnate. But in that case, the spirit calling ritual is unnecessary. It is important to realize that in the United States and quite possible that in other Western countries as well, child birth takes place at the hospital and the placenta is disposed of by the hospital or given away for medical research. It will be very unlikely that the dead will be able to find its placenta and without the placenta the dead is unlikely to be able to reincarnate as they believe that the placenta is necessary for that purpose.

Hmong animism is a very confused religion. Contradictions are the best descriptors of its beliefs and practices.

JESUS THE TRUE SALVATION

Humans are spiritual beings, thus God banished them from His presence after the fall of the first man, but nevertheless they continued to search for ways to reconnect to the spiritual source that created them. Not knowing the truth, they created their own belief systems and hope that these beliefs are the way to reconnect to the spiritual world. Hmong animists believe that Hmong animism is the way that

---

[144] Ibid., 46-47.

connects them to the spiritual source of life. It points Hmong animists directly to Satan (*Ntxwgnyoog*) who they believe is the spiritual source of life. But Satan (*Ntxwgnyoog*) is not the spiritual source of life. He is the spiritual source of death. This is the reason that while Hmong animists worship Satan (*Ntxwgnyoog*) as the life grantor and his demons as their protectors, they also accuse them of causing sickness and death, and dysfunctional to humans.[145] All Hmong animists are encouraged to seriously consider the following passage that Jesus says in Luke 4:18-19:

> "The Spirit of the Lord is on me,
> Because he has anointed me
> to proclaim good news to the poor.
> He has sent me to proclaim freedom for the prisoners
> And recovery of sight for the blind,
> to set the oppressed free,
> to proclaim the year of the Lord's favor."

This passage requires further discussion in order for someone who has little or no Bible knowledge to properly understand its meanings. When Jesus says, ". . .to proclaim good news to the poor," He is not talking about the economically poor people, but He is referring to the people of the world who are spiritually poor because they do not have the loving God. Anyone who does not have the Spirit of the true God is poor in spirit. The good news that Jesus is preaching is the fulfillment of God's promise at the Fall of Man that He will redeem mankind. Humankind, the prized creation in the image of God, was banished from the sight of the Lord after their disobedience to His law. Though God banished them, they were the only creatures that He created in His image. Therefore, He longed to reconcile them to Himself (Genesis

---

[145] Lee and Tapp,31.

3:15). Throughout human history since the Fall of Man, God has been actively working to bring about salvation to humankind. The good news is that Jesus is the promised Messiah, the appointed One that God promised to be the Savior of the fallen world that He has created (Jeremiah 23:5-6). This good news is all about the incarnated person of Jesus Christ, His ministry on earth, His sacrificial death, His triumphant resurrection, and His glorious exaltation in accordance with the Old Testament Scriptures (Philippians 2:6-11). The good news is that God sent Jesus Christ "to proclaim freedom" for the human race who has been the prisoners of Satan and the demons, hope for the fallen mankind because through the reconciliation of the Lord Jesus Christ, mankind can renew their relationship with their Heavenly Father, their Creator God, and relief for the weary due to heavy burden imposed upon them by the power of Satan and the demons. If they come to Jesus and humble themselves before Him, He will set them free from the oppressive power of the dark lords of this world. They will gain freedom from being prisoners of the demons and Satan. And they will receive eternal salvation from Jesus Christ who is the true Lord of mankind. Choosing to accept Jesus Christ as your Lord and Savior is simple, though it is the most important decision you will ever have to make in your life because it will give you freedom from the power of the demons and Satan, save you from eternal wrath of God, and you will be granted eternal salvation. Romans 10:9-10 says:

> If you declare with your mouth, 'Jesus is Lord,' and believe in your heart that God raised him from the dead, you will be saved. For it is with your heart that you believe and are justified, and it is with your mouth that you profess your faith and are saved.

Those that Jesus has set free from the power of Satan and the demons understand that the good news that Jesus Christ is preaching is the message from God the Creator (*Vaajtswv Yawmsaub tug tsim ntuj tsim teb*) that men are sinners, separated from the loving Heavenly Father, and destined for eternal judgment if they do not have Jesus as their Lord and Savior. They understand that salvation is the grace of God, the everlasting life in the Kingdom of Heaven. It is the work of God reaching out to the fallen human race that has been held prisoner by the evil power of the dark lords that rule this fallen world. God completed His redemptive work of the human race through the sacrifice of the Lord Jesus Christ on the cross. Jesus Christ died on the cross to take away our sins. He resurrected from death to justify us, sinners, righteous, and give the believers salvation. It is important to understand that humans are created by God (*Yawmsaub*), so it doesn't matter how far they have drifted away from the Lord God, they still have some sense of the hope that God has promised from the beginning. That is the hope of salvation through redemption. Not knowing the truth, Hmong animists believe that reincarnation is the salvation. It is not. It is only Satan's (*Ntxwgnyoog's*) false promise of salvation for the spirit to steer mankind, particularly the Hmong animists, away from God. Salvation is through Jesus Christ alone. Again, the good news that Jesus Christ brings to the world is the promise "recovery of sight for the blind." This world has been so corrupted by the power of Satan and the demons, so the whole human race is spiritually blinded, but God wants them to have the spiritual sight to see the true God. The message Jesus Christ proclaims to the world is the power of understanding that mankind is hopelessly oppressed by the wicked rulers of this fallen world, but Jesus Christ is the light of the world. The spiritual blindness of the Hmong animists is that though they pay steep prices, they blindly continue to worship Satan and the demons. The more they worship them,

The Belief in the Reincarnation of the Spirit

the more they are being oppressed by them. The more they are being oppressed, the more they pay offerings to appease them. Hmong animists continue to be oppressed regardless of what they do to appease the demons. Those who are being possessed by the demons experienced many undiagnosed physical and mental health conditions, social problems, and even tragic death. However, most Hmong animists, instead of humbling themselves before Jesus Christ and letting Him cast out the demons that oppress them, choose to wear threaded wristbands, necklaces, or ankle bracelets believing that those clothing threads have the power to protect them from demons. In reality, those clothing threads are symbols indicating that they belong to Satan (*Ntxwgnyoog*) and his demons. But all those who turn to the Lord Jesus Christ have been set free from the power of the dark lords. They experience wholeness and freedom from demonic oppression. This passage is very important for the unbelievers. It is the message of hope from God to the unbelievers that He wants to reconcile with them, that the unbelievers are the prisoners of Satan and the demons that they needed the power of the Lord Jesus Christ to set them free, that the unbelievers have been blinded by the power of Satan and the demons from seeing the truth that Jesus Christ is the Savior of the world as God has promised since the day of the Fall of Man,[146] and that the unbelievers have been oppressed by Satan and the demons. However, there is hope because they can break free from such oppression by accepting Jesus Christ as their Lord and Savior.

---

[146] Robert Kolb, *Speaking the Gospel Today: A Theology for Evangelism*, rev. ed. (Saint Louis: Concordia Publishing House, 1995), 21- 69.

CHAPTER 6

COSMOLOGY OF HMONG ANIMISM ACCORDING TO HMONG SHAMANISM

Hmong shamanism forms the second part of cosmology of Hmong animism. It teaches that spiritual cause underlines every illness. There are several reasons why a person is sick. First is that the spirit is lost or departed from the body of the person due to fear. Second is the belief that demons (household or wild demons) has captured the spirit of the person and held it for a ransom. And third is the belief that Satan (*Ntxwgnyoog*) has captured the spirit of the person and raised it as his cattle to be slaughtered to feed himself. Shamans can perform shamanic ritual to diagnose what is going wrong with the person and heal the sick by sacrificing animal to the demons as a proxy for the human spirit and by restoring the spirit back to the person.

This shamanic cosmological view is in direct conflict with the cosmology of the Showing the Way chant. That is, whereas the Showing the Way chant claims that human spirit is immaterial and immortal, Hmong shamanism teaches that human spirit has flesh or spiritual flesh. It holds that the human spirit has a body in the image of a chicken, pig, goat, horse, reindeer, bull, or other kinds of animals and insects. For the reason that they believe that human spirit has body form, they also believe that the spirit is easily scared away from the body, captured by demons and Satan, and it can be killed and eaten. The discussion of core values four to six – the belief in shamanism, the belief in household demons, and the belief in wild demons – in this chapter and in the chapters seven and eight will be based on the cosmological view of Hmong shamanism.

THE BELIEF IN SHAMANISM

Due to the poor structure of Hmong animism, Hmong shamanism sometimes is misunderstood to be a religion by itself. There are at least two contributing factors that have led to this misunderstanding. First, the "ism" after the word "shaman" leads people to believe that shamanism is a religion. In a way, it is a part of a religious belief system, but it is not a religion by itself. Second, Hmong animism is a religion though very unorganized and mainly an oral religion. The parts that make up the whole are not nicely connected together in an oral religion. Therefore, even though Hmong shamanism is a very important part of Hmong animism, its connection is not clearly seen. What is Hmong shamanism? It is the healing arm of Hmong animism. It is that part of the religion that deals with healing.

Hmong animists believe that shamans have the power to heal both physical and spiritual illness. They believe that the spirit of the person has a lot to do with the physical health of the person. If the spirit is separated from the physical body, or if it is captured by the demons and held for a ransom, the person will become sick and could die as a result of the circumstance. The spirit can be detached from the body if the person experiences a sudden fear of something. But fear is not necessarily the only factor that causes the spirit to run away from the body. Hmong animists believe that sometimes the spirit just simply wanders away for an errand and cannot find its way back to reunite with the body. When the spirit is separated from the body, the health system of the body becomes imbalanced and the person gets sick.[147] If the spirit is captured by demons, Hmong animists believe that either the person or someone in the family is guilty of a wrongdoing. It makes no difference whether the violation is intentional or unintentional. If the household demons hold the spirit of the sick person in captivity, Hmong animists believe that someone in the family has done something against the household demons. But if the spirit is seized by wild demons, there are two possible reasons to explain the circumstance. The household demons seized the spirit of the person as a result of a wrongdoing and then barter it to the wild demons for a ransom or the person may have unknowingly violated the personal territory of the wild demons and they capture his spirit and held it for a ransom.[148] A third reason, which Hmong animists tend to believe happened, is that the demons simply seize the spirit of the person out of malicious intent without any wrongdoing from anyone. In any of these cases, the person whose spirit has been seized by the demons could get very sick or die if nothing is done to remedy it. This is when a shaman is called to intervene. Gary Yia Lee and Nicholas Tapp say, "Shamans are traditional religious experts who have the ability to diagnose illness and cure suffering or other misfortunes such as drought or famine."[149]

Of all the writing about Hmong animism, nothing addresses the issue of demonic oppression by means of

---

[147] Anne Fadiman, 100.

[148] Ya Po Cha, 144.

[149] Lee and Tapp, 24.

possessing the person, but this type of oppression commonly happens in the Hmong animist community. The experiences between lost spirit or seized spirit and the person is being possessed by demons are different. Hmong animists believe that if a person gets sick easily or being sick a lot then it must have something to do with the spirit of the person. The spirit is either lost while wandering away from the body, or has been seized by demons. However, someone who is being possessed by demons does not necessarily experience any illness. In this case, the whole being of the person is completely being controlled by the demons. The person may be completely normal when the demons loosen their grip on the person, but the person could experience sudden violent episodes, such as violent shaking, suffocation, or other kinds of physical, psychological, and mental tortures. For Hmong animists, these are the instances when a shamanic ritual is needed. They believe that shamans have the power to heal by bringing the lost spirit back to the body, by bargaining for the release of the seized spirit, or by delivering the demonic-possessed person from the demons. However, based on experiences, rarely is any demonic-possessed person set free from the power of the demons by Hmong shamanic rituals.

The shamanic ritual is a holistic healing system for the well-being of Hmong animists. In addition to what has been discussed above, a Hmong shaman is also called to perform a ritual for a married couple who is infertile. Hmong animists believe that a shaman could invoke the goddess of mercy Guanyin in Chinese or (*Kabyeeb or Nam Puj Dlaabpog* in Hmong) who is believed to be the fertility demon to bring children to the barren couple.[150] Shamans could heal illness in general, which are not necessarily caused by spirit loss or

---

[150] Kao-Ly Yang, "The Meeting with Guanyin, the Goddess of Mercy: A Case Study of Syncretism in the Hmong System of Belief" (*Hmong Studies Journal* 7), 4.

seizure. Shamanic ritual could be performed for the protection of an individual or the whole community. In the case of protecting the community, shamanic rituals are performed when there's an epidemic of illness or a curse befallen the community. For Hmong animists, they could not live as a community without having at least one or two shamans as they are totally dependent on shamans for healing their illnesses.[151]

ORIGIN OF HMONG SHAMANISM

Keith Quincy states, "Shamanism was first practiced by Siberian tribesmen and later spread southward to China, southwest to central Asia and east across the Bering straits to North America." The Hmong probably learned shamanism and adopted into their religious practice when they were in Siberia. This was his assumption about where the Hmong could have learned and adopted shamanism as part of their religious practices. However, he admitted that this assumption does not match the Hmong accounts of the origin of the Hmong shamanism.[152] Depending on whom one asks about the story of the first Hmong shaman, there are different stories about it. One legend put forth by Quincy states that long ago when the world was recently created and mankind was rapidly growing in numbers, though God (*Yawmsaub*) was pleased with the growth of human population, Satan (*Ntxwgnyoog*) hated it, and descended to earth to devour them. When God (*Yawmsaub*) found out about *Ntxwgnyoog's* malicious act, God was furious and sent two of his servants down to earth to hunt down Satan (*Ntxwgnyoog*). But they weren't able to kill him because Satan was able to fly like

---

[151] John McKinnon and Wanat Bhruksasri, *Highlanders of Thailand* (Oxford: Oxford University Press, 1983), 187, 190.

[152] Quincy, 89.

the winds while God's two servants could not. They were unhappy with their inability to kill Satan, so they went back to heaven to report their failure to God (*Yawmsaub*), but God commanded them to return to earth to continue the fight against Satan. In the meantime, they had a child and named him Sheeyee (*Sivyig*). *Sivyig* became the first Hmong shaman when he grew up. God (*Yawmsaub*) purposely sent *Sivyig* to be the healer for the Hmong, but the Hmong initially rejected him when his parents went back to heaven leaving him an orphan. As a young child he needed help, and he first asked the Hmong for help, but they declined, so he turned to a Royal Chinese family who put him to work at their animal farms. One day as he walked around his Chinese lord's palace, he discovered two strangely large eggs. He broke them, but there was nothing in them. He left the broken eggs in the nest, but he discovered that the eggs became whole again the next day when he walked by the spot. He broke them again, but this time he hid himself out of sight and waited to find out how the eggs became whole after they were broken. At dusk a large dragon flew over his head and landed where the nest was. After inspecting the broken eggs, the dragon tore up the ground and kicked up the stones to find the magic healing plant. When the healing plant was found, the "dragon uprooted the plant, separated the tubers from the stalks, crushed them with its talons and placed the pulpy mass in a bowl of water." The dragon raised the bowl up and blew at it spraying the water on the eggs, and the eggs miraculous became whole again. *Sivyig* immediately realized that it was God (*Yawmsaub*) who sent the dragon to teach him the secret of healing and raising people from death. He quickly gathered as much as possible of the magic healing plant and hurried to heal people from their sickness and revive the dead back to life. To match up with Satan (*Ntxwgnyoog*), God (*Yawmsaub*) gave *Sivyig* the flying horse to aid his mobility. Envisioning the enormous battles ahead of *Sivyig*, his Chinese lord gave him "two companies of Chinese soldiers to help him battle Satan." *Sivyig* was able to match up with Satan (*Ntxwgnyoog*) and able to revive every spirit that Satan (*Ntxwgnyoog*) slaughtered. Satan (*Ntxwgnyoog*) eventually realized he could not win the battle with *Sivyig*, so Satan concocted a peace agreement with *Sivyig* and even served as *Sivyig's* servant. Satan's (*Ntxwgnyoog's*) real intention for the peace pact was only to buy time to figure out ways to destroy *Sivyig*. A son was born to *Sivyig* and Satan (*Ntxwgnyoog*) thought that if his son reached adulthood and the two worked together to heal the sick and raise the dead in the world, they would be unstoppable. While *Sivyig* was away from home on a healing duty, Satan (*Ntxwgnyoog*) killed his son and cooked his meat and served it to *Sivyig* upon his return. When *Sivyig* realized that he was eating his son's meat, he was outraged and proceeded to kill Satan (*Ntxwgnyoog*), but God (*Yawmsaub*) intervened. God only allowed *Sivyig* to maim *Ntxwgnyoog* so that he would experience at least some of the pain he caused to mankind. *Sivyig* used his shamanic saber to pierce *Ntxwgnyoog's* eyes and cast him out of his house to be a beggar among mankind. Instead, he found his way back to his fortress in the sky and mustered the demons and renewed the campaign against human beings. Meanwhile, *Sivyig's* power to heal sickness and raise people from death was considerably weakened from eating the meat of his own son. He decided to return to heaven, but promised to return to earth a year later to give his shamanic tools as gifts to mankind so that they would be able to heal themselves. When *Sivyig* returned, no one came to greet him. In anger he threw his shamanic tools to the ground and announced that the tools would never be as powerful in healing as they originally were. The Hmong picked up *Sivyig's* shamanic tools and became shamans.¹⁵³ The aforementioned is one of the several versions of the origins of Hmong shamanism. Another legend of the origin of Hmong shamanism was advanced by Anne Fadiman. In her story,

> The wife of a wicked god named Nyong (*Nyong is an incomplete word for Ntxwgnyoog*) laid an egg as large as a pig house. For three years, the egg did not hatch. Nyong's father chanted to the egg and, in response, heard the jabbering voices of many evil *dabs* (demons) inside it. He ordered Nyong to burn the egg, but Nyong refused. So the egg burst, and out swarmed the *dabs* (demons). The first thing they did was to eat Nyong's wife, down to the last bone, hair, and eyelash. Then, still hungry, they came after Nyong. Nyong opened the door that led from the sky, where he lived, to the earth. Through it flew the *dabs* (demons), as big as water buffalos and as red as fire, with showers of sparks in their wake. Nyong was safe, but from that day on, the people of the earth have known illness and death.

Meanwhile, *Sivyig* spent three years apprenticing with a sorcerer. He learned all the skills he needed to kill the demons. He could even transform himself into an ant or fly like the wind. *Sivyig* was able to heal the sick and raise the dead to life again. He spent many years fighting the demons and healing the sick, but one day *Ntxwgnyoog* murdered *Sivyig's* infant son, cooked his meat, and tricked *Sivyig* into eating it. When *Sivyig* realized that *Ntxwgnyoog*

---

¹⁵³ Quincy, 190-193.

had killed his son and tricked him into eating the meat of his own son, he was stricken with grief and "fled the earth and climbed the staircase up through the sky door into the sky. To avenge his son's death, he pierced both of Nyong's eyes." Satan (*Ntxwgnyoog*) was blinded and lived at the "foot of a mountain in the sky" and *Sivyig* went to live in the "cave at its summit." *Sivyig* did not return to earth anymore, but he also did not want to leave the people without help, so as he entered the door to the sky, he threw his shamanic tools as he spat the holy water on them. The shamanic tools included a saber, a gong, a rattle, and two finger bells. They broke into pieces as they hit the ground, but whoever caught a drop of the water or a piece of the shamanic tools was selected to be a shaman. The shaman has to ride on *Sivyig's* horse, summon his shamanic helpers which according to Jacques Lemoine are more than 170,000 Chinese spirit soldiers and officers,[154] and flying through the sky door to the demon world in order to find the lost or seized spirit.[155]

A third version of the shamanic legend is provided by Vincent K. Her. In this legend, Her states that many of the death songs sung during Hmong animist funerals mention that Satan (*Ntxwgnyoog*) was *Sivyig's* younger brother, but the two were archenemies.[156] With *Sivyig's* ability to heal illness and revive the dead, *Ntxwgnyoog* was jealous. In this version of the legend, Satan (*Ntxwgnyoog*) is not mentioned as the one who cause sickness and death to mankind. It maintains that when Satan's (*Ntxwgnyoog's*) son fell ill, Satan (*Ntxwgnyoog*) sent for *Sivyig* to go over to his house to perform a healing shamanic ritual for his son. While *Sivyig* was in a trance, Satan (*Ntxwgnyoog*) seized

---

[154] Lemoine, 17.
[155] Fadiman, 278-279.
[156] Vincent K. Her, "Hmong Cosmology: Proposed Model, Preliminary Insights" (Milwaukee: *Hmong Study Journal,* Volume 6, 2005), 8.

Sivyig's son's spirit, transformed it into a pig, slaughtered it as a sacrifice and prepared it for *Sivyig*. He knew nothing about what Satan (*Ntxwgnyoog*) had done and ate the meal *Ntxwgnyoog* had prepared for him. He met his son's spirit midway as he returned home and only then learned what Satan (*Ntxwgnyoog*) had done. *Sivyig* quickly returned home and immediately performed a rescue shamanic ritual, but was unable to revive him because he had eaten his son's flesh. Outraged by this, *Sivyig* went to live at a place called "*Toj Tsua Laj Peg Tsua Luv*, or Mountain of Hawks and Swallows, in the upper dimension of the universe."[157] Her contradicts himself at the beginning of next chapter. Her says that *Sivyig* was able to revive his son, but he could not revive the two cows that were slaughtered to feed the people that came to take part of the vigil for his son while he was on a healing mission. The cows agreed to be slaughtered to feed the people only after the family members agreed that they will also be revived when *Sivyig* returned. But they couldn't be revived because the cows' meat was all eaten and their bones were taken by the dogs. The two cows that were slaughtered to feed the people protested against *Sivyig* and argued that it would only be fair for them if his son died as well. Therefore, *Sivyig* allowed his son to die with the cows.[158]

These three shamanic legends are stories Hmong animists believed happened at the beginning of time or at least long time ago, and help them understand why shamanism exists in the Hmong people. However, they cannot agree on who *Sivyig* was fighting against. It is important to recapitulate some of the conflicting points of these stories. Quincy states

---

[157] _____, "Hmong Mortuary Practices: Self, Place and Meaning in Urban America" (PhD diss., University of Wisconsin – Milwaukee, 2005), 100.

[158] Ibid., 129-130.

that Hmong animists believe that God (*Yawmsaub*) sent *Sivyig* to the world to be a healer for the Hmong because Satan (*Ntxwgnyoog*) descended to earth and savagely devoured mankind.[159] In this account, Satan (*Ntxwgnyoog*) was the "Savage One" that *Sivyig* was fighting against. The second legend posited by Anne Fadiman gave a completely different reason. In this legend, even *Ntxwgnyoog* was a victim of his own offspring, the demons. His wife, the mother of the demons, was their first victim, but he escaped their attack by opening the door to earth and let the demons fly down. Sickness and death to mankind began the day that *Ntxwgnyoog* opened the sky door to let the demons descend to earth.[160] In this legend, the demons are the "Evil Ones" who cause sickness and death and *Sivyig* was fighting against them. And the third story advanced by Vincent K. Her is completely different from the first two accounts above. *Sivyig* neither fought against Satan (*Ntxwgnyoog*) nor the demons (*dlaab*), but the sickness and death themselves. In his legend, sickness and death were neither caused by Satan (*Ntxwgnyoog*) nor by the demons. In fact, even Satan (*Ntxwgnyoog*) himself needed the service of the shaman. What is absurd about this legend is that it is like a story written for the kindergarteners. The spirit of *Sivyig's* son whom Satan (*Ntxwgnyoog*) captured and transformed into a pig, slaughtered and prepared for *Sivyig* to eat, was still alive and came to meet *Sivyig* on his way home. Also, the dead cows whose meat and bones were all consumed could still talk and protest against *Sivyig*. These conflicting accounts clearly declared that the *Sivyig* legends are only fictitious myths, and not based on truth.

The contradictions continue as the accounts about how *Sivyig* became the first Hmong shaman differ between the

---

[159] Quincy, 90.
[160] Fadiman, 178.

legends provided by Quincy and Fadiman. Whereas Quincy states that *Sivyig* gained knowledge about how to heal the sick and raise the dead from observing the dragon using the miracle plant to fix the broken eggs,[161] Fadiman states that *Sivyig* became a very powerful shaman after spent three years apprenticing with a sorcerer. *Sivyig* learned all the healing magical powers he needed to heal the sick and raise the dead during the apprenticeship with the sorcerer.[162]

Still other contradictions are found in these three accounts. In Quincy's account, the piercing of Satan's eyes was done on earth before *Sivyig* departed to live in the sky, but in Fadiman's story, this revenge took place after he climbed the staircase to the sky above. Also in Quincy's account, *Sivyig* returned to earth to give his magical shamanic tools as gifts to mankind so that they could heal themselves.[163] But in Fadiman's account, *Sivyig* never returned to earth after the day he climbed the staircase to the sky to avenge his son's death. After piercing Satan's eyes and leaving him blinded, he went to reside in a cave called Nha Yee's Cave[164] believed to be at the summit of the sky. *Sivyig* dropped his magical shamanic tools down to earth from the sky.[165] In Vincent Her's version, *Sivyig* went to live at the *Toj Tsua Laj Peg Tsua Luv* or the Mountain of Hawks and Swallows, not at Nha Yee's Cave after Satan killed his son.

Hmong animists strongly believe that these legendary accounts, no matter how obscure they are, have historical truth and formed the foundation for Hmong shamanism. But if Satan (*Ntxwgnyoog*) dared to rebel against God, his Creator, in heaven and then deceived God's most precious creation whom

---

[161] Quincy, 91.
[162] Fadiman, 178-179.
[163] Quincy, 93.
[164] Lemoine, 14.
[165] Fadiman, 279.

He created in His image on earth to sin against God, the claim that *Sivyig* was able to battle Satan (*Ntxwgnyoog*) and win, and brought him into his house to be his servant is anything but the truth. Conscious people understand that at no time since the beginning of time were humans ever able to physically see and touch Satan (*Ntxwgnyoog*) much less battled against him and subdued him. Only people who know nothing about the power of Satan (*Ntxwgnyoog*) and the conflicts between God (*Yawmsaub*) and Satan (*Ntxwgnyoog*) would believe that *Sivyig* was able to subdue Satan (*Ntxwgnyoog*) and make him his servant. The legends also talk about a skyward staircase that Shaman *Sivyig* purportedly climbed to the sky. Hmong shamanism makes such claim because until recently Hmong believed that the earth was flat and there were points where the earth and the sky came together. These legendary accounts of shamanic origin are nothing more than fictitious stories. But Hmong animists are blinded by the power of Satan (*Ntxwgnyoog*) and the demons (*dlaab*) to see the incredulous claims in these legends. Therefore, they believe that the legends are true and established the authority of shamanism.

For thousands of years, no one cared to know and nothing has mentioned the date *Sivyig* purportedly climbed the staircase to the sky. But a new breed of Hmong shamans who shave their heads, men and women, claim that they know the date was December 16 because their spiritual side, meaning the shamanic demons, told them. They held their first celebration in remembrance of *Sivyig* on December 16, 2014 at Hmong Village, in St. Paul, MN. David Yang, one of the lead shamans, said that they would make December 16 the official date for *Sivyig's* ascension to the sky and will continue to celebrate him as the savior.[166] No one knows

---

[166] 3HmongTV, Kev Teev Hawm Txog Siv Yis Hnub 12/16, view on February 10, 2015. 3HmongTV is an Internet TV channel broadcast in Hmong language.

how the *Sivyig* stories and shamanism came about, but what this group of shamans claims to know and attempts to do is a testament to how shamanism was created long ago. In order to establish shamanic authority over its believers, the creators of Hmong shamanism had to claim special and supernatural authority. The legends of *Sivyig* had to be adorned with supernatural powers given by a good spiritual being. Hmong animists believe that *Yawmsaub* is the good God. In order to be credible in the eyes of its believers, the creators of Hmong shamanism had to claim that *Sivyig* was a man sent by *Yawmsaub* or that he was given the supernatural powers by God (*Yawmsaub*) to heal the sickness and death of mankind. The creators of Hmong shamanism also had to blame the human plight on the evil deity, which Hmong animists believe is Satan (*Ntxwgnyoog*). This created a scenario in which with the powers given to *Sivyig*, he was able to battle against the "Evil One" and human conditions were improved by his work. To quell people's questions about the credibility of *Sivyig*, the creators of the shamanic legend had to create a sad ending to the story that caused *Sivyig* to leave the earth. To the amazement of its believers, *Sivyig*, a human being was able to escape death himself and ascend to live forever in the highest point of the sky. These types of claims of special supernatural powers and authorities given to a human being by a super spiritual deity are not unique to the Hmong. The ancient Egyptian Kings and other Near East ancient rulers also claimed such authority and power. These claims are nothing more than fictitious inventions to legitimize their authority over their subjects. Thutmose III, one of the greatest ancient Egyptian Pharaohs, the Egyptian King who was believed to have enslaved the Israelites, claimed that he had ascent to heaven and was crowned as the king of Egypt. The sun god gave him the authority to rule the people. According to Rodger Dalman, in his coronation inscription, Thutmose III claimed that the sun god had taken him to heaven:

> He opened for me the doors of heaven; he opened the portals of the horizon of Re. I flew to heaven as a divine hawk, beholding his form in heaven; I adored his majesty ____ feast. I saw the glorious forms of the Horizon-God upon his mysterious ways in Heaven. Re himself established me, I was dignified with the diadems which [we]re upon his head, his serpent-diadem, rested upon [my forehead]—[he satisfied] me with all his glories; I was sated with the counsels of the gods, like Horus, when he counted his body at the house of my father, Amon-Re. I was [present]ed with the dignities of a god, with —my diadems.[167]

Again, Hammurabi, the great king of Babylon in 1780 BC claimed that he was called by the God of righteous to rule the people with righteousness and to destroy wickedness. In order to legitimize his authority, power, and Code of Laws over the people, he had to claim special coronation. He made the following claims as his authority:

> When Anu the Sublime, King of the Anunaki, and Bel, the lord of Heaven and earth, who

---

[167] Rodger Dalman, Yahweh's Song: A Handbook for Understanding Old Testament Historical Theology (unpublished handbook, Trinity College of the Bible and Theological Seminary, 2007) 185. Dr. Rodger Dalman was a Trinity College of the Bible and Theological Seminary professor teaching regional courses. The handbook was provided in CD at the regional class in St. Paul, MN in July 2007.

decreed the fate of the land, assigned to Marduk, the over-ruling son of Ea, God of righteousness, dominion over earthly man, and made him great among the Igigi, they called Babylon by his illustrious name, made it great on earth, and founded an everlasting kingdom in it, whose foundations are laid so solidly as those of heaven and earth; then Anu and Bel called by name me, Hammurabi, the exalted prince, who feared God, to bring about the rule of righteousness in the land, to destroy the wicked and the evil-doers; so that the strong should not harm the weak; so that I should rule over the black-headed people like Shamash, and enlighten the land, to further the well-being of mankind.

When Marduk sent me to rule over men, to give the protection of right to the land, I did right and righteousness in . . ., and brought about the well-being of the oppressed.[168]

Was there any truth to these claims? We know there was no truth to these claims. If it was true that in ancient times people could ascend to heaven to receive authority from gods or even God and come back to rule their subjects, leaders should still be able to ascend to heaven to receive authority from god or God today in order to have legitimate authority over their subjects. Similarly, there is no truth to the legend or legends of *Sivyig*, the first Hmong shaman. However, as much as they are untrue, they served their intended purpose well. The Hmong animists believe these

---

[168] Fordham University, "Code of Hammurabi, Ancient History Sourcebook," www.fordham.edu/halsall/ancient/hamcode.asp (accessed August 20, 2013)

stories and submit to their authority. The Hmong animists continue to believe the *Sivyig's* legend or legends and they continue to practice shamanism without question. Even the most educated Hmong animists raise no question about the truth of these stories.

THE PEACEFUL PERIOD

The shamanic myth and the Showing the Way chant both mention about a peaceful period when there was no sickness and death. The Holy Scripture tells us that at the beginning of time the world was very peaceful and life was wonderful on earth. That was the goal God had for mankind. The Scripture in Genesis 1:26-27 says that after God created heaven and earth, plants, animals, birds, sea mammals, fish, and every living creature, God created Adam and Eve. He created them in His own image, in the likeness of God, and gave them the authority to rule over all God's creation. The Bible in Psalm 8:5-6 says this about the mankind God created:

> You have made them a little lower than the angels
> and crowned them with glory and honor.
> You made them rulers over the works of your hands;
> you put everything under their feet.

Genesis 2:8 says that God created a beautiful garden called Eden and placed Adam and Eve there. The Bible says that their lives in the garden were wonderful. There was no sickness and death in the garden. During this peaceful time, everything was in absolute harmony with God. They knew the purposes for which God created them and ordained them and they joyfully fulfilled them. In the cool of the day, God came to meet with Adam and Eve and they walked and talked together in the garden. They thanked God for they were specially created in that they were different from every other creature that God had created. They knew that they were special and precious to God because they looked just like the image of God and they enjoyed the special relationship that they had with God. They could talk to God and God talked to them in normal conversation. They worshipped God and joyously offered their reverence and adoration to God.[169] The Garden of Eden was specially planted by God and for God. It was the heaven on earth, a prestigious place where God dwelled among his creatures and, best of all, His mankind. The nature was the most beautiful among all the natural things God had created. Adam and Eve did not have to work on the soil. They did not have to plant anything: everything was planted by God and all sorts of fruits were their food. Their responsibilities were not only to take care of the garden and the animals, but God gave them the authority to rule the whole world. Adam and Eve were placed in the Garden of Eden because that was where God's earthly dwelling place was. God had good reason for the creation of heaven and earth and everything that was created. He created them for his own glory, Colossians 1:15-16, and God created mankind to glorify God, to worship God, and to have personal relationship with God. That was the primary reason why God put Adam and Eve in the Garden of Eden. This was the reason that God would come to see them, walk with them, and talk to them every day.[170]

During this peaceful period, Adam and Eve did not know sickness and death. They did not know what God really meant when He said to them in Genesis 2:17, ". . .but you must not eat from the tree of the knowledge of good and evil, for when you eat of it you will surely die" because no one had ever died. According to the Bible, mankind did have a period

---

[169] A. W. Tozer, *The Purpose of Man: Designed to Worship* (Ventura: Published by Regal, 2009), 22.

[170] Ibid., 23.

in the distant past that they did not experience sickness and death. They enjoyed life with nature and God (*Yawmsaub*). The reference to this peaceful period in the beginning of time when mankind knew no sickness and death in the Showing the Way chants and the shamanic legends is evident that in the beginning Hmong knew the Creator God (*Yawmsaub tug tsim ntuj tsim teb*). Therefore, no matter how remote they have been from the origin or how far they may have strayed away from God, it may be possible that they still have some trace of knowledge in God.

THE ORIGIN OF SICKNESS AND DEATH

The events that set off the beginning of human sickness and death in the Showing the Way chant and shamanism are different from each other and both are different from the biblical account. Hmong Christians believe that the origin of sickness and death occurred according to the biblical account discussed below. The Scripture in Ezekiel 28:12-15 tells us that Satan was the best created angel of God. His name was Lucifer. He was adorned with the finest and most precious stones: ruby, topaz, emerald, chrysolite, onyx, jasper, sapphire, turquoise and beryl. He was the "model of perfection, full of wisdom and perfect in beauty." The Bible also tells us that he was with God when God created heaven and earth. He also was with God when God created the Garden of Eden and came with God to visit Adam and Eve there in the cool breeze of the day. Lucifer was God's angel of worship. He led the angels in worshipping God in heaven. But one day Lucifer became proud because of his beauty, power and authority, and he wanted to be worshipped instead of worshipping God, so he rebelled against God who created him. Once he rebelled against God, he no longer was called Lucifer; he was called Satan (*Ntxwgnyoog*), the Devil (*tug Ntxeevntxag*), the Serpent (*Naab Txwj Naab Laug*), and the

Great Dragon (*Zaaj Txwg Zaaj Laug*). How do we know that Satan (*Ntxwgnyoog*) rebelled against God? The Scripture in Isaiah 14:12-15 tells us what Satan planned to do in his rebellious mind. The passage says:

> How you have fallen from heaven, O morning star, son of the dawn!
> You have been cast down to the earth, you who once laid low the nations!
> You said in your heart, "I will ascend to heaven; I will raise my throne above the stars of God; I will sit enthroned on the mount of assembly, on the utmost heights of the sacred mountain. I will ascend above the tops of the clouds; I will make myself like the Most High." But you are brought down to the grave, to the depths of the pit.

Then Revelation 12:7-9 tells us that there was war in heaven between God's angel Michael and Satan (*Ntxwgnyoog*). When Satan and his angels lost the war against God in heaven, he and his angels were thrown down to earth. Lucifer became Satan (*Ntxwgnyoog*) and the angels that were thrown down with him became the demons (*dlaab*). If Satan (*Ntxwgnyoog*) was present with God when He created heaven, earth, every living thing, and was there when God picked up a chunk of clay, molded it into humans who looked just like God Himself, and then breathed into the nostrils of Adam and Eve the breath of life and they became living souls. Satan (*Ntxwgnyoog*) could have witnessed God (*Yawmsaub*) bequeathed blessings and giving authority to Adam and Eve saying, "Be fruitful and increase in number; fill the earth and subdue it. Rule over the fish in the sea and the birds in the sky and over every living creature that moves on the ground."[171] If Satan (*Ntxwgnyoog*) was present when God created the Garden of Eden and had visited Adam and Eve there, it would be possible that Satan (*Ntxwgnyoog*) was also present when God (*Yawmsaub*) commanded Adam and Eve not to eat from the tree of knowledge of good and evil, for when they eat of it they will die. "And the LORD GOD COMMANDED THE MAN, "YOU ARE FREE TO EAT FROM ANY TREE IN THE GARDEN; but you must not eat from the tree of the knowledge of good and evil, for when you eat from it you will certainly die.""[172] Then Satan (*Ntxwgnyoog*) became a familiar face to Adam and Eve. Whether he came with God or by himself, Satan (*Ntxwgnyoog*) was not a stranger to them. So what would be the first place Satan (*Ntxwgnyoog*) would go to when he was forced out of heaven? Knowing that mankind was God's most precious creation, what would he do? Satan (*Ntxwgnyoog*) knew that if he was able to trick Adam and Eve to violate God's command, he would be able to pierce God's heart. If his desire was to rule heaven by overthrowing God, what would be his second plan when he lost the battle and was thrown down to earth? Rule the earth. Satan (*Ntxwgnyoog*) came directly to the Garden of Eden and befriended Adam and Eve. Satan (*Ntxwgnyoog*) knew God's usual time when He came to see Adam and Eve, so he came to see them at different times. Then one day Satan entered the serpent and spoke to Eve. This was the first account of Satan and demons possessing a living creature. Since then they not only possessed animals, but also humans and they preferred to possess humans because human beings are God's most precious creation. This is the reason that Hmong animists who do not have God as their Lord are often been possessed by the demons who are supposed to protect them. Now Lucifer who was God's most

---

[171] Genesis 1:28, NIV.
[172] Genesis 2:16-17, NIV.

beautiful and perfect angel who led other angels to worship God became the Father of Lies (*Leejtxiv ntawm kev dlaag*) (John 8:44). He spoke through the serpent to Eve and tricked her into believing that she would not die but would be like God if she ate the fruits of the forbidden tree. The deception of Satan (*Ntxwgnyoog*) created doubts in Eve's mind who then questioned the authority of God to forbid them from eating the forbidden fruits. The question was whether anything God had told them was worth obeying, and whether it would be better to trust and fear God or to believe Satan (*Ntxwgnyoog*). Desiring to be like God, Eve chose to listen to the lie of Satan (*Ntxwgnyoog*) and ate the forbidden fruits and gave some of them to Adam to eat. They did not turn out to be like God, but less human than they were before eating the forbidden fruits because they had violated God's command.[173] When God came to see them as He usually did, they were afraid of God and went into hiding. God knew what they had done, but pretended that he did not know anything, and inquired why they had to hide from Him, and they told God that they had eaten the forbidden fruits. God cursed the ground, passed the death judgment on Adam and Eve according to what God had told them long ago, and banished them from the Garden of Eden (Genesis 3). The peaceful period, the period of no sickness and death became the thing of the past. Adam and Eve soon experienced sickness when Eve gave birth to their sons and death for the first time when one of their only two sons, murdered the other. The violation of God's command not to eat from the tree of the knowledge of good and evil was a universal catastrophe to the whole human race. Mankind has continued to meet the same fate ever since and no matter what they try, they cannot escape the curse that Adam and Eve received from God on the day they violated His command. Every human being that has

---

[173] Kolb, 80.

been born into this fallen world has to die, no one escape death, except Enoch[174] and Elijah,[175] whom, according to the Scripture, were taken to heaven alive by God. The real tragedy of the Fall of Man was not just sickness and death, but the loss of the primary purposes they were created for. Human beings lost their own identities and the purpose of their existence. They did not know who created them and did not know where they came from. Psychologically they may think that they know the purpose of their lives, but these are only the temporary things; spiritually they do not know where they will go after this life.[176] For the Hmong animists, they believe that they will reincarnate. But as much as they believe that the spirit will reincarnate, they also believe that the spirit will remain at the gravesite and in the world of darkness. Furthermore, though they believe that the spirit will reincarnate, Hmong animists also believe that the minute a person dies, his spirit becomes a demon. Though they believe in reincarnation, they do not know for sure, so at best they can only say "if it is true that there is reincarnation." The deception that led Adam and Eve to violate God's commandments did not earn Satan (*Ntxwgnyoog*) a better relationship between Adam and Eve, but it actually created immediate hatred between them. Satan (*Ntxwgnyoog*) may be successful in seizing the authority to rule the earth from Adam and Eve, but he not only became the archenemy of God (*Yawmsaub*), but he also became the archenemy of mankind. This is evident in the belief and practice of Hmong animism that even though they depend on Satan (*Ntxwgnyoog*) for

---

[174] Genesis 5:24 Enoch walked faithfully with God; then he was no more, because God took him away. NIV.

[175] 2 Kings 2:11 As they were walking along and talking together, suddenly a chariot of fire and horses of fire appeared and separated the two of them, and Elijah went up to heaven in a whirlwind. NIV.

[176] Tozer, 25.

granting the dead a new mandate for rebirth to a new life, they also hate and curse Satan (*Ntxwgnyoog*) when there is a death. But what is not known to the Hmong animists is that the idea of reincarnation is nothing more than another lie that Satan (*Ntxwgnyoog*) uses to keep the Hmong from accepting God. But just as humans could not escape the judgment that God pronounced on Adam and Eve, God incarnated in human flesh in the person of Jesus Christ to rescue His human creatures and to point the way for them to return to God. Mankind will continue to suffer sickness and death, but those who accept Jesus Christ as their Lord and Savior are saved from the eternal judgment that God has planned for Satan (*Ntxwgnyoog*) who led the whole world astray. However, those who reject Jesus Christ as their Lord and Savior, deny that God the Father (*Vaajtswv Yawmsaub kws yog Vaaj Leejtxiv*) is the Creator of all things, and blaspheme the Holy Spirit will also face the eternal judgment of God. What is sad is the fact that Hmong animists know that God (*Yawmsaub*) is the Savior of mankind, yet they continue to reject Him, but readily accept Satan (*Ntxwgnyoog*) as the ruler of their lives even though they know that he is the wicked spiritual deity that causes sickness and death to humankind. Rejecting God as the Savior, Hmong animists had to create their own savior and *Sivyig* was believed to be that savior. Rejecting the authority of the Holy Bible, they do not know the truth. Without the truth, their knowledge became distorted. Therefore, even though *Sivyig* was only a fictional character, Hmong animists unequivocally believe in him and no matter how distorted the stories of *Sivyig* are, they believe that all of them are true. We all live as friends and neighbors, as community members and as country-men, and we all are members of the human race coming from the same ancestors, Adam and Eve, and from the same Creator God, but when we depart from this world, some will return to their God who created them, but others will go to the demon world (*dlaab teb*) awaiting the final judgment. Everyone has an equal chance to return to God, their Creator. Which of these two places you want to go after this life? Rejecting the true Word of the Creator, Hmong animists believe anything they have heard regardless of the truth. Everyone has different stories about the origin of sickness and death. Even in shamanism, there are many stories and they contradict one another about how the origin of sickness and death occurred. The Showing the Way chants also have the same problems. Therefore, while some blame Satan and the demons for human sickness and death, others blame human conducts as the root cause of human demises. As discussed above, the legends of *Sivyig* in Quincy and Fadiman blamed Satan and the demons for human sickness and death, but Thomas A. DuBois states that his Hmong informant, a Hmong shaman, told him that Satan (*Ntxwgnyoog*) passed down sickness and death to humans only after they complained about having lived too long. He states the following:

> In the beginning human beings had no disease or death to contend with and thus were blessed with unending life. But this perfect existence bored some people so that they complained to each other about living for so long. A fly overheard their conversation and flew to the heaven, where it reported this view to *Ntxwg (Ntxwj) Nyoog*. *Ntxwg Nyoog* was affronted at human ingratitude and declared that if people were not happy about this living for so long they might as well die. So he sent to earth the *Dab Tsog* (*Dlaab Tsog* in Green Hmong) with an army of assistant

dab (spirits of disease) to bring about an end to human immortality.[177]

The Showing the Way chant also blames humankind's own action as the original cause of sickness and death. Stanza 11 of the Showing the Way chant says:

> What is it now, what happens to the earth? In the beginning, the earth had no sickness and death; it was the people on earth that liked death, killed a worm to conduct a funeral in order to mourn, killed a gibbon to conduct a funeral in order to wail, used a black cow skin to make the drum, and used hemp straws to make the kheng (*qeej*) or reed pipe, beat the drum nine times made nine sounds resounding to Satan's green sky, Satan opened the sky door to look, opened the earth door to see. It seemed the people on earth wanted to die.
>
> Satan *(Ntxwgnyoog)* sent the fly to survey the earth, sent the bee to check the earth, the fly returned and the bee returned. Satan *(Ntxwgnyoog)* opened his mouth to ask, what was happening on earth, why has the sound of drum reached me, *Ntxwgnyoog*, in my orange sky? The fly reported that the people on earth like death. They killed the worm on the path, killed the gibbon on the road. They conduct a funeral for the worm in order to mourn; they conduct a funeral for the gibbon in order to wail. They used a black cow skin to make the drum, and used the hemp straws to make

---

[177] Thomas, A. DuBois. *An Introduction to Shamanism*, (New York: Cambridge University Press 2009), 210.

the reed pipe. They beat the drum nine times making the sound that reach your green sky, beat the drum nine times making resounding noise that reach your orange sky. Therefore, Satan *(Ntxwgnyoog)* dropped sickness onto the earth, and dropped death onto the earth. Satan's sickness had come to the earth for seven generations, but there was no sickness. Satan's death came on the earth for seven years, but there was no death. The earth did not notice the sickness nor did it realize the death. Then Satan opened his sky door to look, opened the earth door to see. Satan saw that his sickness got stuck in the middle of the sky; his death got stuck in the middle of the earth. Satan used a copper scissor to cut the sickness, used a steel scissor to cut the death. The sickness came resting upon the tree branch, the death came resting on a tree trunk.

Now that Tou Jau Laj (referring to the dead) worked his farm at a certain path, others knew how to pick, they picked up Satan's sickness and death put them away in their skirt pouches, but Tou Jau Laj did not know how to pick, picked up Satan's sickness, put it in his liver. Others knew how to pick; they picked up Satan's death and put it in their shirt pocket, you did not know how to pick; you picked up Satan's death and put it in your heart.[178] (Translation is the author's)

---

[178] Bertrais, 23-25.

In this stanza and also in DuBois' story, the origin of sickness and death was sent to mankind by Satan in response to mankind's wish to die. It is totally different from the original cause of sickness and death claimed in the *Sivyig* legends. So which story tells the truth about the origin of human sickness and death? In fact, there is none. Only the Holy Scripture can tell the truth about it.[179]

The roles the fly played in the human plight deserve further discussion. According to DuBois and the Showing the Way chant, the fly had a major stake in the fate of mankind. Satan (*Ntxwgnyoog*) passed the judgment of sickness and death to mankind as a result of what the fly had to tell him. But it is absurd to believe that a fly could understand human language and also was able to speak to Satan (*Ntxwgnyoog*). And even the roles the fly played in this human tragedy are contradictorily described in these two stories. In the DuBois' account, the fly flew to heaven to report to Satan that humans were unhappy about living too long, but in the Showing the Way chant, the fly was said to have been sent by Satan (*Ntxwgnyoog*) from his dwelling place in the sky to earth to find out why there were loud sounds coming from the earth. Which story is true? None is true. Aren't these contradictions clear indication that Hmong animism is far from the truth? These mythical stories may be reasonable for the fools, the simple, and the ignorant to believe, but how foolish it is for the intellectual Hmong animists who expose Hmong animism to the world to believe that these nonsensical and baseless myths are true and accept them as the foundation and principles of their beliefs. Nothing could be truer than Psalm 53:1: "The fool says in his heart, 'There is no God.' They are corrupt, and their ways are vile; there is no one who does good."

---

[179] Genesis 3.

THE HEALING POWER OF THE SHAMANS

Every religion claims to have healing power, not only physical ailment, but also psychological and mental problems. For Hmong animism, shamanism is its healing arm. It is the healing authority of its belief system. Jacques Lemoine, who studied Hmong shamanism in Laos before the country fell to Communism, claims that for a period of one year he recorded 120 successful cases of healing by Shaman *Tsuj Yob* Xiong, an average of two cases a week. He also states that Hmong shaman is not only able to heal Hmong, but non-Hmong as well.[180] Anne Fadiman, reports that while Dwight Conquergood was working on his research project at Ban Vinai refugee camp in Thailand, he was healed of his dengue fever by shamanic ritual.[181] All contemporary shamans continue to claim the power of healing. But not all shamans have good intention. Many shamans also practice black magic. They can "bewitch, poison, or otherwise harm people."[182] According to Cher Chou Kue, they can bewitch people, causing them to be sick. If this is the case, the people who are being bewitched will not be healed unless the bewitching shaman is called to perform the healing shamanic ritual.[183] Not only can shamans harm people, they can also kill people with their evil black magic spells. Many Hmong animists have been demonically-possessed by method of bewitching. Several years ago, a family converted to Christianity because the wife was possessed and they believed that she was bewitched by her relatives. However, after she was delivered

---

[180] Lemoine, 11.

[181] Fadiman, 268.

[182] Robert Jenks, *Insurgency and Social Disorder in Guizhou: The "Miao" Rebellion 1854-1873* (Honolulu: University of Hawaii Press, 1994), 63.

[183] Cher Chou Kue, interview by author, St. Paul, MN, September 4, 2013.

from the demons that oppressed her, the family returned to practice animism again.

Hmong animists believe that spiritual condition underlies health conditions and they believe that the reason someone is sick is because the person's spirit has been seized by demons, Satan, lost when it left the body for an errand or scared away. Even the broken arm is a spiritual problem.[184] The following explanation advanced by Dwight Conquergood is a good example of the belief. While doing his research at Ban Vinai, a Hmong refugee camp in Thailand, he came across a young man who was suffering from chronic malaria. He said:

> The Hmong had a different explanation for the etiology of his illness, however. On the occasion of my visit, the shaman's divination/ diagnosis was that marauding, malevolent spirits were molesting Xiong Houa's lifesoul and trying to carry them off to the sky. If they succeeded in this kidnapping mission, Xiong Houa would die. That night his shaman-grandfather would intervene.[185]

For that reason, it is necessary to conduct a shamanic ritual, at least the diagnostic ritual (*ua neeb saib*), for any sickness or mishap that happen to any family member. But almost all the time, if a shaman is called to diagnose an illness, the result would be some sort of underlying spiritual problem. This is very unfortunate for the Hmong animists who completely trust in their ancestors and household demons for protection. This means that the ancestors and the household demons are not protecting the family. They might be the ones that bartered the spirit of the sick person to the

---

[184] Quincy, 93.
[185] Conquergood, 69.

wild demons. When the family pays a ransom to the wild demons, the ancestors and household demons also get some share of it. The journey to the spirit world is a dangerous adventure. Hmong shamans believe that they alone can't do very much when they enter the spirit world. They also believe that the spirit world is full of malevolent demons and dragons. Therefore, they have to pretend that they are *Sivyig*, the most powerful first Hmong shaman. They have to go into the spirit world with full force of power and might. They have to use *Sivyig's* shamanic tools and his helpers who are both Hmong shamanic demons (*dlaab neeb*) and Chinese imperial soldiers to show their superior power and might, so that demons would really believe that they are the real *Sivyig*. Shamans believe that if they are not careful and if demons know that they are not the real *Sivyig*, demons are not going to be afraid of them or they could even trap the shamans and prevent them from returning to the world of the flesh.[186] There are two groups of shamanic helpers. Among the first group of helpers are the "vernacular spirits." The first is the ancestral shamanic master spirit who was the direct male ascendant of the shaman who passed on his shamanic demons to the current shaman. There are female shamanic demons whose responsibility is to use the iron and silver brooms to clean the shamanic altar where the other shamanic demons will land. There is a magic spider demon that will cast its magic threads symbolizing the road that leads the shaman to *Sivyig's* aboding place that is called the "Nha Yee's Cave" (*Nyaj Yig's* Cave). The first human couple was Gao Jua and Jau Nang (*Nkauj Ntsuab* and *Nraug Naab*). With the help of the Chinese blacksmith, they stretch out a "copper and iron" bridge for the Chinese soldiers to cross over. It is also used metaphorically as a bridge connecting the shaman to

---

[186] Fadiman, 279.

Cosmology of Hmong Animism According to Hmong Shamanism

Nha Yee's Cave, allowing *Sivyig's* spirit helpers to come to aid the shaman. The spider's threads and Gao Jua and Jau Nang's bridge are also used as runways for take-off and landing of the spirit helpers when the shaman commands them to fly out to search for a missing spirit. There are two dragons who "encircle the sky and surround the earth" to stop the spirit from going too far. This dragon couple also represents "imperial power." Next is the "Chinese Imperial Couple." They use their strength to rise to heaven and go to the farthest corners of the earth to block the way and prevent the spirit from going to Satan's palace to seek a new letter of provision for a new life of rebirth.[187] They believe that if the spirit of the sick reaches Satan's palace, Satan's secretary *Nyuj Vaab Tuam Teem* (Nyiu Vang Toua Teng) would grant the spirit a new mandate to reincarnate and it would start to search for a pregnant woman and re-animate as the spirit of that infant. It is important to point out a contradiction here. Hmong animists believe that the spirit of the ancestor can only reincarnate back to the family line, but Hmong shamanism teaches that a spirit can re-animate in any newborn it so chooses and without the performance of the spirit calling ritual. Another shamanic demonic couple is Lady Kaying or Guanyin couple (*puj Kabyeeb* or *puj dlaabpog*). Though she is one of the shamanic demons, her role in shamanism is not so clear. She is believed to be the demon that brings the newborns to their parents and protects the newborns until they are a couple of years old.[188] The second group of shamanic helpers is the more than 90,000 Chinese imperial soldiers and over 80,000 Chinese imperial officers that the Chinese Lord gave to *Sivyig* in his pursuit against Satan. Last but not least are all the 88 generations of Chinese emperors and

---

[187] Lemoine, 14-16.
[188] Kao-Ly Yang, 16-17.

empresses.[189] Combine all of these helpers that the shaman has, they are more than the highest number of military service men and women President Barrack Obama ever sent to Afghanistan to fight against the Afghan Taliban and Al Qaeda forces. It seems a little ridiculous, but this is what the shaman claims to have in his arsenal of power and force. It is important to know that not all shamans claim to have all of these helpers. But those who claim to have them invoke all of these shamanic helpers to accompany the shaman to the spirit world in one shamanic ritual.

By human standards, the shaman has more than enough assistants and military personnel to wage a major war against the demons that have seized the spirit of the sick. The shaman would fly like a strong and most powerful king or a general into the spirit world to search for the missing spirit. When the demons see him going to their world with all of the power and might they should have a reason to be afraid of him. He would not be afraid of any demon or demons that attempted to thwart his effort to find the missing spirit. He would not hesitate to engage in battle with the demons that seized the spirit of the sick. He would use his power to forcibly retrieve the captured spirit from the demons that took possession of it. But that is not the case. The military might and helpers are not for battle against the demons. The shaman needs them all to accompany him so that he would be able to cover all of the earth, the sky above, the underworld beneath, and the demon world (*dlaabteb*) or in other words, the world of the dead (*tub tuag teb*) in his effort to search for the missing spirit. This will make sure that no rock left unturned, no hole left unchecked, or no path left unsearched for the missing spirit.[190] The search will continue and, if necessary, the shaman will leave his shamanic horse

---

[189] Lemoine, 17.
[190] Quincy, 97.

and ride the dead's horse and continue the search into the world of the dead. The shaman will follow the trail to the residential place of the mother of mankind, Gao Ah (*Nkauj Ab*). There she has a pond of sweet water for the spirit that arrives there to wash its face. For any spirit that washes itself with Gao Ah's sweet water, death and rebirth are the results because the spirit has reached the point of no return and has erased all of its memories of the past.[191] Therefore, it is important that the shaman uses some of his helpers to block the way to prevent the spirit from reaching the sweet pond of the mother of mankind.

Here we see contradictions about who Gao Ah really was. In Yang Chong Jai's version of the Showing the Way chant, Gao Ah and Jau Ong (*Nkauj Ab and Nraug Oo*) were identified as the first human couple created by the lady frog.[192] In Yang Chong Chee's version, Gao Ah and Jau Ong were also identified as the first human couple as well as the brother and sister who survived the universal flood.[193] But here, Jacques Lemoine identifies the first human couple as Gao Jua and Jau Nang (*Nkauj Ntsuab* and *Nraug Naab*) and Gao Ah (*Nkauj Ab*) was identified as the mother of mankind.[194] In all, Gao Ah (*Nkauj Ab*) was identified as the mother of mankind, the first human couple, the sister who survived the universal flood with her brother, the mother of *Qas Tuj* and *Tuj Lug*, twin brothers who created heaven and earth, and also the mother of Krang Tu and Krang To (*Qaav Tuj* and *Qaav Taug*), another set of brothers who also were the creators of heaven and earth. Who really was the first human couple? Gao Jua and Jau Nang or Gao Ah and Jau Ong? How confusing is Hmong animism!

---

[191] Lemoine, 28-29.
[192] Bertrais, 61-68.
[193] Ibid., 31.
[194] Lemoine, 14.

When the shaman believes that he has found the demons with the spirit of the sick, he does not engage the demons with the power and might that he brings with him. He does not battle against demons with force, but he turns to the skill of bargaining that he developed over the years as a shaman. The enormous number of aides, the more than 170,000 Chinese soldiers and officers, and the 88 generations of Chinese emperors and empresses that go with him into the spirit world could not offer him any help to bring the captured spirit home. Ironically, they could not even enhance his ability and opportunity to bargain with the demons to release the spirit. There is no guarantee that the sick will be healed. In fact, the shaman does not physically see a demon or demons holding the spirit of the sick person. Even with that many helpers, there is no guarantee that the shaman will be able to find the spirit. He only thinks in his mind that he has found the spirit, which demons have captured, and decides what amount of ransom should be offered to the demons in exchange for the spirit.[195]

The power of the Hmong shaman is nothing more than what is called the "skill of barter." The craftier the shaman, the better chance he can barter with the demons to release the captured spirit. For this reason, some shamans are believed to be more successful in healing than others. Even with those enormous spiritual forces with him, the shaman has no power to forcibly retrieve the captured spirit of the sick person from the demons. What he has to do is to barter another spirit for the captured spirit and usually he barters an animal for the spirit of the sick person. Hmong animists believe that animals also have spirits.[196] To sacrifice an animal for the captured human spirit is to exchange the spirit of the animal for the human spirit. In order for the demons to release the

---

[195] Fadiman, 283.
[196] Lee and Tapp, 27.

captured spirit and in order for the sick to be cured, an animal has to die.[197] In Lia Lee's case, the shaman spoke to the pig that was to be sacrificed for Lia saying, "It would be well rewarded for its work and that at the end of the year its soul would be set free."[198] What kind of animal and how big the animal has to be is dependent on the agreement the shaman has made with the demons. They always have to sacrifice the animal within a certain timeframe, usually within a few days after the shaman has bartered with the demons. They believe that failure to fulfill the agreement is risking the life of the person because the demons will come back to seize the spirit of the person again and it will be more difficult to bargain for the release of his spirit the second time. Not only that the spirit of the sick person is at greater risk, but the spirit of the shaman is in danger as well because demons will take revenge on the shaman.[199] They also have to give the demons certain amount of spirit paper money to please them.

Most anthropologists and ethnographers who wrote about Hmong shamanism claimed that the introduction of Western medicines to the Hmong people did not threaten the healing work of shaman.[200] This is true, but many Hmong animists refused Western medical help due to their belief in shamanism. I personally knew two cases in which the families either refused to follow through with the advice of the medical professionals or failed to seek the help of medical doctor and the end results were tragic for the families due to their beliefs in shamanic healing. The first case was my own half-brother. He grew up as a Christian, attended church every Sunday, joined the youth group and attended youth revival conferences several years. But he married to a wife who was

---

[197] Conquergood, 70.
[198] Fadiman, 285.
[199] DuBois, 46.
[200] Ibid., 61.

an animist. Though she went to church for several years, her faith in God was shallow. All of her family members and relatives were animists. She was more outspoken than my brother. When she developed a brain tumor, the doctors advised them that she had to undergo surgery to remove the tumor, otherwise it would become cancer and she could die. Unknown to me and my oldest brother, he and his wife had already consulted with shamans, and sought advice from the relatives of his mother's side and his wife's family members, all of whom were animists. The shaman told them that her illness was caused by the spirit of our father. The shaman told them that our father wanted a cow from them. When they said that they were going to recant Christianity and revert to animism to perform the ritual, which Hmong animists call the Bull Spirit ritual (*Nyuj dlaab*), my heart sank. I told them that what they were telling us was offensive to us and also to our father who was a good Christian when he passed away. We urged them to listen to the advice of the medical professionals and follow through with the procedure. We urged them not to forfeit their Christian faith, however, they eventually did. They rather listened to the advice of their non-Christian relatives and forgo the surgery. Her younger sister said to my brother and his wife that if they would do what the shaman had told them to do, she would be fine and well. She died two years later with cancer spread all over her body. The second case was a tax client. When they came to do their taxes in 2009, he was already very sick and couldn't remember things well. His illness caused severe headache. The family was animist and had consulted with shamans. The shamans diagnosed him to be a shamanic candidate and said that his illness was caused by the shamanic demons (*dlaab neeb*) that wanted him to be a shaman. For that reason, he and his parents refused to seek medical help. However, shortly before he died, he went to see doctors and he was diagnosed to have brain tumor, but by then it was already too late for the doctors to do anything to help.

JESUS IS THE GREATEST HEALER

Superior to *Sivyig*, the most powerful of any Hmong shamans, and the most powerful demons and Satan, is the Lord Jesus Christ. The story of Jesus healing and raising people from their death is not a myth or legend like the myths of *Sivyig*. It is real and it is recorded as human history. The Bible in Luke 1:26-38 says that Jesus is the Son of God, born of a virgin girl called Mary by the power of the Holy Spirit. He is fully God and fully man at the same time.[201] He is God incarnated in flesh into the world that He created to redeem His precious mankind back to Himself and to proclaim God's Kingdom of Heaven to His lost humankind. However, Jesus did not only preach the Kingdom of Heaven to the people, he healed them from their illness (Mark 2:1-12), cast out demons from people (Mark 5:1-20), and raised the dead to life again (John 11:1-44).

Why does God have to redeem His own created mankind? Genesis 3:4-5 tells us that when Adam and Eve decided to obey the deception of Satan (*Ntxwgnyoog*) and ate the forbidden fruits from the tree of the knowledge of good and evil, they gave themselves and their authority over all creation and the power to rule over the world to Satan (*Ntxwgnyoog*).[202] From that point on they became the properties of Satan, whether they liked it or not. This is the reason why for the Hmong animists, while cursing Satan for causing sickness and death, they also asking Satan to grant new permits of

---

[201] Kolb, 124.

[202] Charles H. Kraft, *I Give You Authority: Practicing the Authority Jesus Gave Us,* (Grand Rapids: Published by Chosen Books, 1997), 20.

reincarnate life for the spirits of the dead. Also, at the same time as they worship their household demons including the spirits of their ancestors, they accuse them of oppression and bartering their spirits to the wild demons. And at the same time as they ask these demons to protect them, they are being possessed by them. Satan gained possession of the whole world from Adam and Eve and this was the reason that Satan had the right to say the following to Jesus:

> The devil led Him up to a high place and showed Him in an instant all the kingdoms of the world. And he said to Him, "I will give you all their authority and splendor; it has been given to me, and I can give it to anyone I want to. If you worship me, it will all be yours" (Luke 4:5-7).

Jesus came to reclaim what was rightfully his, but Satan (*Ntxwgnyoog*) said all of it belonged to him. How much power and authority does Satan have? As we can see from the passage above, Satan probably has a lot. Satan claims that all the kingdoms and authorities on earth were given to him, referring to the day he tricked Adam and Eve into eating the forbidden fruits. Hmong animists believe that Satan (*Ntxwgnyoog*) has the power to cause sickness and death and they are right. This is the reason that no human power including shamans can fight against Satan (*Ntxwgnyoog*) and his demons, but only to bargain with them. However, Satan and his demons do not have all the power and authority over God's creation. Job's story in the Holy Bible tells us that Satan's power and authority are limited by God and he couldn't do anything without God's permission (Job 1). Imagine for a moment what would be like if Satan (*Ntxwgnyoog*) had total control of the world. If Satan had all the power and authority on earth, the whole world would be a lot different today. But thanks be to God who is our Heavenly Father, our Creator, and our Savior, even though Adam and Eve turned over their power and authority to rule the world to Satan, God is still in control of His creation and Satan (*Ntxwgnyoog*) is still subject to God's authority. The supremacy of God's power and authority is evident in the work of Jesus Christ during his time on earth. During Jesus Christ's earthly ministry, he touched and transformed countless lives and made them whole again, whatever their sufferings were. Let us look at the miracle Jesus did for the paralytic recorded in Mark 2:1-12. People were gathering in a house listening to Jesus' preaching, and then four friends carried a paralyzed man over for Jesus to cure. When they could not get the man to Jesus because there were too many people, they decided to climb on the roof, open a hole, and lowered the paralyzed man down in front of Jesus. Jesus said to the paralyzed man, "Son, your sins are forgiven." By these words, the teachers of the laws (Moses' Laws) that were also there were thinking silently to themselves that Jesus was blaspheming God because only God could forgive sins. Jesus immediately responded to them with the following words,

> "Why are you thinking these things? Which is easier: to say to the paralytic, 'Your sins are forgiven,' or to say, 'Get up, take your mat and walk'? But that you may know that the Son of Man has authority on earth to forgive sins. . ." He said to the paralytic, "I tell you, get up, take your mat and go home." He got up, took his mat and walked out in full view of them all. This amazed everyone and they praised God, saying, "We have never seen anything like this."

When Jesus healed people, they immediately felt the cure and became whole from their illness, no matter what it was. Read carefully what Jesus says above . . . "But that you may know that the Son of Man has authority on earth to forgive sins. . ." These words tell us that this paralyzed man's source of illness was sins. Other passages elsewhere in the Gospels of Jesus Christ tell us that illness is either caused by natural conditions or by demonic oppression, but nothing says about the spirit being seized and taken away by the demons as Hmong animists believe happened. It further means that no matter what the source of the illness was, Jesus has the power to cure them all. Jesus did not have to negotiate with any spiritual force like the Hmong shamans have to negotiate with the demons to release the spirit of the sick person. Again Jesus does not have to sacrifice any animal or use anything to exchange for the spirit of the sick person. When He commanded, no matter what the source of the illness was, whether it was sin, natural cause, or demonic oppression, it had to obey His command and the sick person was immediately healed. What does the passage above tell us? It tells us that Jesus is fully God in human flesh.[203]

As pointed out above, shamans have no authority over demons. Though Hmong animists and shamans alike believe that during the trance, the shamans have entered into the spirit world. Quincy states, "only the shaman had the ability to leave his body, enter the spirit world, and deal directly with the spirits, demons, and genies."[204] One might believe that the shaman would see himself leading his team of spirit helpers, the thousands of Chinese spirit soldiers and the emperors and empresses into the spirit world. But the truth is such claim is untrue and it's only in their imaginations. According to Jacques Lemoine, Hmong shamans do not

---

[203] Kolb, 125-127.
[204] Quincy, 93-94; DuBois, 45.

actually see the spirit world, but while remaining blind behind the veil, they think that they see the spirit world in their minds. They do not actually see any demon holding the spirit of the sick. They believe in their minds that they receive the information about what caused the illness "through the constant narration of their seer-spirit" (*leejnkaub*).[205] A former shaman, Cher Chou Kue, who practiced shamanism for over six years before converting to Christianity reports that while in a trance, he did not see anything, and there was nothing to indicate that he was entering the spirit world. Unlike what Lemoine claims that it is the "seer-spirit" that guides the shaman and gives him narration during the trance, Kue states that the narration during the trance was learned phrases from years of practicing shamanic ritual. In fact, he says, even at the end of the shamanic ritual, the shaman doesn't really know what the real cause of the illness is. What the shaman tells the family about what caused the illness is only guesswork. Though he has to make the family believe that what he says is what he learned during the trance. This is why after the diagnostic shamanic ritual the shaman has to tell the family of the sick person to wait for several days to see if the person recovers from the illness. If the illness does not go away then it means that his diagnosis is incorrect and the family is free to summon a different shaman to conduct another diagnostic ritual. Kue says that no shaman would admit that what he tells the family about what caused the illness is only speculation. The shaman also has to plant fear in the minds of the family that if they don't follow through with what the shaman tells them to do then the demons would do more harm to the family as well as to the shaman. Kue says what kind of animal to be sacrificed and its size, the amount of spirit paper money to be burn to the demons, and the fee for conducting the shamanic ritual are determined solely by

---

[205] Lemoine, 15-16.

the shaman, but he has to say that they are determined and required by the demons in order for the demons to release the captured spirit so that the family would follow through with the requirements. Kue says that he was not only a shaman. He was also a psychic who knew what would happen in the future. Having a divine rock in his hand, he could predict what might happen in the future. However, while practicing shamanism and psychic, he kept thinking to himself "These things don't make sense." He then started to read the Bible to find out if there was any truth in the Bible. As he read the Bible more it made more sense to him and so he converted to Christianity. He is no longer a shaman and psychic, but a preacher.[206] The Lia Lee case that Anne Fadiman discussed extensively in her book "The Spirit Catches You and You Fall Down" is an example of how Hmong shamans misdiagnosed or are unable to diagnose what causes illness and their failure to cure the illness by shamanic rituals.[207]

Now, let us turn our attention to Jesus' authority over Satan (*Ntxwgnyoog*) and demons (*dlaab*). What does Jesus say in response to his disciples who reported to Him that demons had submitted to them in Jesus's name? Jesus says "I saw Satan (*Ntxwgnyoog*) fall like lightning from heaven" (Luke 10:17-18). To understand what Jesus really mean by seeing "Satan (*Ntxwgnyoog*) fall like lightning from heaven," we have to refer to Revelation 12:7-9. This passage tells us that Satan (*Ntxwgnyoog*) rebelled against God and there was war in heaven between God's angels and Satan (*Ntxwgnyoog*) and his demons. Then Satan (*Ntxwgnyoog*) and his demons lost the war and were thrown down to earth. But the most important meaning of the passage in Luke 10:18 is that Jesus wants to tell us that He is God in heaven. He is the one who

---

[206] Cher Chou Kue, interview by author, St. Paul, MN, September 4, 2013.

[207] One has to read the entire book in order to understand the perspective of the Hmong animists in regards to the underlying cause of illness.

hurled Satan (*Ntxwgnyoog*) and his demons down to earth from heaven. Therefore, Jesus has full authority over Satan (*Ntxwgnyoog*) and the demons wherever they are and He is God wherever He is. Jesus is omnipresent. The Bible records many accounts of Jesus casting out demons. Let us look at one of them in depths to know what kind of authority Jesus Christ has over Satan and demons. In Mark 5:1-17:

> They went across the lake to the region of the Gerasenes. When Jesus got out of the boat, a man with an impure spirit came from the tombs to meet him. This man lived in the tombs, and no one could bind him anymore, not even with a chain. For he had often been chained hand and foot, but he tore the chains apart and broke the irons on his feet. No one was strong enough to subdue him. Night and day among the tombs and in the hills he would cry out and cut himself with stones.
> When he saw Jesus from a distance, he ran and fell on his knees in front of him. He shouted at the top of his voice, "What do you want with me, Jesus, Son of the Most High God? In God's name don't torture me!" For Jesus had said to him, "Come out of this man, you impure spirit!"
> Then Jesus asked him, "What is your name?" "My name is Legion," he replied, "for we are many." And he begged Jesus again and again not to send them out the area.
> A large herd of pigs was feeding on the nearby hillside. The demons begged Jesus, "Send us among the pigs; allow us to go into them." He gave them permission, and the impure spirits came out and went into

the pigs. The herd, about two thousand in number, rushed down the steep bank into the lake and were drowned. Those tending the pigs ran off and reported this in the town and countryside, and the people went out to see what had happened. When they came to Jesus, they saw the man who had been possessed by the legion of demons, sitting there, dressed and in his right mind; and they were afraid. Those who had seen it told the people what had happened to the demon-possessed man and told about the pigs as well. Then the people began to plead with Jesus to leave their region.

The *Sivyig* legends that portrayed him fighting against Satan (*Ntxwgnyoog*) and winning are nothing but myths. There is no evidence anywhere to prove that *Sivyig* even really existed. But Jesus is real. He is the incarnated God coming down from heaven. The scriptural passage above proves that Jesus is God. It is much harder for people who are not Christians to accept that Jesus is God and the Savior of humanity[208] than for the demons to proclaim that Jesus is the "Son of the Most High God." This demon-possessed man had lived a solitary life in the tombs or at the cemetery for a long time. His dwelling place was the graves among the dead. The man was tormented and he cried out for help day and night. His family and relatives loved him and had tried their best to help, but even steel chains could not prevent him from breaking loose because the power of the demons that was in him made him very strong. Other gospel tells

---

[208] Ramesh Richard, *Preparing Evangelistic Sermons: A Seven-Step Method for Preaching Salvation* (Grand Rapids: Baker Book, 2005), 79.

us that the man was fit in violence and people who passed through the area had been attacked by him. But when Jesus arrived, the demons could not do anything, but ran toward Him and fell on His feet and worshipped Him, begging Him not to punish them. When Jesus asked for his name, instead of giving his real name, he said his name was Legion, a description of how many demons were in him. Legion is a military term and a legion of military personnel during Jesus' time was more than 5,000 soldiers. When the man replied to Jesus saying his name was Legion, he actually told Jesus that there were thousands of demons, like a legion of armed soldiers, in the man. In this passage, we see that no matter how many demons and how powerful they may be, they have no power over Jesus Christ. They couldn't do anything but beg for mercy by asking Jesus Christ not to send them to hell because it wasn't time yet for God to punish them. In the presence of the Lord Jesus Christ, they could not do anything without His permission. Unlike Hmong shamans, Jesus did not have to bargain with the demons to release the man. Jesus issued his command and the demons had to comply immediately.[209] They had to obey Jesus' command and come out of the man. They wanted to go into the herd of pigs, but they needed permission from Jesus Christ. Therefore, they had to beg Jesus and only when Jesus gave them permission then they went into the pigs.

This passage reveals the amazing power and authority of our Lord Jesus Christ over Satan (*Ntxwgnyoog*) and demons.[210] However, it also reveals that demons are very strong and powerful and can do anything they want to do to people who are not shielded by the power and authority of the Lord Jesus Christ. This is the reason why Hmong

---

[209] Kraft, 242.

[210] John M. Frame, *A Theology of Lordship: The Doctrine of the Christian Life* (Phillipsburg: P & R Publishing, 2008), 22-23.

animists who put complete trust in their household demons and ancestors for protection are constantly being tortured by them. People deserve to know that Jesus is Lord of all lords and He has authority and power over everything. In this world one either has Jesus Christ as his Lord or Satan as his lord, there are no other choices. Those who do not accept Jesus Christ as their Lord and Savior, their Master is Satan, a cruel and tyrannical lord.

Paul Vang, a church member gave testimony about why he decided to convert to Christianity. He said that prior to their conversion to Christianity he had no interest in knowing God and he kept wondering why Christians go to church every Sunday. He believes that if his family did not experience the terror of demonic oppression, he would never have thought to become Christian. He and his family were oppressed to the point that they felt the presence of the demons in the house, were depressed and thought of suicide, and were very afraid to stay in the house alone. He was the first to experience demonic oppression, then his wife, and his daughter. They did all that they could as any Hmong animists would do to cast out the demons, but nothing worked. Hmong animists believe that the peach tree branches could hit demons and have the power to scare them away. His father-in-law, who is an animist, used a handful of peach tree branches to conduct a ritual called "whip the demons" (*nplawm dlaab*) to clear the demons from the house, then threw them in the trash bin after the ritual, and the garbage truck had hauled them away; but the same bunch of peach tree branches showed up at his doorstep again the next morning. They eventually sought help from their only Christian friend and gave themselves to the Lord. They continued to experience the demonic oppression for some time after their conversion, but as they grew in faith and with much prayer from church members and Christian friends, they have been free from the power of the demons.[211] He is gracious and is amazed by the power of the Lord Jesus Christ that he and his family are free. This testified that God has vested the power of casting out the demons to the believers of Jesus Christ. Not only can Jesus Christ and his disciples cast out the demons, but in the name of Jesus Christ, Christians can cast out demons just as Jesus did. The first conversions of Hmong animists to Christianity in Laos also testified to this statement. According to Naolue Taylor Kue:

> The mass movement drama began in this way: While the entire Alliance mission staff was absent, attending the annual field conference in Vietnam on May 12-23, 1950, Nai Kheng led a thousand Hmong to Christ. When they returned, the Andrianoffs found an amazing state of affairs. This was reflected in a telegram which Mr. Andrianoff sent to Mr. Roffe in Luang Prabang: "Over a thousand converts – Come over and help us."
>
> The first Hmong who opened his heart to Christ was Boua Ya Thao, a sorcerer, one of Kheng's neighbors who Dr. Roffe said he was watching and wondering how he, Nai Kheng, could live in a haunted house without harm. The sorcerer then began to ask Kheng, "How is it that you can live in a haunted house and suffer no harm?" Nai Kheng took this opportunity to witness to him about the Lord Jesus, the supreme God of all deities. To make the

---

[211] Paul Vang, personal testimony, Lake Elmo, MN, November 23, 2013. Paul Vang and his wife gave very emotional testimonies at their Thanksgiving party about how grateful they were to the Lord for saving them from the power of the demons.

story short, as a result, Nai Kheng prayed in Laotian, Boua Ya prayed in Hmong, Ted Andrianoff prayed in poor Laotian and Ruth Andrianoff prayed in English. After this, Boua Ya had the fetishes removed from his house and yard and burned. Boua Ya became the first believer in early May of 1950.[212]

Historically, Hmong converted to Christianity only after they had done everything but still were unable to cast out the demons from oppressing them. This is still true today. Hmong animists would turn to God (*Yawmsaub*) and humbled themselves before the name of Jesus Christ as a last resort and only after they realized that their household demons are unable to protect them or that their household demons are the ones who oppressed them. Most Hmong animists are not physically possessed by demons, but they never truly experience the freedom from Satan and his demons either. But those who come to Christ and when Jesus sets them free, they are truly free, as Jesus says in John 8:36, "So if the Son sets you free, you will be free indeed." They never truly experience the freedom from demons because they worship Satan (*Ntxwgnyoog*) and the demons who are the destructors of God's creation, as Jesus says in John 8:38, "I am telling you what I have seen in the Father's presence, and you do what you have heard from your father" *who is Satan* (added emphasis is the author's).

---

[212] Naolue Taylor Kue, *A Hmong Church History,* (Thornton: Hmong District, 2000), 62-63. Mr. Kue was a pastor in several Hmong Alliance Churches before became a missionary. He was sent to Thailand, first to the Thai people in Thailand, then as a professor and administrator of the Christian & Missionary Alliance Bible Institute in Thailand. He is currently a missionary to an ethnic minority in Thailand. He was also elected as District Superintendent of the Hmong District of the Christian & Missionary Alliance.

In the *Sivyig* legend, it is said that *Sivyig* was able to raise people from their death, but that is only a myth.[213] If there was a real *Sivyig* who had that much power to battle against Satan (*Ntxwgnyoog*), to cure the sick, and to raise people from their death, the killing of his son would only prompt him to do a lot more against Satan, his archenemy. He wouldn't just abandon his fellow mankind to be slaughtered by Satan as the legends claim to have happened. In real life, people do not simply give up and accept defeat when life and death is on the line. This *Sivyig* myth cannot be taken as a true story and as the foundation of one's belief and hope.

But if there is one human being that has that much power to raise people from their death, that man is Jesus Christ. During his earthly ministry preaching the Good News of God's Kingdom of Heaven, Jesus not only cured the sick and cast out the demons, but He also raised people from their death to life. The Scripture in John 11:1-44 tells a very dramatic and emotional event when Jesus raised a man by the name of Lazarus who had been dead for several days from his tomb. Starting from verses 21 to 44:

> "Lord," Martha said to Jesus, "if you had been here, my brother would not have died. But I know that even now God will give you whatever you ask." Jesus said to her, "Your brother will rise again." Martha answered, "I know he will rise again in the resurrection at the last day."
>
> Jesus said to her, "I am the resurrection and the life. The one who believes in me will live, even though they die; and whoever lives by believing in me will never die. Do you believe this?" "Yes, Lord," she replied, "I

---

[213] Vincent K. Her, 101.

believe that you are the Messiah, the Son of God, who is to come into the world."

After she had said this, she went back and called her sister Mary aside. "The Teacher is here," she said, "and is asking for you." When Mary heard this, she got up quickly and went to him. Now Jesus had not yet entered the village, but was still at the place where Martha had met him. When the Jews who had been with Mary in the house, comforting her, noticed how quickly she got up and went out, they followed her, supposing she was going to the tomb to mourn there.

When Mary reached the place where Jesus was and saw him, she fell at his feet and said, "Lord, if you had been here, my brother would not have died." When Jesus saw her weeping, and the Jews who had come along with her also weeping, he was deeply moved in spirit and troubled. "Where have you laid him?" he asked. "Come and see, Lord," they replied. Jesus wept. The Jews said, "See how he loved him!" But some of them said, "Could not he who opened the eyes of the blind man have kept this man from dying?"

Jesus, once more deeply moved, came to the tomb. It was a cave with a stone laid across the entrance. "Take away the stone," he said. "But, Lord," said Martha, the sister of the dead man, "by this time there is a bad odor, for he has been there four days." Then Jesus said, "Did I not tell you that if you believe, you will see the glory of God?"

So they took away the stone. Then Jesus looked up and said, "Father, I thank you that you have heard me. I knew that you always hear me, but I said this for the benefit of the people standing here, that they may believe that you sent me." When he had said this, Jesus called in a loud voice, "Lazarus, come out!" The dead man came out, his hands and feet wrapped with strips of linen, and a cloth around his face. Jesus said to them, "Take off the grave clothes and let him go."

Death is the one thing humans wish to avoid or escape, but as much as they hate it and try to escape it, death is what they all move toward each and every day. For some, the pace moves slower than others, but no matter what the pace is for each person, everyone will reach that end point. Beyond that is death and for mankind death is the ultimate suffering, the final separation from loved ones, and it's the eternal departure from this earthly realm. God knew from the beginning of time that death was an unbearable suffering and that's why He warned Adam and Eve not to eat from the tree of the knowledge of good and evil because once they ate of it the violation was irreversible and mankind would suffer death. In the same general area in the Garden of Eden, God planted a tree of life and God did not prohibit them from eating from it (Genesis 2:9). However, instead of eating from the tree of life, they ate from the forbidden tree and humans have continued suffering death ever since. But Jesus is not only Lord for the living, He is the Lord for the dead as well. For Him death is not the end of life. It actually is the beginning of eternal life. Life is in His hands, so no matter how long a person has been dead, He can still bring him back to life and that's what he did with Lazarus. Jesus can do this because He is the supreme God, the Creator of the universe, and the Supreme Being from whom every form of life originated.

He is life and life is He. He could lay down His life and take it back again (John 10:17). People might ask why He didn't raise everyone who died back to life while He lived on earth. He could and He did raise many more people back to life, but life in the flesh would eventually end anyway. What He offers for mankind is a lot better than the physical life. That is eternal life with Him in His Kingdom of Heaven. God is not like what Lee and Tapp portrayed him to be – "an absentee god,"[214] – but He is as John H. Frame rightly described, "As Lord, God is, first of all, personal." Though supreme, God is "a person: one who thinks, speaks, feels, loves, and acts with purpose and to his own glory." He is transcendent and separated from mankind because of his holiness, but He is intimately close to us and not beyond our reach. It's not like the *Sivyig* story that even his believers admit to be a myth, a make believe story, but Jesus is recorded in world history and only the ignorant deny Him. Unlike Satan (*Ntxwgnyoog*) who enjoys seeing mankind suffer, God loves mankind because they are His precious creation and He takes on human flesh in the person of Jesus Christ to feel the pain of human suffering and redeem them from eternal death.[215] Do you have Jesus Christ as your Lord and Savior?

No one knows how long Hmong have been practicing shamanism, but there is evidence that Hmong shamanism has been heavily influenced by non-Hmong belief practices.[216] As stated above, the majority of shaman helpers were Chinese figures. Hmong animism also incorporated religious practices of other ethnic groups and nationalities as part of its belief system wherever they live.[217] Evidence of Hmong animism and shamanism adopting other religious

---

[214] Lee and Tapp, 31.
[215] Frame, 20.
[216] Lee and Tapp, 38-44.
[217] Kao-Ly Yang, 7.

practices is the incorporation of the Lao blessing ritual called "Baci." At the Baci ritual, people tie white threads on the person's wrist while bequeath blessing words to the person. There are several reasons a Baci ritual would take place. For example, the sick person who just went through the healing shamanic ritual is likely to receive these blessing threads. Another sign of a major adjustment to their belief is that some Hmong animists started to guide their dead to heaven (*ntuj ceebtsheej*), the same heavenly place Hmong Christians believe is God's Kingdom of Heaven, instead of to the world of darkness which Hmong animists also called the "parched sky dried land, frozen sky darkness land" (*ntuj qhua teb nkig, ntuj txag teb tsaus*), where their ancestors reside and which Satan (*Ntxwgnyoog*) is the lord and ruler. Though they don't want to believe in God and don't want to accept Jesus Christ as their Lord and Savior, they know that God's Kingdom of Heaven is a better place than the world of darkness, so Hmong animists have started to send their dead to heaven as well.[218]

Just as Hmong animism has adopted other religious beliefs and practices, it is reasonable to speculate that the *Sivyig* story could have been borrowed from the Bible, specifically the life story of Jesus Christ. This is not a far fetch speculation, as Hmong in China had been exposed to Christianity since the early 17th century.[219] Anyway, for the powers ascribed to *Sivyig*, no conscious person would believe that a human being would be able to physically fly, much less with a horse, like the birds or wind, be transformed into anything he wanted, and climb or fly to the sky to live there forever. Also, no reasonable person would believe that a person would have the power to raise the dead to life again. Only the depraved mind due to lack of knowledge of truth

---

[218] Hmongism, the Showing the Way chant.
[219] Quincy, 16.

would consider such myths to be true and base his belief and hope on them.[220] These powers and authorities belong to God alone and only the Lord Jesus Christ who is fully God and fully man could exercise them.

---

[220] Frame, 363.

CHAPTER 7
WORSHIP OF THE HOUSEHOLD DEMONS

Hmong refer to the spiritual beings as follows: the immortal spirit of the person is called *ntsujplig* or simply *plig*. They called demons - *dlaab*, Satan – *Ntxwgnyoog*, and God –*Yawmsaub*. Hmong animists called the protective household demons – *dlaab vaaj dlaab tsev*. But most writers of Hmong animism preferred to use the term "household spirits," a translation of *"plig vaaj plig tsev"* to refer to the Hmong term *"dlaab vaaj dlaab tsev"* or "household demons." I believe that these writers chose the term "household spirits" because it conveys a softer tone and exhibits a nicer image of the household demons than if they used the term "household demons." But by that they have mistranslated the term "household spirits" from the Hmong term *"dlaab vaaj dlaab tsev."* I will use the term "household demons" as it is the correct translation of the Hmong term *"dlaab vaaj dlaab tsev."* The word *"dlaab"* is a generic term for demon or demons. It can further be classified as "tamed demons" (*dlaab nyeg*) or "wild demons" *(dlaab qus)*. Hmong animists further divide the household demons into two groups. First, the spirits of the ancestors that are also called the "demons of the deceased parents" (*dlaab nam dlaab txiv*), demons of grandparents (*dlaab puj dlaab yawm*), demons of great grandparents (*dlaab pujkoob yawmkoob*), and so on. Second are the demons that have been adopted by the ancestors as their household demons. Together they form the household demons.[221]

THE HOUSE IS NOT ONLY FOR THE LIVING

Every written account of Hmong animism portrays the household demons as the family protectors who have good intentions for the family. The purpose of this study is to reveal the truth, the tyranny and cruelty these household demons exhibit towards the Hmong animists. But first, we should discuss who these demons are and where they belong in the house. Hmong animism teaches that household demons reside in every corner and post of the house. They are the protectors of the family. Hmong animists believe that when these household demons are properly worshipped, the family will prosper in wealth, have good health, and have harmony in the family. On the other hand, if there is disharmony in the family, if the family has health problems or is suffering, or if the family is struggling financially, they believe that the household demons are not properly worshipped. Therefore, the household demons have caused these problems in order to get attention from the family, especially the head of the household. The house of a Hmong animist is not just a living space for the family, but it also is the family's place of worship. The house is not just for the living, but it is also for the spirits of the ancestors as well as for the tamed household demons. Therefore, in a house of a Hmong animist, one

---

[221] Ya Po Cha, 141.

would see the fetish, the family altar, and if there's a shaman in the family, a shamanic altar. One would also see silver colored paper money pasted to the entrance door frame, various walls inside and outside of the house, the stove, kitchen cabinets, and even the bedroom door frame to signify the sites of abode of each of the household demons. Some herbalists even erect altars for the herbal medicine demons.[222]

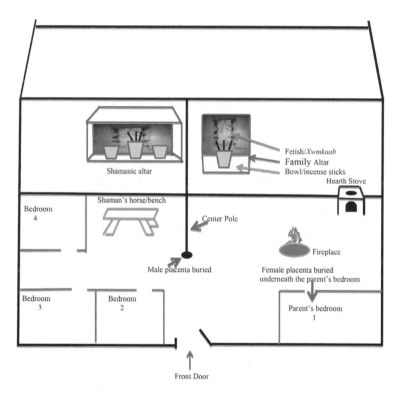

Figure 7.1: Schematic diagram of a traditional layout of a Hmong animist's house. This diagram represents a traditional Hmong house and the altar and fetish represent a Hmong family whose religion is animism. The shaman's altar and shaman's horse or shamanic bench, indicate that someone in the family is a shaman. Only families who have a shaman would have the shaman's altar and the horse or the shamanic bench. The

---

[222] Lee and Tapp, 29.

shamanic altar usually is more elaborately decorated than what showed above. A shaman would require other shamanistic gear, but due to limited space in the drawing, I deliberately chose not to show them. Every place and pole in the house is religiously significant and a different household demon is designated to occupy each site.

The household altar that also includes the fetish (*xwm-kaab*) is the most visible symbol of Hmong animism. The altar is hung on the wall directly opposite to the main door in the main living room. The family altar is the central theme of animistic worship. It is the place where incense sticks are burned as fragrance, and fruits, food, and wine are presented as thanksgiving offerings to all the household demons. But some families do not have the family altar. They only have the fetish hanging on the wall.

The legends about the family altar are many, but three are discussed below. One of the legends goes like this: A long time ago in China there was a Hmong king named Vang Kang (*Vaaj Kaav*) who won every battle against the Chinese. He was feared by the Chinese but loved by the Hmong as their king and protector. In order to be safe from the Chinese, each Hmong family had to hang a painted picture of the King *Vaaj Kaav* on the wall. When the Chinese soldiers saw the picture they knew that the family belonged to the Hmong King and those who did not have the picture of him were tortured and in many cases killed. King *Vaaj Kaav* promised the Hmong that he would deliver his pictures to all Hmong families at each new lunar year. In return, each Hmong family who received a picture of him had to give a rooster to the King as household tax. However, years later when King *Vaaj Kaav* was killed by the Chinese soldiers, all Hmong families who had the pictures of the king became the target of torturing and killing. Therefore, instead of hanging his picture, Hmong started to hang silver paper with several rooster feathers. When the Chinese soldiers asked, they told them that the altar and the fetish were built for ancestral worship. But actually, the family altars were built to honor the king and his spirit was invited to dwell in the fetish. In accordance with his annual giving of his pictures for the protection of the Hmong families, Hmong started to pay offerings at the lunar New Year to him, with each family sacrificing a rooster and the feathers pasted to the fetish and the altar.[223]

A second version of the legend of the family altar is provided by Timothy T. Vang. It is similar to the first legend discussed above, except that the name of the person being worshipped is different. It states as follows:

> In a Hmong animist's house, one would quickly notice a raised altar by the wall. That altar is called *xwmkaab*. When an older Hmong person speaks about *xwmkaab*, he would also say that it is "*Xwmkaab Los Yej*." Legend has it that in the old days, there was a Hmong brave general who was petrified by the Chinese. His name was *Los Yej* (Lo Ye). His followers would often hang his painted picture by the wall of their houses. Whenever a Chinese intruder came into the house, he would quickly notice *Los Yej's* picture on the wall and refrain from harassing the family. Later, after *Los Yej* was tricked and killed by the Chinese, any family that had his picture on the wall would easily be identified and subjected to torture or kill. The Hmong decided to take *Los Yej's* picture off the wall and erect an altar in its place with burning incense, boiled eggs, paper money, and an uncooked rice bowl on that altar in

---

[223] Timothy T. Vang, 96.

dedication to *Los Yej*. The belief was that when *Los Yej* was alive he was the protector, and even though he had died, his spirit would still be able to protect them. When he was still alive, *Los Yej* always wished four things would become reality for the Hmong. 1) That each Hmong family would have a full house of children (*"Muaj tub muaj ki puv vaaj puv tsev"*). 2) That their livestock would increase, filling the hills and plains (*"Muaj tsajtxhu puv toj puv peg"*). 3) That they would have money filling the family treasury (*"Muaj nyaj muaj txaj puv naas"*). And 4) that they would have grains filling the silos (*"Muaj qoob loo puv txhaab"*). These wishes are of military and political importance. The strength of a nation depends on the number of people available to serve in military service and good economy provides fund to equip and support for national defense. Having these four things will help in time of war against the Chinese, but the lack of these will only lead to defeat. Therefore, these are the wishes of the Hmong General *Los Yej*. Today, when the Hmong speak about these wishes, they refer to them as *Xwmkaab Los Yej*, which means the fourfold wishes of *Los Yej*. The word "*xwm*," which pronounced "*xwj*" or xu" in Chinese, is four. The word "*kaab*" in Hmong means, policy or guideline (*kaabke*). *Xwmkaab Los Yej* means the fourfold policies or guidelines of *Los Yej*. The family altar in a Hmong animist's house is erected to pay respect to the grave Hmong General *Los Yej* and to commemorate his fourfold wishes or policies for the Hmong.[224]

A third legend is offered by Patricia V. Symonds from the Hmong in Thailand. The legend has it as follows:

> Long ago Puj and Yawm Saub (Grandmother and Grandfather God) sent a baby to the world. They placed it on the junction of three paths. They sent this child because they wanted to test the people in the area. Puj and Yawm thought the Hmong would pick the child up and take it home. The child was crying. A Hmong man went by but did not pick the child up. A Lao man went by; he did not pick the child up. A Chinese man went by, and, seeing the crying child, he picked it up and carried it home. When the man reached home, the child disappeared, but Saub told the man to make an altar to the child, and as long as he honored the altar, they would be rich. Puj and Yawm Saub sent the same message to the Lao and the Hmong man saying they must also keep and honor altars, but they would never be as wealthy as the good Chinese man.[225] (Add emphasis is the author's).

---

[224] _____, personal communication by author, Maplewood, MN, October 8, 2014.

[225] Patricia V. Symonds, *Calling in the Spirit: Gender and the Cycle of Life in a Hmong Village* (Seattle and London: University of Washington Press, 2004), 13-14.

All three legends seemed to suggest that the family altar is built for prosperity and wealth and to pay respect for Hmong heroes. They believe that by worshipping these brave men, their spirits will protect and bless the Hmong animists. The spirits of these men will help the Hmong animists build wealth through good crops and an increase in livestock, and will prevent wealth from leaving the house.[226] Hmong animists depend on the demon of the family altar for everything, i.e. protection, good health, blessings, prosperity, and so on, but it rules the family with absolute power. It is the most tyrannical and cruel household demon. It rules the family with an iron rod ready to strike at anyone at any time unless the family completely submits to its authority with fear and obedience. It demands proper respect and worship. Any mistreatment, even by accident, could result in serious consequences. A family friend of ours shared a story about an incident that happened to one of their animist relatives a few years ago. One day a young child accidentally sprayed water at the family altar. A day later, the house was full of maggots. The parents thought that flies must have come into the house and laid eggs on the food, so they cleaned up the maggots and went about their business. The next day, they found more maggots in the house. They realized that something was wrong. They cleaned up the maggots and then called a shaman over to do a diagnostic ritual to find out what happened. The shaman told the family that the spray of water at the family altar was a violation and disrespectful to the demon of the family altar (*dlaab xwmkaab*). The shaman told the family that in order to avoid any further disastrous event the family had to appease the household demon with offerings.[227]

---

[226] Lee and Tapp, 36.
[227] Gaoxee Yang and Doua Yang personal testimony during one of the "New Believers' Class" sessions that I taught at their residence.

In a house of a Hmong animist, every corner, pole, beam, and tool has religious significance, but some are more important than others. The center pole of the house is very important for the male members of the family. It is where the placentas of all male infants are buried. This is where the Showing the Way chant instructs the spirit of the deceased male member of the family to find his placenta, or golden jacket, to wear in order to be able to be reborn. According to Lee and Tapp, this center pole is thought to be the central nerve of the patrilineal of the family.[228] The living family connects to the ancestors through this center pole, implying that the spirits of the ancestors live in the center pole. However, Ya Po Cha offers a somewhat different version of religious significance of the center pole. He states that the center pole is the dwelling place of the household guardian demons or the tame demons. In the same way that the center pole supports the house, the guardian demons are the protectors of the family. If the center pole is cut down, the house crumbles and if the guardian demons are toppled by wild demons, the family is "thrown into disarray."[229] The family members are sternly warned not to chop the center pole. They can touch it, but no one can use a knife or any tool to chop or chisel even a very small piece of it. As a young animist, my parents had to remind me every so often not to cut the center pole. No one can use a stick to strike at the center pole, nor can anyone use a rope to whip it. If that happens, the family had better be prepared to make a huge sacrifice to appease the center pole demons or else a family member could get sick or worse die. Nhia Toua Khang reported that when he was young and

---

> My wife and I were appointed as mentors and taught the "New Believers' Class" to them. This story was shared with them by the family who was affected by the event.

[228] Lee and Tapp, 37.
[229] Ya Po Cha, 138.

before his family converted to Christianity, he was struck by the center pole demon. He said that he woke up one morning with a serious bleeding nose. When his father conducted a diagnostic consultation with the household demons, he was told that the demon of the center pole was offended because his feet pointed straight toward the center pole during sleep. He said that the house was newly built and the bedroom was constructed just about a week earlier, but the bedroom had to be torn down.[230]

WHO THE DEMONS ARE

Though Hmong animists believe in the presence of household demons in every corner and post of the house, they do not necessarily agree on which demons belong at each place. Here are some examples of conflicting beliefs among the Hmong animists. Lee and Tapp define the household demon of the main door (*dlaab txhajmeej*) as the "spirit of wealth and richness,"[231] while Cha defines it as the demon of the "guardian of reputation,"[232] and Symonds claims that it is the demon that guards the main door.[233] Three writers presented three conflicting explanations about what the demon of the main door (*dlaab txhajmeej*) is doing for the family. Furthermore, for Lee and Tapp, the *dlaab roog* (no English translation is possible) is the demon that guards the main door. This *dlaab roog* is the demon that protects "all entrances to the home."[234] While the demon of the main door

---

[230] Nhia Toua Khang, interview by author, St. Paul, MN, June 21, 2014.

[231] Lee and Tapp, 36; Nicholas Tapp, *The Hmong of China: Context, Agency, and the Imaginary* (Boston: Brill Academics Publishers, Inc., 2003), 190.

[232] Ya Po Cha, 140.

[233] Symonds, 13.

[234] Lee and Tapp, 37.

(*dlaab txhajmeej*) dwells on the red and white rope with several jags protruding through it and hangs on the main door lintel, the *dlaab roog* "resides within the framework of the main door." Symonds described this *dlaab roog* as the demon of the bedroom door. It resides inside the house on a gourd on the bedroom wall and guards the bedroom door, especially the bedroom of the parents or married couple of the head of household because this household demon *dlaab roog* is responsible for the fertility of the family and of the family's livestock.[235] But Cha describes *dlaab roog* as an annual religious ritual. It is neither a demon of a main door as Lee and Tapp claim nor a demon of a bedroom door as Symonds describes. Cha states that during *dlaab roog* ritual, domestic animals are killed and cooked to offer to the household demons and the spirits of the ancestors. This is part of the ancestral annual worshipping ritual and as was historically done, women of the families and non-Hmong are not allowed to participate, and no other language than Hmong is spoken during this ritual.[236] According to Conquergood, his informant reported that the reason only the Hmong language is to be spoken during the ritual is because the first pig that was used for the sacrifice was a stolen swine.[237] These conflicting explanations indicate that though Hmong animists worship these demons, they don't know exactly who these demons are and what function they perform for the family.

Besides the demons of the family altar, center pole, front door, main door, and bedroom door, there are still other household demons. There are the demons of the hearth oven (*dlaab qhovtxus*), cooking fireplace (*dlaab qhovcub*), demon

---

[235] Symonds, 13.
[236] Ya Po Cha, 141.
[237] Dwight Conquergood, "I Am A Shaman: A Hmong Life Story with Ethnographic Commentary," (Minneapolis: University of Minnesota, Center for Urban and Regional Affairs 1989), 25-27.

of the loft (*dlaab nthaab*) that protects the granary loft,[238] demons of the bedrooms including the guest bedroom, and many unnamed demons for utensils and household tools. Furthermore, there are still countless shamanic demons (*dlaab neeb*) if there is a shaman in the family and herbalist demons (*dlaab tshuaj*) for the herbalists. Hmong animists never realize that there are too many demanding demons in their houses. Though they constantly live in fear of demonic oppression, they continue to worship them. They never realize that they cannot appease every one of them. This is the reason why Hmong animists have to sacrifice animals time after time to these demanding demons, but they still live in fear of them. Though they always live with fear, Hmong animists continue to believe that these demons really are their protectors rather than their oppressors.

VIOLATION OF THE RITUALS

There are repercussions for not conducting the rituals correctly. To perform a ritual properly means to perform it the same way it has always been done in the past. Any deviation in the performance of the ritual will be considered a violation and the household demons could turn against them. For the *tso plig* (release of the spirit) ritual, the names of the ancestors have to be correctly called lest someone in the family lineage will become blind.[239] Ya Po Cha states that if these rituals are not performed properly, not only will the household demons will not protect the family, they will "barter the soul of a family member to evil spirits, making that person sick."[240]

---

[238] Lee and Tapp, 37.
[239] Symonds, 149.
[240] Ya Po Cha, 142-143.

When it comes to Hmong religious beliefs, whether they are good or bad, Hmong animists are prohibited to ask the question, "Why?" Hmong animists cannot ask the question "Why" because Hmong animism is a religion of fear. Fear is the power of Satan (*Ntxwgnyoog*) and the demons (*dlaab*). Every ritual Hmong animists do for the spirits, whether for the household demons, the wild demons, or the spirits of the ancestors, they do to appease them so that they will not cause harm or death to the family.[241] Fear is the rule of Hmong animism and there are a lot of reasons to be fearful of these demons because they actually can do a lot of harm. If anyone asks any question, the response from parents or the religious leaders usually is one with a very negative connotation and cursing. The typical response is "Don't you dare to ask any question, for if demons hear, they will make you sick and die." Another reason no one cares to ask the question "Why" is that when ask they will get the typical response, "This is the grandmother's path, the grandfather's way, grandmother has done it, grandfather has done it (*Puj ua kaab, yawm ua kev, puj ua tseg, yawm ua ca*). You cannot question what has been done by the ancestors." In other words, this is the practice that our ancestors have done and left for us – don't question it.

TRUE DELIVERENCE

God (*Yawmsaub*) says in Isaiah 45:23 "Let all the world look to me for salvation!
For I am God; there is no other."[242] Hmong long for the deliverance from demonic oppression, but Hmong animists believe that they can be delivered from such oppression by

---

[241] Ibid., 47-70.

[242] The Book is a special edition of the New Living Translation, published by Tyndale House Publishers, Inc, Wheaton, IL.

the invocation of one demon to fight against another. Cha acknowledges that God (*Yawmsaub*) is the "savior of the human race," but Hmong animists refuse to accept Him as their Savior. Cha also states that Hmong animists believe that *Yawmsaub* was a man. This belief is consistent with the Holy Scripture in that God (*Yawmsaub*) revealed himself to human beings in human flesh. God (*Yawmsaub*) incarnated in the person of Jesus Christ to reveal God's authority, love, and mercy to His human creatures[243] and to renew the "vertical relationship" between God (*Yawmsaub*) who is our Heavenly Father and His fallen human race.[244] However, Hmong animists reject Jesus Christ as their Lord and Savior. The true story that God (*Yawmsaub*) incarnated as human in the person of Jesus Christ to become the Savior of the human race is nothing more than a laughingstock for the Hmong animists. But the fictitious human characters such as Chi Tu (*Cis Tuj*) and Tu Blu (*Tuj Nplug*), Tou Chi Tu (*Tub Cis Tuj*) and Tou Chi Blu (*Tuj Cis Nplug*), *Qas Tuj* and *Tuj Lug*, *Qaav Tuj* and *Qaav Taug* who are credited as the creators of heaven and earth, the mythical character of *Sivyig* who claimed to be the first Hmong shaman, and the false promise of reincarnation are very real for them. This God (*Yawmsaub*) is not important in the lives of the Hmong animists as they believe that *Yawmsaub* is just "an absentee god." But for those who realized that the yoke of Satan (*Ntxwgnyoog*) and the demons (*dlaab*) is too burdensome, you are invited to come to Jesus. You will experience God's amazing power and grace. He will deliver you from the power of Satan and the demons when you put your trust in God (*Yawmsaub*) and accept Him as your Lord and Savior. For Jesus says,

---

[243] Kolb, 64-65.
[244] Ibid, 131.

"Come to me, all you who are weary and burdened, and I will give you rest. Take my yoke upon you and learn from me, for I am gentle and humble in heart, and you will find rest for your souls. For my yoke is easy and my burden is light" (Matthew 11:28-30).

By being constantly oppressed and ruled over tyrannically by the household demons who were supposed to protect them, Hmong animists should know that demons, be it the household demons or wild demons, are not true lords and saviors. If they are, they would be gentle, sympathetic, and forgiving to those who worship them.

The Bible says that those demons that Hmong animists worship are the rebellious angels that God has thrown down to earth with Satan (*Ntxwgnyoog*) after they rebelled against God (*Yawmsaub*) in heaven. For this reason, they are enraged and by knowing that their time is short before God brings them to their eternal judgment in the lake of fire, they rule the earth tyrannically. Revelation 12:7-9 tells us who the demons are. It reads,

> Then war broke out in heaven. Michael and his angels fought against the dragon (*zaaj txwg zaaj laug*), and the dragon and his angels fought back. But he (*zaaj txwg zaaj laug*) was not strong enough, and they lost their place in heaven. The great dragon (*zaaj txwg zaaj laug*) was hurled down – that ancient serpent (*naab txwj naab laug*) called the devil (*tug ntxeevntxag*), or Satan (*Ntxwgnyoog*), who leads the whole world astray. He was hurled to the earth, and his angels with him.

It is important to know that those household demons are not their true protectors; only God is. Those demons are the fallen angels that teamed up with Satan to rebel against God in heaven, and as fallen angels, they no longer are called angels, but demons (*dlaab*) because they no longer belong to God but Satan. The Bible tells us in Genesis 1:1 that God (*Yawmsaub*) created the universe and everything in it and human beings are his most precious creation, but Genesis 3:1-7 tells us that this Satan (*Ntxwgnyoog*), who God hurled down to earth, betrayed the first two human beings God created to rule this earth and they sinned against God. However, with God's love for the human beings, God promised in Genesis 3:15 that He would send the Savior to save them. Jesus was that promised Savior. For anyone who decides to accept God (*Yawmsaub*) as their God and Jesus Christ as their Lord and Savior, God will deliver them from all of their tyrannical household demons and they will forever be free from the oppression of the household demons. God's Holy Spirit will dwell in those who belong to Him and He will protect them. They will no longer be tortured by Satan (*Ntxwgnyoog*) and the demons because God alone is the true and loving God who will protect those that belong to Him.

Hmong animists believe that Satan (*Ntxwgnyoog*) has the power to give life and renew life through reincarnation, but that isn't true. He neither has the power nor will he give life to humans. Satan (*Ntxwgnyoog*) is the life destroyer, not a life giver. The power and authority to give life is God's alone. The Showing the Way chant teaches that Satan (*Ntxwgnyoog*) is the one who causes sickness and death to human beings, that is true and that's all Satan does. Satan's (*Ntxwgnyoog's*) main goal on earth is to cause sickness and death to God's most precious creation, the human beings. Satan is God's main enemy in heaven and on earth. But human beings are God's most precious creation. Therefore, by destroying human beings, Satan knows that he is striking at God's heart. Hmong animists may wonder how Satan (*Ntxwgnyoog*) is destroying them. This is not hard to find out. Hmong animists cannot deny the fact that many of them have been possessed or oppressed by their own household demons or wild demons and they cannot deny that such oppression does not happen to them. If they would think back to those times when they were told that the reason someone in the family was gravely ill or that the reason a tragedy happened to the family was because their household demons caused it, or that they had to do certain things or sacrifice certain animals, otherwise someone in the family would die, they would know that their household demons are not their protectors, they actually are their oppressors.

Hmong animists are unable to understand that Satan (*Ntxwgnyoog*) is the ruler of the world of darkness and the demons that they adopted as their household protectors are Satan's (*Ntxwgnyoog's*) own agents on earth. The Bible says that Satan (*Ntxwgnyoog*) is actively working in full force with his demons to oppress mankind.[245] Hmong animists who worship the demons are at the same time also afraid of them, but Hmong Christians should give thanks to God for they no longer are afraid of the demons. Hmong Christians are not afraid of Satan (*Ntxwgnyoog*) and demons (*dlaab*) because they worship God (*Yawmsaub*) alone as their household protector. God is gentle but most powerful and through His protection, Satan and his demons cannot touch those who belong to Him because God has power and authority over Satan and the demons. The Bible tells us that Satan (*Ntxwgnyoog*) was God's most powerful angel in heaven until he rebelled against God. Ezekiel 28:12-19 reads as follows:

---

[245] 2 Corinthians 4:4 "The god of this age has blinded the minds of unbelievers, so that they cannot see the light of the gospel that displays the glory of Christ, who is the image of God."

"...You were the seal of perfection, full of wisdom and perfect in beauty. You were in Eden, the garden of God; every precious stone adorned you: carnelian, chrysolite and emerald, topaz, onyx and jasper, lapis lazuli, turquoise and beryl. Your settings and mountings were made of gold; on the day you were created they were prepared. You were anointed as a guardian cherub, for so I ordained you. You were on the holy mount of God; you walked among the fiery stones. You were blameless in your ways from the day you were created till wickedness was found in you. Through your widespread trade you were filled with violence, and you sinned. So I drove you in disgrace from the mount of God, and I expelled you, guardian cherub, from among the fiery stones. Your heart became proud on account of your beauty, and you corrupted your wisdom because of your splendor. So I threw you to the earth; I made a spectacle of you before kings. By your sins and dishonest trade you have desecrated your sanctuaries. So I made a fire come out from you, and it consumed you, and I reduced you to ashes on the ground in the sight of all who were watching. All the nations who knew you are appalled at you."

Though Satan and his demons still have the power to oppress mankind, they don't have power over God. Therefore, true deliverance is when someone accepts God as their God and Jesus as their Lord and Savior. In that instant, Satan (*Ntxwgnyoog*) and the demons (*dlaab*) have no power over him because God's power is protecting him.

Only then will he experience the complete freedom from Satan (*Ntxwgnyoog*) and the demons (*dlaab*). Do you want to have the experience of complete freedom from Satan and the demons for yourself?

CHAPTER 8

ANCESTRAL WORSHIP

The spirits of the deceased parents, grandparents, and great grandparents become the family's ancestors. During the funeral, all three spirits of the dead are instructed to leave the house, one to the grave, another one to the "parched sky dried land, frozen sky darkness land" or the demon world, and a third to be reincarnated. But Hmong animists continue to believe that the spirits of their ancestors reside inside the house and worship them as part of the household demons. According to Ya Po Cha, every place in the house belongs to the tamed demons, but the horizontal cross beam that touches the center pole of the house is the dwelling place for all the spirits of the family's ancestors.[246] But Lee and Tapp believe that the center pole, not the cross beam, is the dwelling place of the ancestors. They say the living family connects to the ancestors through the center pole.[247] However, Anne Fadiman and Patricia Symonds state that the four corner poles, rather than the center pole or the cross beam, of the house are the dwelling places of the

---

[246] Ya Po Cha, 138.
[247] Lee and Tapp, 37.

Ancestral Worship

ancestral spirits.[248] From Vincent K. Her's perspective, the ancestral dwelling place is neither the center pole, the cross beam, nor the four corner poles, but the family alter itself. Her states:

> For the Hmong traditionalist (animists), we worship by remembering the deceased members of our family, including our children, siblings, parents, grandparents, and ancestors. We build altars in our homes for this purpose. We offer food and incense regularly. In the home, we also have domestic guardians we called 'dlaab vaaj dlaab tsev.' These, together with our ancestral guardians, help to protect and ensure that we live healthy, productive lives.[249] (Added emphasis is the author's).

Five scholars of Hmong religion of animism offer four different places as the dwelling place of the spirits of the deceased family members and ancestors. This shows that Hmong animism is truly a religion of confusion. No two persons have similar explanation about the same subject.

Ancestral worship is important and required. Worshipping the dead starts during the funeral service, but only if the dead is an elderly person who has children and grandchildren, as Hmong animists believe that only the children would worship their parents and grandparents. During the funeral service and usually during the blessing sessions of the services, the children and grandchildren as well as the children of relatives would sit on the floor in front of the reed pipe (Kheng) player and the drummer. When it's time to bow down in propitiation to the dead, the reed pipe player

---

[248] Fadiman, 282; Symonds, 12.
[249] Vincent K. Her, 18.

would signal to the people and they would bow down. The purpose of it is that when they bow down in propitiation to the dead, the dead blesses them. Worshipping the dead is part of the belief that their ancestors will continue to bless them. Lee and Tapp say that "the ancestral spirits must be paid respects in order for the living to obtain good health and to prosper."[250] Symonds says that "the ancestors and household spirits, who are the tame spirits, must be treated with honor and respect. They must be cared for, or the result can be bad crops, illness, or even death in the household."[251]

Figure 8.1: This photo was taken on February 8, 2015 at the funeral of a cousin. These are the children and grandchildren. They worshipped their father during a blessing session. The two men stood in front of them were the bequeathers. They represented the father to bequest blessings to the children. Usually the bequeathers are paid thousands of dollars for such performance.

---

[250] Lee and Tapp, 36.
[251] Symonds, 18.

Ancestral Worship

An integral part of ancestral worship is the belief that spirits have to eat. Therefore, they believe that they have the obligation to feed the spirits of their ancestors. Feeding the dead starts from the funeral service and will continue for as long as it possibly can. During the funeral service, the dead is fed three times a day – breakfast, lunch, and dinner. After the funeral service, the family will deliver breakfast for the spirit to eat, starting the first morning after burial. The delivery of breakfast to the dead is to be repeated three mornings consecutively, but no lunch and dinner are delivered. Then on the 13th day after death or burial, the family has to perform the *xw plig* (xu-plee) ritual, as discussed above, to bring the spirit back home for a more lavish feast. The family will continue to deliver food, fruits, drinks, and flowers to the grave for this spirit for years afterward. Even those who believe that this spirit is also reincarnated after the *xw plig* ritual, they still bring food, fruits, drinks, and other things to the grave anyway. Hmong animists believe that if they don't feed their ancestors, they will be hungry, and in turn will withhold blessings and protection. As a result, the family will be cursed, become poor, have bad health, and face other undesired consequences, including tragic death. Lee and Tapp say that the names of the ascending three generations of ancestors have to be called individually, but ancestors beyond three generations could be called to join the feast without naming their names.[252] The belief that the spirits of the dead have to eat and depend on the living to feed them, and the fear that failure to feed their ancestors will cost them blessings, has caused the majority of Hmong to feel the obligation to remain animists. This is one of the most important reasons why Hmong animists refuse to convert to Christianity.[253]

---

[252] Lee and Tapp, 36.
[253] Conquergood, 20.

Though Hmong animists believe that spirits have to eat in order to survive, they only feed them a few times a year. If the spirits of the dead needed feeding from the living, occasional feeding wouldn't be enough. As humans, we have to eat on average three meals a day, so how could the spirits of the dead survive on feeding only 3 to 4 times, or even less, a year? Shouldn't they be fed 3 to 4 times daily if they really have to eat in order to continue to survive as spirit? There are only a few occasions a year that Hmong animists invite their ancestors to join them in ritual festivities. These are: the New Year's celebration; first crop harvest; wedding; funeral; at the newborn's spirit calling ritual; and other unspecified occasions. Many of these rituals are not regularly recurring events. The two regularly recurring occasions are the New Year and the first crop harvest, but the Hmong in the United States no longer farm for subsistence. This eliminates one of the important ritual occasions at which time the ancestors could be fed. And not all non-Christian Hmong in the United States believe in animism and have stopped practicing it, which includes ancestral worship. If the spirits of the dead really depend on the living family members to feed them in order to survive, they are in great trouble, as many of the non-Christian Hmong in the United States no longer make offerings to their ancestors. The fact that Hmong animists feed their dead only 3-4 times a year clearly indicates that the spirits of the dead do not need feeding. And if the spirits of the dead need feeding, all human spirits of all races should need feeding as well, not just the dead spirits of the Hmong animists.

While worshipping and feeding the spirits of the dead, Hmong animists cannot agree on which of the three spirits they are worshipping and feeding. Some say that the spirit to be worshipped and fed is the one that stays at the grave, but others believe that it is the one that stays with the ancestors in the world of darkness. Vincent Her, Lee and Tapp, and Ya

Ancestral Worship

Po Cha are among those who believe that the spirit that stays with the ancestors in the world of darkness is the one to be worshipped and fed.[254] Her says that the living families have to feed the spirits of the dead because those spirits that reside in the world of darkness "suffer constantly from hunger and starvation."[255] The contradiction is that the Showing the Way chant only provides one-way instruction for this spirit to go to the world of darkness. It is told to stay there forever with its ancestors, and it is also warned to never come back to the house of the living, but some Hmong animists still believe that this is the spirit that they worship and invite back home to join the living family at festivals. It is inconceivable that Hmong animists continue to believe that this spirit still can come back to the house of the living to participate in the feasts. Stanza 22 of Yang Chong Chee's version of the Showing the Way chant affirms this argument. It says:

> . . .now that you have arrived in the parched sky dried land, the frozen sky darkness land, but your grandmother and grandfather will say that you lived on the earth and you belonged there. The earth is good for farming and it is good for producing clothes, why are you coming, what do you have with you? You will say that you have nothing, but only the instruction of the way. Your grandfather and grandmother will ask you to show them the instruction of the way. The instruction of the way only shows you the way to the parched sky dried land, the frozen sky darkness land and you are coming to stay forever and

---

[254] Lee and Tapp, 36; Vincent K. Her, 100; Ya Po Cha, 149.
[255] Vincent K. Her, 100; Ya Po Cha, 149.

never know the way to return home...².⁵⁶ (Translation is the author's.)

There are other Hmong animists who believe that the spirit to be worshipped and fed is the one that stays at the grave. Vang Vang states that Tou Yer Lee, a Hmong animist leader in Minnesota, reports that the spirit that stays at the grave is the one to be worshipped and fed. Vang reports:

> One spirit rules the body, the second one rules the breath, and the third one rules the blood. Upon death, the first spirit that rules the body stays with the body and remains at the gravesite. Later he comes back to help the family he left behind. This is the spirit that the living children and descendants must feed and worship. The second spirit who rules the breath reincarnates, but can only reincarnate to be a child of the same clan. And the third one is to be escorted to the ancestral world or Hades, where his ancestors have gone.[257]

The last funeral ritual is the *tso plig* (release the spirit) ritual, which takes place about six months or later after the death of the person, is also a form of ancestral worship. The spirit of the dead is again invited to visit its home. The spirit of the dead is represented by a winnowing tray covered by a shirt of the dead. The spirit of the dead is lavishly served with food, alcohol, spirit paper money, flowers, and more.

---

[256] Bertrais, 53-54.

[257] Vang Vang, "Hmong: From Animism To Christianity," (PhD diss., Vision International University, 2002), 23. Currently, Dr. Vang is the senior pastor of the True Life Church, a Hmong Christian & Missionary Alliance Church, in North Carolina.

Relatives and friends of the dead gather together and feast with the spirit of the dead. This is the last occasion which the living family members would invite the spirit of the dead to visit the family alone. After this the family will continue to invite the spirit to come to join the family on special occasions, but other ancestral spirits will also be invited.

The contradiction is that though all three spirits have been sent out of the house during the funeral ritual and at no time which the family invites the spirit of the dead to return to live at home, Hmong animists continue to believe that the spirit of the dead resides in the house as household guardian to bless and protect the family.[258] While believing that the spirit of the dead resides inside the house, they deliver food to the grave. And while claiming that the spirit resides at home, Hmong animists believe that the spirit that comes to eat with the family during festivals is either coming from the grave or the world of darkness.

FEAR THAT THE DEAD MIGHT BECOME BAD DEMON

Although Hmong animists worship their dead, they are also fearful that their dead might become bad demon and cause distress to the family. Yvonne Lee, a co-worker talks about how her brother's house became haunted. This house was built by the family and it was only a few blocks away from our house. I knew him personally as well. She states that her aging parents lived with her brother's family. Her father was frightened by many unusual experiences at the house. She says that there were times when he felt the presence of the demons in the house. At one occasion, he saw a young man wearing orange clothes came to the door and rang the doorbell, but when he opened the door, there

---

[258] Ya Po Cha, 138; Fadiman 282.

was no one at the door. Then he had a dream seeing the same young man with the orange clothes saying to him that he was coming to get him. Lee says that Hmong animists believe that if one sees oneself or someone else wearing orange clothes in a dream, that is a bad sign and it usually means that the person might die. For that reason, her father was fearful of what he saw in his dream. He shared these experiences with his relatives and asked them for help. She says that her father passed away not long after he reported these fearful experiences that he had. She says that the night after his death many relatives came to the house to plan for his funeral. Many of them were on the porch and they saw a man sitting by himself in the dark at the bonfire in the backyard. They believed that he was her father because the man looked and sat exactly like her father. One of the men was going to go to the bonfire to see who that man was, but the rest of the men who were with him wouldn't allow him to go there. As soon as they came inside and looked out the window toward the bonfire, the man that was there a few moments earlier had disappeared. She also says that her father usually planted lemongrasses in the small garden in the backyard every spring and he had a bundle of them ready to be planted, but he died before planting them. All of the lemongrasses were untouched and remained where he left them, but two days after his death, the family discovered that all of the lemongrasses had been planted in the garden. They asked one another to find out who planted them, but no one had. How these lemongrasses were planted was very strange because the lemongrasses were just tucked into the surface of the soil and there was no footprint on the freshly tilted dirt. They believed that their father planted the lemongrasses after his death. Her brother's house became haunted after his death. They experienced many strange activities in the house such as hearing movement and lights being turned on and off when there was no one there, but they continued to live

Ancestral Worship

in the house until one night when her brother felt someone grabbed his arm as he came out of the shower. They left the house that very night and never returned to live in the house. She further says that a few months after they moved out of the house, her brother, sister-in-law, and their 14 year-old daughter went back to the house to pick up two dining chairs and a few other things from the house. Their daughter ran upstairs to pick up a few of her things, but she immediately ran down scared and cried and said that she saw her grandfather wearing some white clothes in the bedroom. Two nights later, he had a dream seeing his father and his father said to him, "Where have you all been for so long? I have been looking for you, but I couldn't find you. Now that I have found you, I'm coming to stay with you." Her brother was tragically murdered not long after all of these experiences. The families believe that their own father might have come back to haunt their brother's family.[259]

Hmong Christians do not believe that spirit becomes demon after death, capable of returning to haunt and cause tragic death to family members, or plant things after death. They believe that Ecclesiastes 12:6-7 provides a very clear understanding concerning where the spirit goes after death. Ecclesiastes 12: 6 "Yes, remember your Creator now while you are young, before the silver cord of life snaps and the golden bowl is broken. Don't wait until the water jar is smashed at the spring and the pulley is broken at the well. 7 For then the dust will return to the earth, and the spirit will return to God who gave it."[260] However, because not everyone believes in God, therefore, Hmong Christians believe that only some of the spirits will return to God in heaven to enjoy the presence of its Creator and others will go to the world of darkness awaiting judgment. The demons

---

[259] Yvonne Lee, interview by author, St. Paul, MN, December 22, 2014.
[260] New Living Translation.

that haunt the Hmong animists are the household demons that they worship. They pretend to be the family's dead person so that they will not be accused of causing calamity to the people that worship them. It is unfortunate that Hmong animists continue to refuse to believe in the power of the Lord Jesus Christ. If they are willing to accept Him, He will definitely deliver them from such demonic oppression. Their house will not be haunted, they will not be tortured, and there will be no more tragedy due to the power of the evil household demons. It is important for the Hmong animists to know that Hmong Christians do not experience such demonic oppression, something Hmong animists long for, but never receive it.

HMONG CHRISTIAN PERSPECTIVE ON ANCESTRAL WORSHIP

For the Hmong Christians who know about both Hmong animism and Christianity, it makes no sense to believe that the spirits of the deceased parents and ancestors continue to need feeding from the living. A saying that Hmong animists often throw at Hmong Christians is, "You Hmong Christians, because you don't feed and worship your parents and ancestors, you will not be blessed because they are hungry." Another saying is about sacrifice of animals and offering of spirit money to the dead at funeral. They say, "Because you did not sacrifice any cow and burn any spirit money to your dead, your love one will be poor in the demon world (*dlaabteb*)." Hmong Christians believe that the spirits of their passed away members are going to heaven to be with their God who created them. They are not going to the world of darkness, which Hmong call "parched sky dried land, frozen sky darkness land" (*ntuj qhua teb nkig, ntuj txag teb tsaus*) where hunger is a constant fear. Therefore, they do not need feeding nor do they need animals sacrificed to them by their living family. Hmong Christians usually kill a few cows as food for the guests, but not for the purpose of sacrifice to the dead. God takes care of them and provides everything they will ever need in heaven. Hmong Christians do not sacrifice animals and burn paper money to the dead, but they, unlike Hmong animists, never experience any incident or sign to indicate that their deceased parents or any deceased family members are hungry and in need of feeding. They never experience any threats of harm or death from the spirits of their dead family members for failure to feed and worship them. Nor do they experience any haunted spirits in their houses. Hmong Christians continue to respect and honor their deceased members, not only their parents and grandparents, but every family member that passed away, including their children and other descending family members. However, they believe that God alone is to be worshipped and not their deceased family members. They accept the Lord Jesus Christ as their only God and trust in His saving power for salvation, blessing, and protection,[261] not the spirits of their deceased parents and ancestors or the household demons that, instead of protecting them, threaten to harm those who worship them.

WORSHIP OF PROMINENT HMONG FIGURES

Hmong animists not only worship their own ancestors, they worship prominent Hmong figures. One of the family fetish stories discussed above was about the worship of a brave Hmong leader *Lo Yej*. According to Nicholas Tapp, Hmong in China regularly make sacrifice to Yang Tu Ku Teng (*Yang Tw Kw Teem*), who was a prominent Hmong leader. The legend has it that long ago there was a Hmong leader

---

[261] Kolb, 62.

named Yang Tu Ku Teng (*Yang Tw Kw Teem*) and his brother Yang Shoua (*Yang Suab*) was his army general. Yang Shoua (*Yang Suab*) had a dragon heart and he was very brave and a fierce fighter. He fought many battles against the Chinese and won every one of them. When the Chinese realized that they could not win battles against the Hmong unless they could get rid of *Yang Suab*, they then tricked the Hmong leader *Yang Tw Kw Teem* into a peace deal. The two sides were in peace and even became good friends. They invited one another to festivities. One day the Chinese invited the two Hmong leaders to a feast. *Yang Suab* helped the Chinese cook for the feast, but at the dinner, they accused him of stealing the pig's heart. With that accusation, his brother *Yang Tw Kw Teem* was furious at *Yang Suab* for having humiliated him before the Chinese. When the two of them returned home, *Yang Tw Kw Teem* killed *Yang Suab* and scooped out his heart and delivered it to the Chinese. As soon as the Chinese received the heart of the brave warrior general, they launched a fierce attack on the Hmong. Without the brave general, the Hmong were defeated and they had to flee in a hurry in order to survive. *Yang Tw Kw Teem* committed suicide by jumping into the Yellow River as a result of the defeat. The Hmong had nothing but an old pig. When the pig could not go any further, they sacrificed the pig in honor of *Yang Tw Kw Teem*. Since then, this sacrificial offering has been performed regularly for the "Spirit of Heaven" in hope that the family will receive blessings.[262]

Another Hmong figure that Hmong people have been worshipping is Shong Lue Yang. However, not all Hmong animists worship him. Shong Lue Yang claimed to be an illiterate person who became a Hmong messiah in 1959 when he claimed that he was sent by god to save the Hmong and the Khmu peoples. Although he was an illiterate, he was

---

[262] Tapp, 193-196.

able to create two written languages, one for the Hmong and the other for the Khmu, which it was his mother's native language. As a result of the creation of the written languages, he earned or gave himself the title of "Mother of Writing." He claimed to have the ability to foretell what would happen in the future. According to Chia Koua Vang, one of his remaining disciples, people flocked to learn his writing and his teaching. The written languages that he created were named "Pahawhs." Vang stated that Shong Lue Yang claimed that he himself had been born two times as a Hmong and as the savior of the Hmong and Khmu peoples. Shong Lue Yang claimed that his heavenly father god picked him out of the 12 sons to be born as a savior for the Hmong and Khmu. He said that he agreed to be born only after his heavenly father agreed to give the "Pahawhs" to the Hmong and the Khmu. His heavenly father promised that his two younger brothers would bring the writings to him when the time was right. He was born, grew up, married, and had five children, but his heavenly younger brothers did not come to give him the Pahawhs, so in disappointment he died. On the way back to heaven, he inadvertently reincarnated as a boar and remained a boar for years until he was killed by a farmer. He then went back to heaven and found out that his two younger brothers were still there. He asked his heavenly father why his younger brothers did not deliver the Pahawhs to him and his heavenly father said that it wasn't the right time yet. His heavenly father was angry at him for returning to heaven too soon. Therefore, his heavenly father ordered him to reborn. He was born again on September 15, 1929 in Vietnam, by his earthly father Chong Chi Yang and mother Kong. They named him Shua Yang and when he got married and had children, he was renamed Chia Shua Yang according to Hmong tradition. However, he gave himself the name of Shong Lue Yang later. He claimed that the name Shong Lue was the name given to him by his first set of parents when he was born the first time. During his early life he had to move from place to place between Vietnam and Laos. He became an orphan at a very young age and suffered many more tragic losses of family members including his siblings, during the Vietnam War. In April of 1959, his heavenly father told him that he was giving him the Pahawhs, but he had to start smoking opium, build a round house as a house of worship, build an altar to place flowers and candles on as incense offerings, and not sleep with his wife at night. On May 15, 1959, Shong Lue started to smoke opium and separated himself from his wife. That midnight when his wife and children were all asleep, two young men came to his bedroom and taught him the two Pahawhs, one for the Hmong and the other for the Khmu. These two young men kept coming night after night to teach him the Pahawhs. Then on September 15, 1959, his wife gave birth to twins. After the birth of his twin sons, the two young men stopped coming to teach him the Pahaws at night. The first born lived for only seven days and the younger son lived only seven more days and died. When the younger son, Xa, died he left him a message saying that they had been with him every night for seven months (from May 15 to September 15 of the same year was only four months, but Shong Lue Yang claimed it was seven months, a miscalculation by three full months) and they had taught him all that he had to know about Pahawhs. Therefore, he should start to teach the Pahawhs to other Hmong and Khmu. The message also said that whoever accepted his teaching and the Pahawhs would be blessed, but if the Hmong did not accept his writings and teaching, they would continue to be oppressed, poor, and be servants for other nations for "the next nine generations."[263]

---

[263] Chia Koua Vang, Gnia Yee Yang, and William A. Smalley, trans. Mitt Moua and See Yang, *The Life of Shong Lue Yang: Hmong "Mother of Writing," Southeast Asian Refugee Studies, Occasional*

Ancestral Worship

To make a long story short, Shong Lue was in great trouble with the Communist government in Vietnam by teaching his writings to the Hmong and Khmu and sought help from General Vang Pao. He eventually moved to Laos under General Vang Pao's protection. In Laos, he had the freedom to teach his writings and Chia Koua Vang was one of his disciples. Not long after he moved to Laos under the protection of General Vang Pao, there was a rift between him and the General. The troubles started to pop up again, but this time they were not the problems of teaching his writings to others. Shong Lue became more prophetic in his teachings. Many times when he prophesied that on certain day and at certain time the Communist soldiers were going to attack General Vang Pao's armies, they happened. General Vang Pao became suspicious of him, thinking he was a spy for the Communists. Part of Shong Lue's messianic preaching was the proclamation that a Hmong king was about to come to establish a Hmong kingdom. General Vang Pao was also angry at Shong Lue that he was recruiting the General's soldiers to join him as his security army. When the Lao King and the prime minister heard that Shong Lue was going to establish a Hmong kingdom, they were furious about it and ordered General Vang Pao to stop his movement. Shong Lue did not heed the repeated warnings, so General Vang Pao ordered the bombing of his compound. According to Tchuyi Vang, former chief of intelligence officer for General Vang Pao, Shong Lue was warned that if he did not stop proclaiming the establishment of a Hmong kingdom then his compound would be bombed. When the day passed without bombardment, Shong Lue told his followers that his "Father Hmong King" (*Txiv Vaaj Moob*) was too powerful and rendered General Vang Pao's fleet of T-28 planes inoperable.

Papers, Number Nine, (Minneapolis: University of Minnesota, 1990), 11-191.

That's why no airplane flew over to bomb his compound. The truth was that General Vang Pao did not want to bomb him. But when his secret agents that were among the followers of Shong Lue at his compound reported back to General Vang Pao what Shong Lue had said, he ordered the bombing of Shong Lue's compound the next day and it was destroyed. [264] Shong Lue was jailed several times, but each time his followers would bribe the jailors to secretly discharge him. Shong Lue was assassinated in 1971, allegedly by General Vang Pao's secret agents. Today the Hmong Pahawh is still being taught in the United States, but only a very small number of Hmong animists are interested in studying the writing. This writing is not only a form of writing; it is a religion of its own. One could remain an animist, but anyone who studies the Pahawh writing also has to believe in his messianic teaching that Shong Lue Yang was the 9th son of god and worship him as the savior of the Hmong.[265]

The most recent Hmong prominent figure that Hmong animists have started to worship is General Vang Pao, who died January 6, 2011 in Clovis, California. He earned the title the "Father of the Hmong" and he surely deserved that title for the love he gave to the Hmong. The Hmong were granted resettlement in the United States as refugees because of his involvement with the CIA during the Vietnam War. He was the most important and powerful Hmong man in this generation, therefore, Hmong animists believe that after death his spirit has the power to bless them if they worship him. At Hmong Village, a shopping center, owned by Hmong, an altar is erected for General Vang Pao. People worship him by offering food, fruit, and drinks on the altar, (see figure 8.2 below). He is being worshipped in part to pay respect for him

---

[264] Tchuyi Vang, interview by author, St. Paul, MN, November 4, 2013.
[265] Chia Koua Vang, Gnia Yee Yang, and William A. Smalley, trans. Mitt Moua and See Yang, 11-191.

Ancestral Worship

as the most important Hmong father figure and in part as an ancestor of the Hmong.[266] At the first ever national Hmong 18 Clan Council Conference in Minnesota on October 18-20, 2013, a Hmong animist leader prayed to General Vang Pao to bless them and give them wisdom.[267] The Scripture in Exodus 20:12 says "Honor your father and mother, so that you may live long in the land the Lord is giving you." Our parents, whether they still live or have passed away, deserve our respect and honor. We should always be grateful for them, respect them, and give them the honor they are due, but we should never worship them. General Vang Pao was a great and very important Hmong man and no one, Hmong and non-Hmong who knew him, would deny his contributions for the plight of the Hmong and also for his services for the United States during Vietnam War. He should continue to be respected and honored for what he has done and for whom he was, the same way the United States gives respect and honor to George Washington, Abraham Lincoln, and Martin Luther King Jr., but he should not be worshipped.

---

[266] An altar was erected with a big picture of General Vang Pao on the common hallway wall at Hmong Village, a shopping center that is owned by several Hmong families in St. Paul, MN. This altar was erected to make offerings to his spirit.

[267] "Hmong 18 Council Conference," A Hmong animist leader was praying to General Vang Pao to bless, guide, and give answers to them during the conference, St. Paul, MN, October 18-20, 2013, viewed on Hmong TV, an Internet TV program, October, 30, 2013.

Figure 8.2: This is an altar erected with a huge picture of General Vang Pao on the wall of a common hallway at Hmong Village, a shopping center owned by several Hmong families in St. Paul, MN. This altar is erected for the purpose of making offerings to his spirit. On the altar is a bowl with several mangoes. This bowl is occasionally refilled with different fruits, such as bananas, plums, and so on, and sometimes chicken eggs are placed there as well. The biggest bowl contains the incense sticks. Normally these joss sticks would be burned if the altar is at private home or outdoors. There are two candle lights, though they are not on. There are two flowery lights on each side of the altar, but the light bulb of the one on the right side is broken and has not been replaced for about a year. And there's a tall cup containing drinks.

CHAPTER 9

WORSHIP OF THE WILD DEMONS

Hmong animists believe that wild demons (*dlaab qus*) are everywhere beyond the door of the house. They believe that wild demons form hierarchic governing system similar to the human's governmental system. In order to live in harmony with the wild demons (*dlaab qus*), they have to worship the demons, particularly the leader of the territorial wild demons. Beyond the territorial wild demons, they also believe that every major natural feature such as a river, mountain, or rock, and even big tree, are possessed by a wild demon. Hmong animists believe that there are as many wild demons as humans living everywhere, not only in the forests, but also in cities and towns. If not careful one could accidentally walk into the personal space of a wild demon. Hmong animists believe that a lot of sickness is due in part to incidents like those described here. If a wild demon felt violated because someone unknowingly invaded its personal space, the wild demon could capture the spirit of that person and hold it for a ransom causing the person to be sick. In order to recover from the illness, a shaman has to perform the shamanic ritual and bargain with the demon to release the person's spirit. The family has to pay whatever price the shaman is able to bargain with the demon.[268] Most of the times, it will be some spirit paper money, one or two chickens, a pig, or in an extreme case, a cow or a water buffalo, sacrificed to the demon. Due to the fear that one might unknowingly violate a wild demon's territory, to appease the demon or demons, Hmong animist hunters would normally invite the demons of the area to feed with them. Before eating, an elder person of the group would scoop a spoonful of rice and pick up a piece of meat, then say something like this: "We are hunters in the area, we want your protection and want peace with you, we want you to provide us with some animals, therefore, we invite you who govern or oversee the territory to eat with us." The rice and meat are then thrown down to the ground, and then the group could start to eat. Even though Hmong animists have regularly done this type of peace offering, there have been instances when they felt the presence of wild demons while hunting. There was an incident that was widely discussed about. While a hunter was alone on the tree stand, apples were thrown at him and landed on the tree stand when no one else was nearby or no apple tree was around. A relative of mine reported one of his experiences while hunting. It was already late so he returned to the car. He knew where his car was, but after making a couple of circles around, he could not find the way back to his car. He realized something was wrong and decided to shout out for his hunting partners. He made an all-out yell for them and his eyes immediately opened and saw that his car and his hunting partners were only about 50-70 yards away from him. His hunting partners said to him that they saw him walked past them and the car earlier, but they did not realized that he was in trouble, so

---

[268] Ya Po Cha, 144.

they did not call to him. There had been cases when one hunting partner saw the other hunting partner as a wild animal, such as a bear, bull, or a deer, and took a shot at the animal, but it turned out to be his hunting partner that he shot and killed. They believed that instances like these are the work of the wild demons. No Hmong Christian hunters ever experienced any instance of feeling the presence of demons, thanks to the power and protection of the Lord Jesus Christ. There were two incidents that even though they happened back in Laos when I was very young, the memories of the incidents are still very clear in my mind today. These two incidents will affirm why Hmong animists are fearful of wild demons. In the midst of the Vietnam War, probably in 1971, we had to move from place to place to avoid the conflict of war and built temporary villages along the way. We settled in an area for a few months. One day, a man, his name was Chong Chao Vang, went hunting by himself. He came home frightened, exhausted, and was already very sick. He informed his family and several neighbors surrounding his house that he had encountered wild demons while hunting. He was dragged downslope while struggling with the wild demons. Whenever he grabbed onto the trees, the demons would force opened his hands and pull him away and down the slope again. He said that he was dragged by the demons the whole morning. He died three days later. All the villagers knew about this incident as it was openly discussed at his funeral.[269] Extreme cases like this one were rare, but they did

---

[269] Youa Hang Khang, interview by author, Rudolph, WI, October 9, 2013; Wang Sher Khang, interview by author, Minneapolis, MN, October 5, 2013. Author's note: To make sure that the memory of this event was accurate, my older brother, Youa Hang Khang, and my cousin Wang Sher Khang were interviewed and both affirmed the story. This family was related to us by marriage. Two brothers (sons of Chong Chao Vang) were married to two sisters who were my cousins.

happen. In cases like these, Hmong animists believe that he unknowingly wandered into the wild demons' territory and the wild demons he encountered were vicious ones. They believe that the demons had captured his spirit and caused his death. There was another incident and this one was personal. It happened at the same village about a month after the incident mentioned above. One day a few of us young children were playing in the little creek near a cousin's house. The rest of them had left the creek and gone inside the house except for me who was still playing in the water. Suddenly I saw a hand rise up from behind some thick bushes about 20 yards away. The hand was first shown with two fingers, then lowered down, and re-appeared with three fingers, and then four. I watched the display of the hand for a few minutes then got scared and ran into the house and told the people in the house that there was a demon outside. Some adults and several children who were playing in the creek with me earlier immediately ran back to see what or who was behind the bushes. Behind the bushes, the area was clear and no one was seen around. The bushes were tall enough that without climbing on something, no one would be able to raise their hand above the bushes.

WORSHIP OF TREES

Hmong animists not only believe that wild demons govern natural features, they actually worship those features. The object they worship could be a big stand-alone rock, a river, or the biggest and tallest tree in the area. One of the most common practices is the adoption of the biggest and tallest tree or sometime a cluster of trees as the divine trees (*ntoo xeeb*) and invite the most powerful wild demon (*dlaab xeebteb xeebchaw*) of the area to live in the tree. They worship the divine tree and promote the tree as the supernatural authority of the village believing that the tree would have the power to protect the village from enemies, promote peace and tranquility among the villagers, bless the village with good crops and livestock, and prevent disasters from happening to the village. In order to adopt a tree or a cluster of trees as the divine tree or trees (*ntoo xeeb*), the head of the village and several Hmong animist leaders have to search for the right tree or trees in the forest and when found, they all have to agree to it. Once they agree to adopt the tree as the divine tree, they have to hold a meeting with the villagers and inform them about it. They set up a day for the tree to be consecrated, and what to bring as offerings for the tree. The religious leaders have to prepare two roosters, some spirit paper money, joss sticks and candles as an offering to the tree. Other villagers are also required to bring their own spirit paper money, incense sticks, and any other items they could bring to offer to the tree. After the tree is adopted, no one is allowed to cut down the tree, not even the surrounding trees that might fall onto it. People are prohibited from hunting near it in case it might be shot at, defecated near it, or urinated on it. Anyone who knowingly or unknowingly violates the tree will be punished by the village leaders. They believe that if a violation was done, but no one knew about it, the violator could get a major disaster from the demon, the village animistic religious leader who was supposed to protect and care for the divine tree could get sick, the village as a whole could have poor crop yields, poor livestock production, or the village could face situations such as disagreements, murder, and the like. They also believe that similar situations will occur to the members of the village as well if the divine tree is neglected. Some Hmong animist communities even believe that the divine tree (*ntoo xeeb*) is bigger and more powerful than God the Creator and force Hmong Christians that live among them to take part in their propitiation. After the adoption, the villagers have to make annual pilgrimages of offering during the New Year's celebration, but the offerings are not just a couple of roosters, they have to bring a pig and more spirit paper money, joss sticks, fruits and produce to make offering to the tree.[270] Hmong animists and local governments in Thailand have used this method of adopting divine trees as a way of forest conservation and it works well for them because after the consecration of a tree, the whole area of forest was off limits for hunting, cutting for fire woods, or clearing for farming.[271] If one looks at these things that Hmong animists do to themselves, there is no wonder why Hmong animists are living in constant fear of the demons. They cannot control their own behavior, they cannot follow the rule of human law; therefore, they have to invoke the evil demons to rule over them. The consequences for violating the human rules are monetary fines, but the consequences of violating the demonic rules are sickness and death. Oh Hmong animists, how much longer will you subject yourselves to these curses? Do you know that God (*Yawmsaub*) is the Creator of the universe? Why not worship Him instead of the tree? Why not rely on Him who created you to protect you from harm instead of the evil demons?

WORSHIP OF CAST METAL STATUES

Not only do they worship natural objects, Hmong animists also worship cast metal statues made by human hands. Though Hmong animists never make any object for the purpose of worship other than the family altar, fetish, shamanic altar, and other kinds of altars,[272] Hmong animists

---

[270] Nicholas Tapp, Jean Michaud, Christian Culas, and Gary Yia Lee, *Hmong/Miao in Asia,* (Chiang Mai: Silkworm Books), 2004, 340-141.

[271] Ibid., 344.

[272] Exodus 20:4-6, "You shall not make for yourself an idol in the form of anything in heaven above or on the earth beneath or in the waters

have no problem worshipping idols made by other religions, specifically Buddhist statues. Also Hmong animism has no conflict with any other major religions that allow pantheistic worship and the worship of cast metal idols, except for Christianity because Christianity teaches its believers to completely separate themselves from worshipping Satan, demons, family's ancestors, household demons, divine trees, cast metal objects, and the list goes on.

FIGHT AGAINST THINGS THEY WORSHIP

Though Hmong animists worship these demons that live in the natural objects or objects made by human hand, they also fight against them at the same time. Unlike Christians who yearn to be fully filled by the Holy Spirit, Hmong animists would do everything possible to cast out the demon that possesses a person. Whenever a demon turns against them, they fight back with shamanic ritual, magical power, or even the invocation of another demon to fight against it. At the same time as they worship these demons, Hmong animists accuse them of causing sickness and death. If there's any death in the family, they blame it on Satan (*Ntxwgnyoog*), the household demons (*dlaab vaaj dlaab tsev*), the wild demons (*dlaab qus*), or all of them. Hmong animists do not understand the concept of lordship. Their way of worshipping these demons is more in the form of worship-servant. Hmong animists worship these demons and pay offerings to them not because they are their gods and lords, but only because they hope that these demons would be their servants to provide safe protection and receive blessing from them.

---

below. You shall not bow down to them or worship them; for I, the Lord your God, am a jealous God, punishing the children for the sin of the fathers to the third and fourth generation of those who hate me, but showing love to a thousand [generations] of those who love me and keep my commandments."

BELIEF IN GEOMANCY

Hmong animists not only believe in the blessings of the divine tree, they also believe in the blessing of a good geomantic location. Hmong call it "*memtoj*," which means underground live vein or "*loojmem*," underground live vein of the dragon. Chinese call it "*feng shui*." Hmong animists believe that the earth has underground live veins and whoever lives or buries a dead parent near or on a vein will be blessed. Normally, Hmong animists will not buy or build a house where its location is not believed to be geomantically significant. Hmong animists believe that a bad geomantic site will negatively affect the family that lives in the house. They may be sickly, become poor, experience chaos in the family, be socially disadvantage, be intellectually lacking, and so on. But a good geomantic location will help the family to have good health, prosper in whatever they do, and advance in social status and be intellectually better. In other words, the earth vein can bless the people who live near or on it. By the same belief, Hmong animists also believe that a good geomantic burial site for an elderly parent is very important. The descendants whose dead parent is buried near or on the earth's vein will be blessed. Lee and Tapp say, "The descendants of an ancestor will therefore benefit by having his grave located in a favorable place, just as the fortunes of the living may be affected by where their houses or villages are situated."[273] When an elderly person dies, the sons and relatives of the dead will spend several days looking for a perfect geomantic site. They even hire an expert to help them identify a perfect geomantic burial site. The cost is not important, but a good geomantic site is necessary. When we were looking for a burial site for our mother, my brother-in-law, who is an animist, made a lot of suggestions about

---

[273] Lee and Tapp, 127.

which sites were geomantically good, but we had to tell him that, as Christians, we did not consider it important. This is evidence that people who refuse to believe in God and His blessings will believe in the blessings of everything and usually from things that can't do anything. If it is true that the earth has underground live dragon veins and earth veins and such veins are of blessings for those who live on them or who buried their dead parents on them, then the Hmong would have been the richest people on earth, most advanced in everything, and they should be the first to have landed on the moon. But the opposite is true. The fact that Hmong animists depend on the blessings of everything else but God is a curse for them. Hmong lost their lands and independence to the Chinese, being persecuted and oppressed wherever they live, being one of the poorest peoples on earth, and being oppressed by the very demons that they believe to be their protectors. All these are evidence that Hmong are not being blessed by the tree, the underground live veins and the dragon veins, by their ancestors, household demons, wild demons, and other things that they believe and worship. These are the abominable practices that God prohibits people to do and whoever practices them will be cursed.

WORSHIPPING BEINGS

God created humans as worshipping beings, but because Hmong animists deny God's truth and refuse to acknowledge God's glory, they are left without the true God, but as worshipping beings, they must worship something. Refusing to worship the true God, they worship Satan (*Ntxwgnyoog*), demons (*dlaab*), rock, tree, river, mountain, cast metal statue, and so on. They practice idolatry, exactly what God strongly prohibits his human creatures to do. The Hmong, as being part of the fallen human race, deny God's truth and instead of worshipping the true God and seeking His protection and blessing, they believe that a tree will give them protection and the underground live veins will bless them. They believe that the tree is God and God is nothing. For Hmong animists, created things are promoted as God and God the Creator is demoted to be non-existence. This is exactly what Apostle Paul says in Romans 1:25, "They exchanged the truth about God for a lie, and worshipped and served created things (trees) rather than the Creator. . ." They exchanged glory for shame, incorruption for corruption (Romans 1:23).[274]

---

[274] Frame, 243.

CHAPTER 10

IS GOD A STRANGE GOD?

Hmong animists not only believe that *Yawmsaub* is the Creator, but they also believe that He is the good God and every good thing comes from Him. Lee and Tapp claim that God (*Yawmsaub*) is an "absentee god." While claiming that God (*Yawmsaub*) has been long absent from human affairs, they acknowledge that He has appeared in points of history to help mankind, and will also appear to help when people call upon Him.[275] This indicates that they do not totally deny that God (*Yawmsaub*) has no interest in human affairs. They only expose their own contradictions. Hmong animists deny Him because they do not want to glorify Him. However, in the midst of confusion and denial, Hmong animists have no doubts in their minds that *Yawmsaub* is the good God and he will punish the wrongdoers. When they are alone and thinking of doing something bad, illegal, or otherwise improper, they often think to themselves that even though no one sees them, "heaven sees" (*ntuj pum*), referring to God (*Yawmsaub*) as heaven, and that heaven will punish (*ntuj yuav tsau txim*) if they commit the wrongdoing.

---

[275] Lee and Tapp, 31; Timothy T. Vang, 103.

Hmong animists think that the Christian God in the Bible is a totally strange God that the Hmong as a group of people never know, but that is not true. The fact that God (*Yawmsaub*) revealed himself to the people of Israel first does not mean that He is not the God of the Hmong. The *Yawmsaub* whom all Hmong know to be the good God is the very God in the Bible. He is the God that revealed himself to the Israelites as the Creator God, the God of Abraham, Isaac, and Jacob, but He also revealed himself to the Hmong as the Creator God (*Yawmsaub tug tsim ntuj tsim teb*) and that He is the good God that the Hmong could depend on in times of crises. If anyone else other than the Israelites knows God well, it may have to be the Hmong. The only problem that Hmong animists refuse to accept God as their Lord and Jesus Christ as their Savior is because the Hmong were not God's chosen people at the beginning and that Jesus was not born into the Hmong, and that the Hmong were not the ones who wrote the Bible or the Word of God. But considering that Hmong animists never knew the Bible, their beliefs about God (*Yawmsaub*) and Satan (*Ntxwgnyoog*) are not too far off from the Bible. Samuel R. Clarke, who was a missionary to the Hmong in China for more than 30 years from the late 19th to early 20th centuries, stated that even though the Hmong have been living in close proximity with the Chinese for thousands of years, they did not worship the same spiritual being *Shang-ti* that the Chinese considered to be the Supreme Being, Buddhist, or Taoist idols that the Chinese people worshipped. According to Rev. Kong Hee, *Shang-ti* is the name of the Supreme God in the Bible in Chinese, the same way that Hmong Christians believe that the name of *Yawmsaub* is the name of the Creator God in the Bible in Hmong.[276] Mr.

---

[276] Kong Hee, "God in Ancient China: Discover the Similarities Between the History of China and the Christian Scriptures," http://youtube.com/watch?v=1kkxUyMAMXQ&feature=plcp (accessed June 28, 2014).

Is God a Strange God?

Clarke further reported that the Ahmao Hmong believed that a "Heavenly King" called "Vang-vai" created heaven and earth, but they did not worship him either.[277] The Hmong animists in the United States, Laos, and Thailand know very well that *Yawmsaub* is a good God and that he is the Creator God, but they too choose not to worship Him. They rather worship Satan (*Ntxwgnyoog*) and the demons that they know well to be the cruelest and most wicked deities.

When a Hmong animist converts to Christianity, he does not convert into believing in a totally unknown God. All that he has to do is accept that God (*Yawmsaub*), whom he has always denied, is the Lord of his life and Jesus as his Savior. At that same moment he will have to deny Satan (*Ntxwgnyoog*) and the demons (*dlaab*) that he has always worshipped. He will no longer worship Satan (*Ntxwgnyoog*), demons (*dlaab*), and ancestors, but will believe and worship God (*Yawmsaub*) alone. Just as he used to believe in Satan and the demons as his protectors, providers, and saviors and denied to glorify God (*Yawmsaub*), he now will deny them and accept *Yawmsaub* as his God, his Lord and Savior. When Hmong animists understand that the God in the Bible is the *Yawmsaub* that they already knew, it is easy for Hmong animists to accept and believe in God because they know that *Yawmsaub* is the good God. Even so the transition is not a simple decision. It is a dramatic and life-changing experience for the new convert because he will have to totally abandon what he knew and start believing in what he has always denied and rejected. He will be required to give up everything that is related to Hmong animism. The family altar, the shamanic altar and all shamanic tools, and everything else that is used for demonolatry, ancestral worship, or the worship of idols have to be removed from the house

---

[277] Samuel R. Clarke, *Among the Tribes in South-West China, 1911*, reprint (London: Forgotten Books, 2012), 62-63.

and burned. He has to get rid of every valuable item such as the golden Buddha statue and anything else that symbolizes Hmong animism, Buddhism, or non-Christianity. Lee and Tapp claim that the practices of burning family altars, forbidding ancestral worship and practicing traditional funeral rites are a form of intolerance of traditional Hmong culture by Hmong Christians.[278] No, this is not cultural intolerance, but it is the conversion process. In order to be a Christian, one has to get rid of the old things and adopt the new things. He has to put into his house the Bible and other Christian materials. He has to train his mind to believe, trust, and rely on God. He has to realize that the lords of the family are no longer the household demons, the spirits of the ancestors, and Satan, but that Jesus Christ is now their Savior and God (*Yawmsaub*) is the Lord of the family. Therefore, the transformation from animism to Christianity is quite dramatic, but it is an eternal life-saving change – a transition from the darkness world of the dead to the Kingdom of Heaven.

SIMILARITIES

Hmong animism, a religion that is wholly satanic and demonolatry and completely denies the existence of the God in the Bible, contains several accounts of events similar to the various accounts recorded in the Bible. Similarities discussed here do not necessarily mean similarities in beliefs and practices as in the Scripture. This section will explore some of those accounts in more details. As discussed above, Hmong are probably among the very few groups of people that have a story about the universal flood. Samuel R. Clarke, who was a missionary to the Black and Ahmao Hmong in China at the turn of the 20th Century, reported that even the Chinese people who have co-existed with the

---

[278] Lee and Tapp, 41.

Hmong for thousands of years don't have a story about the universal flood.[279] Hmong celebrate the first crop and the New Year as part of the celebration after the gathering of the crops (Exodus 23:16). The most striking account is the similarity in the beliefs between God (*Yawmsaub*) and Satan (*Ntxwgnyoog*). There are still many other things that Hmong animists appear to have borrowed from the Scripture to use as part of the shamanic rituals. For example, animals are sacrificed for the purpose of saving life and as offerings of thanks. Rare, but it has been done, is the sewing of three crosses on the back of a shirt to be worn by a person who is possessed, sickly, or gravely ill believing that when demons see those crosses, they would leave the person alone.

UNIVERSAL FLOOD

The universal flood account as recorded in Genesis 6 states that God (*Yawmsaub*) deeply regretted that He created mankind. They had become so evil and wicked that God decided to wipe them from the face of the earth. But Noah was righteous and blameless in the sight of the Lord so He saved Noah's family from destruction. God decided to re-create mankind and re-populate the earth after the universal flood, beginning with Noah's family. Therefore, God instructed Noah to build a very big ship for his family and animals and birds. God eventually brought down a flood that destroyed a whole generation of the wicked human race, but Noah's family was saved. Genesis 6 states:

> ⁵ The LORD saw how great the wickedness of the human race had become on the earth, and that every inclination of the thoughts of the human heart was only evil all the time. ⁶

---

[279] Clarke, 50-59.

The Lord regretted that he had made human beings on the earth, and his heart was deeply troubled. [7] So the Lord said, "I will wipe from the face of the earth the human race I have created—and with them the animals, the birds and the creatures that move along the ground—for I regret that I have made them." [8] But Noah found favor in the eyes of the Lord.

[14] So make yourself an ark of cypress wood; make rooms in it and coat it with pitch inside and out. [15] This is how you are to build it: The ark is to be three hundred cubits long, fifty cubits wide and thirty cubits high. [16] Make a roof for it, leaving below the roof an opening one cubit high all around. Put a door in the side of the ark and make lower, middle and upper decks. [17] I am going to bring floodwaters on the earth to destroy all life under the heaven, every creature that has the breath of life in it. Everything on earth will perish. [18] But I will establish my covenant with you, and you will enter the ark—you and your sons and your wife and your sons' wives with you. [19] You are to bring into the ark two of all living creatures, male and female, to keep them alive with you. [20] Two of every kind of bird, of every kind of animal and of every kind of creature that moves along the ground will come to you to be kept alive. [21] You are to take every kind of food that is to be eaten and store it away as food for you and for them."

[22] Noah did everything just as God commanded him

Is God a Strange God?

It is amazing that Hmong who know nothing about the universal flood in the Bible have legends about the universal flood. The Showing the Way chant states that it was Satan (*Ntxwgnyoog*) who, with a cruel heart and desired for human destruction, flooded the earth, but Gao Ah (*Nkauj Ab*) and Jau Ong (*Nraug Oo*) sought advice from God (*Yawmsaub*) to learn what to do about it. God or Grandmother God (*Pujsaub*) and Grandfather God (*Yawmsaub*) told them that when the flood came, the whole earth would be inundated with waters and all mankind would perish. God (*Pujsaub and Yawmsaub*) instructed Gao Ah and Jau Ong to build a wooden drum in preparation for the flood. The story says that all mankind perished in the flood except the brother (Jau Ong) and his sister (Gao Ah), who survived in the wooden drum.[280] There are many legends about the flood. One of which was recorded by Samuel R. Clarke from the Ahmao Hmong as follows:

> Two brothers ploughed a field one day, and next morning found the soil all replaced and smoothed over as if it had never been disturbed. This happened four times, and being greatly perplexed they decided to plough the field over once more and observe what happened. In the middle of the night while the brothers were watching, one on one side of the field and the other on the other side, they saw an old woman (a different legend recorded by Timothy T. Vang stated it was an old man)[281] descended from heaven with a board in her hand, who, after replacing the clods of earth, smoothed them with board.

---

[280] Bertrais, 28-29.
[281] Timothy T. Vang, 106.

The elder brother at once shouted to the younger one to come and help him to kill the old woman who had undone all the work. But the younger brother suggested that they should first ask her why she did this and put them to so much trouble. So they asked the old woman why she had acted so, and made them labor in vain. She then told them it was useless for them to waste time in ploughing land as a great flood was coming to drown the world. She then advised the younger brother, because he had been kind to her and prevented the elder brother killing her, to save himself in a huge wooden drum. . . She told the elder brother, because he had wished to kill her, to make for himself an iron drum.[282]

When the flood came, the iron drum that the older brother was in sank and he died, but the younger brother survived. His sister who rode in the wooden drum with him also survived. Though the legends are many and they describe the flood slightly differently from one another, they recorded the same story and though the story told is different from what is stated in the Bible, it still is considered a universal flood because it says that the whole earth was destroyed by the flood.

CELEBRATION OF THE FIRST-FRUITS OF CROPS

The celebration of the first-fruits of crops is the occasion when people give thanks to God for His blessing. The Bible instructs the Israelites to make offerings as a way of

---

[282] Clarke, 50-51.

honoring and acknowledging God as the source of blessing. The commandment prohibits the Israelites from eating any of the new crops before they make offering of thanks to God. Leviticus 23:9-14:

> ⁹ The LORD said to Moses, ¹⁰ "Speak to the Israelites and say to them: 'When you enter the land I am going to give you and you reap its harvest, bring to the priest a sheaf of the first grain you harvest. ¹¹ He is to wave the sheaf before the LORD so it will be accepted on your behalf; the priest is to wave it on the day after the Sabbath. ¹² On the day you wave the sheaf, you must sacrifice as a burnt offering to the LORD a lamb a year old without defect, ¹³ together with its grain offering of two-tenths of an ephah of the finest flour mixed with olive oil—a food offering presented to the LORD, a pleasing aroma—and its drink offering of a quarter of a hin of wine. ¹⁴ You must not eat any bread, or roasted or new grain, until the very day you bring this offering to your God. This is to be a lasting ordinance for the generations to come, wherever you live.

It is certain that other groups of people would most likely make offerings of thanks for first-fruits of crops as well, but not everyone gives thanks to God who created these crops as food for mankind. The Hmong have been faithfully observing the first-fruits of crop offerings, but for the Hmong animists, even though they often call a few relatives and neighbors to join them in celebration, it is a familial affair rather than a communal celebration, and instead of giving thanks to God the creator of the crops, they give thanks to ancestors and the household demons.²⁸³ The most important crops offering is the rice offering. Hmong families always grow a small plot of early rice. This rice always ripens early, ahead of the rest of the field. They use this early rice as the crops offering. Similar to the Levitical passage above, Hmong animists do not eat the fruits of the new crops until the head of the family makes the offerings of thanks (*laig dlaab*) to the ancestors and the household demons. Hmong Christians also celebrate the occasion and give thanks to God (*Yawmsaub*) who created these crops as food for humans. As traditionally observed, Hmong animists do not sacrifice a pig, goat, cow, or water buffalo, but they sacrifice at least two capon roosters.²⁸⁴ Capon roosters are raised specifically for this event and castrated pigs are raised particularly for the New Year celebration.

NEW YEAR CELEBRATION

The Hmong New Year celebration traditionally takes place in the 12th lunar month, which is the calendar month of November. However, Hmong New Year celebrations in the United States span the months of November to December. It is not to be celebrated on the same day, and each village, city or town celebrates on different days to allow folks from different locations to come to join the festivities. This creates some confusion for the non-Hmong people. Though all Asian nations that Hmong are living in celebrate New Year in April, Hmong celebrate New Year in November and December. This clearly indicates that ethnically and culturally the Hmong are different from the rest of Asian peoples.

---

[283] Ya Po Cha, 61.
[284] Ibid., 61

Is God a Strange God?

The Hmong New Year celebration is the holiday that marks the end of the harvest season[285] and it is a time of enjoyment to welcome the New Year. There are two aspects of the New Year celebration. First and probably the most important part of the celebration is the religious aspect of it. Second, it is the time for social gathering. Most important is the opportunity for the young men and women to come out in the public square to seek each other's affection and find a life-long mate. The Hmong New Year celebration appears to include several religious aspects similar to that which stated in Leviticus 23:15-43. It includes the celebration of food, atonement, and the day of rest and renewal. The traditional Hmong New Year celebration is divided into two dimensions – the private and public. The private dimension of the celebration is further divided into three parts. The first part of the New Year celebration is the festivity of food. In Leviticus 16:15-43, God commanded Moses to tell the Israelites to offer burnt offerings of lambs, rams, goats, bulls, and grains to the Lord. The Hmong do not make such offerings, but they celebrate the end of the harvest with a lot of eating from house to house. In countries where people raise their own livestock, this is when the castrated or neutered pig is slaughtered. For several days, people invite one another to eat and they go from house to house. They eat, drink, and are merry. This is also the time when the shamans burn the jaws of the animals they sacrificed to the demons as substitutes for the human spirits to release them from their duties.[286] This is the reason that Hmong animists have to sacrifice animals to save lives every year because the spirits of the sacrificed animals are released from their duties at the end of the year. The shamans also have to renew the relationship with the

---

[285] Paul Hillmer, 27; Geddes, 76-77.
[286] Fadiman, 281.

shamanic demons for another year; otherwise, they cannot continue performing shamanic rituals. Similar to the Israelites' day of atonement of sins, the Hmong animists also gather together for atonement. This is the second aspect of the Hmong New Year celebration. Leviticus 23: 26-32 says:

> ²⁶ The LORD said to Moses, ²⁷ "The tenth day of this seventh month is the Day of Atonement. Hold a sacred assembly and deny yourselves, and present a food offering to the LORD. ²⁸ Do not do any work on that day, because it is the Day of Atonement, when atonement is made for you before the LORD your God. ²⁹ Those who do not deny themselves on that day must be cut off from their people. ³⁰ I will destroy from among their people anyone who does any work on that day. ³¹ You shall do no work at all. This is to be a lasting ordinance for the generations to come, wherever you live. ³² It is a day of Sabbath rest for you, and you must deny yourselves. From the evening of the ninth day of the month until the following evening you are to observe your Sabbath."

Atonement in the Old Testament is to confess sins to the Lord and to reconcile themselves with the Lord with the blood and burnt offerings of animals and grains.[287] For the Hmong animists, the concept of atonement is completely different. It is neither about confessing one's sins, as Hmong animists do not understand biblically what sin is, nor reconciling oneself to one's lords as they do not consider

---

[287] J. D. Douglas and Merrill C. Tenney, *Zondervan Illustrated Bible Dictionary* (Grand Rapids: Zondervan, 2011), 474.

their household demons, ancestors, and Satan their lords even though they worship them. But it is about reconciling one's own spirit to oneself so that the body is whole again. Atonement also means to cast away from the family all evil and wild demons, all other evil forces, and bad lucks that may have secretly crept into the house that can possibly cause misfortunes, unhealthy relationships, illnesses, and death to the family to vanish with the passing year. And the household guardian demons who are the spirits of the ancestors and tamed demons are invoked to return to take their positions in the house to protect and bless the family. On the Day of Atonement, the Hmong animists gather all their clan members, who share the same ancestral root of household demons (*thooj dlaab koom qhua*), together for an atonement ceremony (*tusub*). A person who does not share the same ancestral root of household demons (*tsi thooj dlaab koom qhua*) cannot participate in this ritual even if he shares the same last name and lives among them. If they knowingly or even unknowingly allow someone who does not share the same line of household demons to join the ritual, there is a chance that there will be great consequences. The first atonement ritual is called *lwmsub* and it starts at home. Every family has to prepare a bundle of bamboo leaves (in US, any bundle of fresh leaves of tree branches is fine as bamboos are unavailable in most parts of the country). The ritual starts with the father or the eldest male of the family waving the bamboo leaves everywhere inside the house with the intent of casting out the evil and wild demons, all other evil forces, and bad lucks from the family. The lady of the family will also sweep the floors after the man. Now the ritual is called *tusub* (some groups continue to call *lwmsub*), which every family member has to gather together at an appointed place. If someone is unable to attend the ritual, a shirt belonging to the absent person has to be brought to the ceremony to represent the person; otherwise, the household demons will not protect that person. A tree is cut and planted at the appointed place and a rope made of woven straw grass is tied to the tree, one end higher up and the other end on the ground. Some clans will require that all bundles of the bamboo leaves from every family are brought to the gathering place and be tied to the tree with red fabric strings, some clans will just leave them on the ground beside the tree, but other clans do not bring them to the gathering place at all. In this case, every family is instructed by the religious leader how to dispose of them. They believe that all evil forces are swept and are stuck in the bundle of leaves, so if it's not carefully dispose of them, these evil forces can return to the house. At the gathering place, everyone, young and old has to walk in circle around the tree inside the loop of the grass rope, several times each way. The rope crossing symbolizes crossing from the old year to the New Year. While walking in a circle, the religious leader who conducts the ritual waves a rooster over people's heads and utters words to cast out evil and wild demons, all other evil forces, and bad lucks from the people. He bequeaths blessings of good health and prosperity to the people for the coming year. He also invokes the household guardian demons, the spirits of the ancestors, and the wild demons that rule the area to come to watch over them and protect them from harms and tragedies, and to bless them with peace, good health, and prosperity in the coming year. When the walk is complete, the performer of the ritual slashes the throat of the rooster and sprinkles the blood on the grass rope, the tree, and the bundles of the bamboo leaves to signify that the people are protected by the sacrificed blood of the rooster.[288] Some groups will throw the sacrificed rooster over the people from one side to the other to forecast how the fortunes of the people in the coming year will be like. If the rooster lands with the head pointing away

---

[288] Ya Po Cha, 51.

from the people, the right or left side of the people, they believe that they will have a good luck, healthy, and prosper year, but if the head of the rooster points toward the people, the coming year is not good. There is also a public aspect of the *tusub* ceremony which everyone can participate in the ritual of walking around the tree and inside the loop of the rope, which both Hmong and non-Hmong can participate.

Third, as Moses' Law commands the Israelites to sacrifice burnt offerings of food and animals to the Lord, the Hmong animists also sacrifice animals, not to God, but to their household demons and ancestors. This annual sacrifice serves two purposes: first as thanksgiving offerings and second as atonement to the spirit. The animals they sacrifice are not lambs, rams, bulls, and goats, but chickens and eggs. As a way of showing their appreciation for the blessings and protection they have received, roosters are sacrificed to the demons of the family altar, their ancestors, and the household demons. The family altar gets a new makeover and the fetish is replaced with brand new money paper and new rooster feathers. Hmong animists believe that spirits can be captured by demons and Satan, detach from the body when triggered by fear, or it simply wanders away in an errand. Not only that the spirits of the family members might have been absent from the body, but the spirits of the ancestors and the household guardian demons might be forced to leave the house by evil wild demons and other evil forces that invaded the house. Hmong animists believe that illness, mishap, and misfortunes are signs of the spirit being absent from the body as well as the absence of the ancestral spirits and household demons from the house. Therefore, New Year celebration is the occasion for the annual family atonement in which the spirit calling ritual is performed for the whole family as well as the call for the return of the spirits of the ancestors and the household guardian demons to take their places in the house, to protect, and bless the family again. The wealthy families will sacrifice a rooster for each family member, but one or two roosters can be sacrificed for all family members if the family cannot afford one for each. The less fortunate families that cannot sacrifice even a single rooster can use eggs instead. According to William Geddes, the festivity of the sacrificed roosters is so private that only the family members can eat.[289] Leviticus 23:28 says, "Do not do any work on that day, because it is the Day of Atonement, when atonement is made for you before the Lord your God." Hmong animists also prohibit work during this atonement period. During this atonement period, not only are the people prohibited to do work, but all family tools, including crossbows and guns are marked with the paper money and they are not to be used for three days. Not only that they cannot do any work, they are prohibited to cook as no pot or pan can be used for cooking. But prior to the three days of rest, Hmong animists have to prepare enough sticky rice patties, some of which are offered to the household demons and ancestors, but most of them are for the family to eat during the three days of rest.[290] The term "days of rest" is used, but the Hmong term for this occasion means "days of restriction or prohibition," (*caiv*) as no one is allowed to do any work, no tool can be used for any type of work, and so on.

The second dimension of the Hmong New Year celebration, traditionally, is the occasion for social gathering. This is the occasion when the single young men and women spend time out in the public square to find their soul mates. For a whole month, they go from town to town or village to village to participate the ball-tossing games to find their lifelong soul mate and many get married after the New Year celebration. Hmong girls are taught to be passive, shy, and to withhold their feelings toward boys, but during the New

---

[289] Geddes, 77.
[290] Ya Po Cha, 50-51.

Year celebration a Hmong girl can show her feelings for a boy by initiating the tossing of the ball to the boy she feels attracted to.[291] It is not only the occasion for the young men and women to find mates, but it is also the occasion for their parents to choose their sons-in-law or daughters-in-law. While the young men and women toss the balls to each other in courtship game, their parents are watching and observing and giving their approval or disapproval to their sons or daughters at the end of the day.

The Hmong New Year celebration in the United States is no longer an occasion for the young men and women to find their mates, but it is an occasion for entertainment such as beauty contests, talent shows, night life entertainment, and it is an opportunity for vendors to sell their products. The event is supposed to be a great opportunity for the non-profit organization(s) to raise tens of thousands of dollars to fund their programs, but it also is the best opportunity for some crooked individuals who run the event to pocket thousands of dollars from the proceeds of the event. The men and women who line up to toss the balls are not only the young folks who are looking for their lifelong mates, but many of them are the middle-aged people who either have been divorced or are looking for an opportunity to engage in an extra-marital affair. As Hmong are more modernized and globally connected, the New Year celebration has become an international affair. Every year, thousands of middle-aged men and women, many of them married men and women, travel from the United States to Laos, Thailand, Vietnam, and China to participate in Hmong New Year celebrations. As a result, marriage problems in the Hmong community have reached an epidemic proportion never before seen in Hmong history. Now not many young people are getting married,

---

[291] Paul and Elaine Lewis, *Peoples of the Golden Triangle* (London: Thames and Hudson Ltd, 1984), 126; Hillmer, 30.

but instead many married couples are getting divorced after the New Year celebration is over.

ANIMAL SACRIFICES

Animal sacrifice serves four general purposes in Hmong animism. First, it is the thanksgiving offering as is done during the first-crops offering and New Year celebration as discussed above. Animal sacrifices at these annual events show appreciation for the blessings and protection the people believe they have received from their ancestors and household demons. The second type of animal sacrifice is the sacrifice of animals for the deceased during funerals. Hmong animists believe that the more animals and spirit paper money they sacrifice and burn to the dead, the richer the dead will be in the world of darkness. In poor countries like Thailand, Laos, China, Vietnam, and Myanmar, sacrifice of one or two pigs, and a cow or a water buffalo, is sufficient. In the United States and in other rich countries, cows are the most common animals to be sacrificed to the dead. For an elderly man or woman and particularly those who were former leaders, as many as 20-30 cows are sacrificed. Ironically, Hmong animists feel the obligation to sacrifice many big animals to their elderly parents,[292] but they have no obligation to sacrifice any big animal to their young child who passes away before them. As discussed before, they don't even have the obligation to give a proper funeral service and burial for an infant who dies before the naming or spirit calling ritual. If they sacrifice a big animal for their dead child, they do it out of love, not out of obligation. Animal sacrifice to parents during the funeral is the single most important lineage obligation the sons have for their parents. For Hmong animists, obligation is more important than love. The sacrifice of big animals to

---

[292] Vincent K. Her, 129.

their parents is not necessarily out of love, but it's because of obligation. Therefore, regardless of financial situation, each son of the elderly parent must meet the minimum obligation of sacrificing at least one cow to his deceased parent. This is part of the reason that Dia Cha and Gary Yia Lee charge that Christianity is a threat to the Hmong animistic traditions because Hmong Christians refuse to meet the Hmong communal responsibility of sacrificing animals to their elderly parents and relatives who are animists.[293] But this lineage obligation can be very detrimental to many, especially for the poor sons of elderly parents. This is when the poor son who cannot afford to sacrifice a cow to his deceased parent will hear his relatives say, "we will tie a rope around your neck and tie the other end to the pole, see if you can make a sound like cow." This means that if he can make a sound like cow, he will be sacrificed to his deceased parent, but if he cannot make a sound like cow, then he better get a cow to be sacrificed to his deceased parent, no matter how poor he is.

Figure 10.1: This photo was taken on June 28, 2014 at the funeral of an aunt. This photo contains a house made of golden spirit paper money and several golden spirit paper money flowers. These are the spirit money that she will be using in the world of darkness. With a lot of

---

[293] Dia Cha, 4; Lee and Tapp, 42.

these spirit paper money, some of which look like those contain in the photo below, the family believes that she will be very rich in the demon world (*dlaabteb*) or the world of darkness. They believe that her house in the world of darkness will be made of gold, resembling what is made for her here.

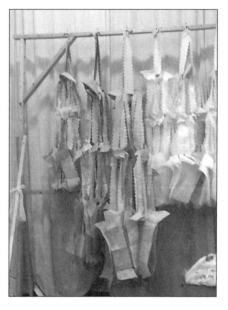

Figure 10.2: This photo was taken on August 18, 2013 during the funeral of another aunt. These are another type of spirit paper money that Hmong animists offer to their dead. They believe that the dead will be using them in the world of darkness. These are the spirit paper money that Hmong animists believe that the spirits of the dead of Hmong Christians will be poor in heaven because the living family members do not provide for their dead. If it is true, the spirits of the dead of Hmong animists will never need the support of the living family members because they are millionaires and billionaires in the world of darkness. But the opposite is true. The spirits of the dead of Hmong animists continue to need feeding from their living family members, but the spirits of the dead of Hmong Christians never return to cause illness or tragic death to their living family members if they do not get what they want from them.

Ralph F. Wilson states that "Nearly every culture throughout the world has employed sacrifice, usually animal sacrifice, to somehow appease the anger of the gods."[294] Hmong animism does exactly that. This is the third type of animal sacrifice Hmong animists performed. It is done to appease the angry demons, whether they are the household demons, the ancestors of the family, wild demons, or Satan, that are believed to have caused calamity in the family. Hmong animists consider this type of sacrifice as restitution for offenses they either knowingly or unknowingly committed against the demons. Hmong animists are very well aware that every conduct has ritualistic consequences and they are fearful of it. For example, they believe that whipping or cutting the center pole of the house could cause the offender or even the head of the family to be blind, sick, or face other form of consequences. They are careful not to offend the demons, not out of love and respect for them, but out of fear because sometimes the consequences are quite great and unbearable. Sometimes, burning spirit paper money is sufficient to appease the offended demons. But in most cases, animal sacrifice is required. In the Old Testament, God commanded the Israelites to sacrifice animals to Him as offerings for sin atonement for individual or for the sins of the whole community, offerings of fellowship, and thanksgiving offerings. These sacrifices are done as part of worshipping and in reverence to God. They are required so that the sinful human beings can reconcile themselves to God who is Holy. Without justification by the blood of the sacrificed animals, they cannot continue to enjoy a good relationship with God, and continue to receive God's favor and mercy of forgiveness.[295] But the concept of animal sacrifice in Hmong animism is not so that they would continue to enjoy good relationship with their household demons, ancestors, wild

---

[294] Ralph F. Wilson, *Lamb of God: Jesus' Atonement for Sin,* Loomis: Jesus Walk Publication, 2011, 15.

[295] Leviticus 4:1-35; 23:26-32; Douglas and Tenney, 474.

demons and Satan. It is quite the opposite. It is done so that the demons and Satan would leave them alone.

The fourth type of animal sacrifice is probably the most important one for Hmong animists. As discussed above, sacrifices performed by shamans are either for the protection of the spirit of the individual or the spirits of the entire family members from evil demons[296] or to secure the release of the spirit of the sick person whose spirit is believed to have been seized and held captive by the demons. This type of sacrifice is a lifesaving sacrifice, similar to the concept of Jesus, as the Sacrificial Lamb, being crucified on the cross to take the place of our eternal death. As Isaiah prophesied the work of the Sacrificial Lamb in Isaiah 53:4-5:

> Surely he took up our pain
> and bore our suffering,
> yet we considered him punished by God,
> stricken by him, and afflicted.
> [5] But he was pierced for our transgressions,
> he was crushed for our iniquities;
> the punishment that brought us peace was on him,
> and by his wounds we are healed.

Just as Jesus Christ suffered for our transgression by being the substitute for our death,[297] the sacrificed animal is to pay for the debt, bear the pain, and suffer death as a substitute for the person whose life is in danger of death. Hmong animists believe that without sacrificing the animal to the demons, the person is sure to die. The life or spirit of the sick person is redeemed by the life or spirit of the sacrificed animal. The Hmong term for such animal sacrifice is *"tua tsaj theej txhoj"* which translates as "sacrifice animal

---

[296] Fadiman, 282.
[297] Wilson, 27.

Is God a Strange God?

to take the place of the guilty." The word "*theej*" means to "take the place of or redeem" and the word "*txhoj*" means "guilty or in a dire position." It usually refers to someone who is guilty of something or someone who is in a very bad situation in which he is mired. It always refers to a situation that requires the use of another person or another thing to take the place of that guilty person in order for that person to be released. When the term *theej txhoj* is used, it implies the use of one thing to redeem another thing such as sacrificing the animal to redeem the person whose life is in danger of death. But the sacrifice of animals does not carry the same meaning as stated in Hebrew 9:22 ". . .without the shedding of blood there is no forgiveness."[298] The purpose of the animal sacrifice is to use the animal as a proxy for the captured spirit so that the demons would release the spirit and leave him alone. And the implication of animal sacrifice is not to be saved from eternal death as it is implied in the sacrificial death of Jesus Christ on the cross. Its purpose is only to redeem the affected person from physical death, as Hmong animists do not know that there is also eternal death beyond the physical death. Even after such sacrifice, there is no definitive evidence that the recovery from illness is due to the redemptive work of the sacrificed animal. Many die anyway after the redemptive sacrifice of the animal.

It is with great sadness that the majority of the Hmong are still in the dark. They haven't seen the light of the Lord Jesus Christ and have not been saved by the blood of the Sacrificial Lamb.[299] Hmong animists believe that animals can save life, but actually no animal life can save a human life. If an animal

---

[298] Robert L. Reymond, *The Lamb of God: The Bible's Unfolding Revelation of Sacrifice* (London: Christian Focus Publication, Ltd, 2006), 39.

[299] John 1:29 The next day John saw Jesus coming toward him and said, "Look, the Lamb of God, who takes away the sin of the world. . ."

life could save a human life, then human life is only worth as much as the animal's life. Human life is worth too much to be saved by animal. However, that's exactly what Hmong animists believe and do. For Hmong animists, their savior is the pig or cow that they raise in their animal barn or that is bought from the slaughter-house. They sacrifice animals year after year to save their lives, but they are not being saved. It is only a false hope, a form of false promise, the household demons, ancestors, and Satan employed to enslave Hmong animists. The more they sacrifice animals to the demons, the more animal sacrifices the demons demand from them. Who taught the Israelites to sacrifice animals for atonement of sins? It's God. However, if animals can save life then God wouldn't have planned for the Lord Jesus Christ to be crucified on the cross as a Sacrificial Lamb to save human life. Human life is too precious to be redeemed by animal life. Only the Lamb of God, the Lord Jesus Christ, the Son of God and Son of Man, can save human life. Physical death does not end one's life, but the impending eternal judgment of God will be unbearable for those who are without the Lord Jesus Christ, the Lamb of God, as their Savior. Do not rely any longer on the redemptive work of animal sacrifice. Come to the Lord Jesus Christ all Hmong animists,

> [18] For you know that it was not with perishable things such as silver or gold that you were redeemed from the empty way of life handed down to you from your ancestors, [19] but with the precious blood of Christ, a lamb without blemish or defect. [20] He was chosen before the creation of the world, but was revealed in these last times for your sake. [21] Through him you believe in God, who raised him from the dead and glorified him, and so your faith and hope are in God, 1 Peter 1:18-21.

Is God a Strange God?

See, Hmong Christians do not sacrifice animals year after year to redeem life, but they are not being oppressed by demons, ancestors, and Satan. For all who come to God (*Yawmsaub*), the blood of the Sacrificial Lamb that was shed on the cross has paid for the price of their eternal death in full.[300] For it is written:

> Salvation is found in no one else, for there is no other name under heaven given to mankind by which we must be saved (Acts 4:12).

Animal cannot save life. Only the blood of Jesus Christ, the Son of God and Son of Man, who is fully God and fully man, the "God-man," can save life.[301] Jesus says in John 6: 40:

> For my Father's will is that everyone who looks to the Son and believes in him shall have eternal life, and I will raise them up at the last day."

---

[300] Wilson, 30.
[301] Ibid, 77.

CHAPTER 11

OPPRESSION AND PERSECUTION IMPACTING HMONG CHRISTIANS

John 15: [18] "If the world hates you, keep in mind that it hated me first. [19] If you belonged to the world, it would love you as its own. As it is, you do not belong to the world, but I have chosen you out of the world. That is why the world hates you. [20] Remember what I told you: 'A servant is not greater than his master.' If they persecuted me, they will persecute you also. If they obeyed my teaching, they will obey yours also. [21] They will treat you this way because of my name, for they do not know the one who sent me. [22] If I had not come and spoken to them, they would not be guilty of sin; but now they have no excuse for their sin. [23] Whoever hates me hates my Father as well. [24] If I had not done among them the works no one else did, they would not be guilty of sin. As it is, they have seen, and yet

they have hated both me and my Father. [25] But this is to fulfill what is written in their Law: 'They hated me without reason.'

As Christians throughout history have been oppressed and persecuted for no reason other than the name of Jesus Christ, Hmong Christians worldwide have also experienced similar oppression and persecution. In democratic societies, Hmong Christians are being psychologically oppressed and persecuted through social isolation and ostracism. But in communist countries, Hmong Christians also face physical torture, forced recantation of faith in Jesus Christ, imprisonment, and many murder, just in the name of Christianity. The following report is just one of the countless accounts of persecution that Hmong Christians face in various Communist countries. On October 11, 2007, BosNewsLife reported the killing of 13 and imprisonment of Hmong Christian leaders by the Laos Communist Government. The report states:

> Most of the leaders of Laos Evangelical Church in Ban Sai Jarern village in Bokeo province in northwestern Laos are still imprisoned, said Compass Direct News, which investigates reports of persecution.
> In addition many other believers, including women and children, are still in prison, local Christian sources said, although estimates of the number detained were apparently unavailable. Only up to 30 believers still meet, three months after government forces detained 200 Hmong Christians "falsely" accused of being separatist rebels.
> Police and other security forces killed at least 13 Christians in the region since July,

an unprecedented number in the area, which observers said had been free of both separatist activity and government interference in churches. But last year, sources said, authorities pursued Hmong who had fled religious or political persecution in Vietnam and had taken refuge in Ban Sai Jarern.[302]

Hmong Christians who travel to Asia, particularly Vietnam and China, reported that Hmong Christians are most persecuted in areas where Hmong animists hold higher local and provincial government positions.

INTOLERENCE LEADS TO PERSECUTION

The most misleading label of Hmong Christians by Hmong animists is the social stigmatization of Hmong Christians as the poor, uneducated, and unintelligent people. Dia Cha says that Hmong converted to Christianity because they were poor and could not afford the traditional shamanic rituals, funerals, and ancestral worship. And they converted to Christianity because they were poor and could not afford education for their children, but the missionaries provided education for them.[303] The truth is the reason Hmong are the poorest among the poor in the world is the curse that Hmong worship everything but God. Lee and Tapp even argue that the mass conversion event of the Ahmao Hmong in China at the turn of the 20th century was only the results of several confused beliefs. 1) The Ahmao Hmong converted to

---

[302] BosNewsLife, "Laos Government Crackdown on Christians Continues; Several killed And Detained," www.bosnewslife.com/3217-3217-laos-government-crackdown-on-christians (accessed December 30, 2013.)

[303] Dia Cha, *Hmong American Concepts of Health, Healing and the Conventional Medicine,* (New York and London: Rutledge, 2003), 1.

Christianity simply because they were confused by the messianic message of the second coming of Jesus Christ given by the missionaries with the Hmong's mythical belief that a Hmong king will come and he will gather all Hmong under his rule[304] and will give the Hmong a country. The truth is that Hmong Christians have the Bible as their principle of belief. They do not believe in such a groundless myth. Those who teach and believe such a myth are the Hmong animists themselves who do not know the truth about the coming King. Shong Lue Yang, a Hmong animist and a self-proclaimed messiah for the Hmong, was one of the Hmong animists who taught this mythical message. Who believed his message? Only the Hmong animists believed him. According to Tchuyi Vang, a former chief of intelligence officer for General Vang Pao, the reason General Vang Pao ordered the bombardment of Shong Lue's compound was the very reason that he taught that a Hmong king was coming soon to establish a Hmong kingdom.[305] Keith Quincy's following statement proves my argument that Hmong animists are those who believe in such mythical messianic message. Quincy states:

> According to Hmong legend, man and God once communicated freely, but now only the shaman retains the power, if not to speak directly to God, to communicate with Shee Yee (*Sivyig*) and, through him, Yer Shau (*Yawmsaub*) who cares about mankind. It is this aspect of Hmong shamanism that has helped to sustain the Messiah myth, the belief that Yer Shau (*Yawmsaub*) will one day

---

[304] Lee and Tapp, 40-41.
[305] Tchuyi Vang, interviewed by author, St. Paul, MN, November 4, 2013.

send the Hmong a king who will rule over an independent Hmong nation.[306]

Hmong Christians do not believe such teaching as they have their faith solidly grounded in the teaching of the Bible. 2) The creation of the written language for the Ahmao Hmong was a fulfillment of the "prophecy that one day the lost form of Hmong writing would be restored to them." Lee and Tapp claim that Ahmao Hmong converted to Christianity as a result of the creation of the Ahmao Hmong writing. According to Rev. Pollard, the writing was created in response to the need that a native written language was required to further the teaching and training of these new Christians in the knowledge of the Scripture, the Lord God, the Savior Jesus Christ, and the Christian catechism after the mass conversion of Ahmao Hmong to Christianity.[307] The conversion was not the result of the creation of the writing, but the creation of the writing was the result of the conversion. Who created the most popular form of writing called the "Romanized Popular Alphabet" that currently in use worldwide by both Hmong Christians and Hmong animists? They were the missionaries sent to Laos in the 1950s. They were Father Yves Bertrais, a French Roman Catholic missionary, and Dr. G. Linwood Barney, a missionary from the Christian & Missionary Alliance of the United States.[308] All Hmong, both Christians and animists, should be thankful that after generations of the Hmong being marginalized and oppressed by the local majority peoples, the missionaries with the love of Jesus Christ cared enough about the Hmong to do something good for them. The Hmong surely are

---

[306] Quincy, 95.
[307] Samuel Pollard, *The Story of The Miao*, (London: Henry Hooks, 1919), 173-175.
[308] Naolue Taylor Kue, 67-68.

indebted to them. Regrettably, many Hmong animists who have direct benefit from the education, writing system, and other programs provided by the missionaries, are those most critical about Christianity. 3) Gary Yia Lee and Nicholas Tapp discussed the mass conversion of the Ahmao Hmong in China to Christianity at the turn of the 20th Century as follows, "There can be no doubt that converts at this time were in a desperate economic and political position and welcomed the teachings of Christ as a beacon of hope in their misery." Sure, Rev. Samuel Pollard, the missionary who led the mass conversion of the Ahmao Hmong in Yunnan Province, described in depth the poor conditions of these people, but nothing in his book, "The Story of The Miao" stated that economic desperation was the main reason for their conversion to Christianity. Pollard stated that these people trotted through many days of treacherous paths and sometimes in the soaking rain to come to see him, expecting nothing, but to learn more about the true Savior Jesus Christ. He said, they asked nothing, but "their one request was, give us books and teach us about Jesus."[309] In fact, Rev. Pollard reported that after the Ahmao people became Christians, these poor people were able to pool their own money together to build churches and schools for themselves and their children, something that Hmong animists haven't been able to do even today. They were poor, but that was not the reason for their conversion to Christianity. If poverty was the reason for their conversion to Christianity, Ahmao Hmong Christians wouldn't have survived the cruelest form of persecution the Communist Chinese government lodged against them. They converted to Christianity because they found the true Lord who loved and saved them from the demons of their ancestors, Satan, and their household demons, the tyrannical lords that had oppressed them generation after generation.

---

[309] Pollard, 38.

Those who refuse to accept Jesus Christ as their Lord and Savior continued to enjoy the blessing of the world – the warm and good treatment of the flesh, but they are physically and spiritually oppressed by Satan and the demons. Lee and Tapp miscontextualized Rev. Pollard's words to claim that he was in "considerable grief and upset" that many of the new converts took the Bible too literally "believing that the Day of Judgment was already at hand and the Messiah, whom they identified as a Hmong one, was shortly to be born... In one case a Miao woman claimed to be the sister of Christ and went around winning converts."[310] I read the book, "The Story of The Miao," through and through, but did not find that particular assertion. The book contained several unfavorable incidents in which Rev. Pollard indicated his disappointment, from which Lee and Tapp drew their assumptions from. First, a man by the name of Wang-lao-ta, a "wizard in the old days," who with ill intention went about distant villages misrepresenting himself as the "deputy of the missionary" and claimed that he had the authority to receive anyone to the church and baptize anyone who wanted to be baptized. For personal financial gain, he charged these unsuspecting new converts large sums for an opportunity to be baptized. However, he died of severe smallpox shortly after these wicked deeds and the "natives all looked upon this as the judgment of God on an arch-deceiver." A second incident happened when a group of people, many of them women, went about to spread rumors that Jesus was about to come. They even gave dates and misled a lot of people to wait for the second coming of Christ on those dates, but when He did not come as they prophesied the people were disappointed, discouraged, and many "returned to the blackness and despair of the old life."[311] Rev. Pollard

---

[310] Lee and Tapp, 40.
[311] Pollard, 112-113.

stated that these people, not because they took the Bible too literally as Gary Yia Lee and Nicholas Tapp claimed, but missed the point of the very message that he kept telling them that "of that hour knoweth no man." There were so many wonderful things that the missionary was able to do for the Ahmao Hmong, not only for the converts but also for the non-believers, including the establishment of schools that for the first time in their lives, children had the opportunity to attend school. But Lee and Tapp chose to discuss the few unfavorable incidents that were considered the least important among all the good things Rev. Pollard had done. The Ahmao Hmong through their resiliency and audacity are the strongest Hmong Christians in China despite the Communist Government's oppression, thanks to the Lord Jesus Christ and Rev. Pollard's love for these people. Lee and Tapp concluded that conversion to Christianity is an unfortunate mishap that happened to the Hmong because Christianity breaks down the Hmong traditional way of life, negatively impacting the Hmong communal and kinship relationships.[312] Even now in the United States, Hmong animists continued to look down on Hmong Christians as the poor, uneducated, and unintelligent people.[313] The fact is almost all Hmong Christian pastors have at least bachelor degrees, most have Master's Degrees, and a large number of them have Doctorate Degrees, but it is hard to find a Hmong shaman or a chanter of the Showing the Way chant with a bachelor degree, not to mention graduate degree. Hmong Christians own their own church buildings, pay their own pastors, and run ministry programs locally and overseas by their own self-supported funding, but Hmong animists have nothing to prove that collectively they have done anything good for the Hmong community, except probably the annual

---

[312] Lee and Tapp, 40-44.
[313] Teng Lo, radio program, preaching against Hmong Christians.

Hmong Animism

Hmong New Year celebrations that are often ripe with corruptions, bickering, in-fighting, and envy among the key players and opposing parties. Hmong animists often say that Christianity is a religion of intolerance of other non-Christian religious practices. Lee and Tapp alleged that the practices of burning the family altar, forbidding ancestral worship, and disallowing the practice of traditional funeral rites are a form of intolerance of traditional Hmong culture by Christianity.[314] The truth is these practices are not cultural. They probably are confused by what is cultural and what is religious. These practices are strictly Hmong animistic religious practices that must be abandoned if one is to convert to Christianity. In fact, no Hmong cultural aspect is untainted by the Hmong religion of animism, but Hmong Christians have not abandoned Hmong culture. Hmong animists use these occasions to worship demons, Satan, and their ancestors, but Hmong Christians use them to worship God and give thanks to the Lord. For example, New Year celebration is a time to give thanks, which Hmong Christians give thanks to God, but Hmong animists give thanks to their ancestors and household demons. At funeral, Hmong Christians use the time to worship God and thank God for the life and legacy of the person who passed. But traditional funeral is about worshipping the dead, demons, Satan, and the spirits of their ancestors and also to glorify themselves. This is why when they thank the people who give financial support, they have to say among other things the words "to serve the demons and provide for the guests (*tam dlaab ntaa qhua*)." A traditional Hmong funeral for an elderly person is completely controlled by the relatives, not by the children of the deceased, so financial limitation of the family is not as important as to make sure that the funeral meets the highest expectation of obligations the

---

[314] Lee and Tapp, 41.

children have for their parent. The children of the deceased have to come up with the amount of money demanded by the relatives who run the funeral. For many, the children end up in great debt after the funeral of a parent. To recapitulate a statement I made earlier, this is the time the poor children, especially the son or sons, of the dead elderly parent will hear, "We will tie a rope around your neck and tie the other end to the pole, see if you can make a sound like cow. If you cannot make a sound like cow then you must produce a cow to be sacrificed to your parent." Does this sound like love? The average cost of a traditional Hmong funeral in the United States is over $45,000. The more a funeral costs, the better the funeral is for the dead, and the more glory to the relatives who run it.

Dia Cha even goes further to allege that "Christianity represents a threat to Hmong communal harmony." [315] The real threat to the Hmong communal harmony is the unrelenting spreading of disrespectful, harmful, and hateful messages against Christianity and Hmong Christians. That is the real threat to Hmong communal harmony. Hmong Christians worship God, but Hmong animists worship demons, Satan, and ancestors. Whatever Hmong Christians do, Hmong animists look down on them as untraditional and inferior, but Hmong animists impose whatever they do upon Hmong Christians. If Hmong Christians do not participate then Hmong animists accuse them of breaking the communal norm and creating disharmony. Just as Hmong Christians never coerce their Hmong animist relatives to worship God, Hmong animists must cease forcing their Hmong Christian relatives to participate in the worship of demons, Satan, and ancestors. Just because Hmong Christians do not participate in those demonic, satanic, and ancestral rituals does not mean that Hmong Christians have abandoned their non-Christian

---

[315] Dia Cha, 3.

relatives. There is nothing that a Hmong animist does ritually that does not involve demonic worship. Even the wedding ritual of a Hmong animist involves the worship of household demons and ancestors. Communal harmony will be achieved only when Hmong animists are willing to accept that Hmong Christians will not participate in the satanic, demonic, and ancestral worship and stop coercing them to do what is against the will of their God and the principle of their beliefs. Informed Hmong Christians will not participate in Hmong animistic rituals, for as the Apostle Paul says in Galatians 5:1:

> It is for freedom that Christ has set us free. Stand firm, then, and do not let yourselves be burdened again by a yoke of slavery.

Demonolatry, ancestral worship, and shamanic rituals are slavery to demons and Satan that Hmong Christians who have been set free by the blood of Jesus Christ would not choose to be burdened again by the yoke of Satan and the demons. How could one be a Christian by continuing to worship ancestors, practice demonolatry, or conduct funerals the same way Hmong animists do or continue to participate in every aspect of Hmong animism? Hmong Christians do participate in all aspects of communal functions that do not involved animistic ritual.

Dia Cha also charges that Christianity is a threat to Hmong animist's health care.[316] How is it that Hmong Christian's refusal to participate in shamanic healing rituals a threat to the health of Hmong animists? Isn't the slavery of shamanic, demonic, satanic, and ancestral rituals the very reason Hmong Christians became Christians? If they continued to want to rely on shamanic power for healing

---

[316] Ibid., 3.

they wouldn't have converted to Christianity. Since they no longer believe in the power of shamanism, they will not seek shamanic healing ritual for their non-Christian relatives. There are two reasons Hmong animists decided to convert to Christianity. They are: 1) illness, and 2) demonic oppression. Most Hmong Christians had practiced animism and many were shamans themselves prior to conversion. They knew very well that shamanic rituals did not cure illness. The very reason they converted to Christianity was that they were fed up with this dark life of slavery to demonic rituals. According to Vang Vang, 80% of the people he surveyed stated that their reason for converting to Christianity was sickness and "demonic torment;"[317] sickness not from natural cause, but being tormented by the very household demons they worshipped as their protectors. Paul Vang's story of demonic torment discussed earlier is testimony to the reason that Hmong Christians who are set free from the power of the lords of darkness by the Lord Jesus Christ would not get their hands dirty again with the evil demons by participating in Hmong animistic rituals.

Dia Cha further charges that "devotion to the Christian faith tends to weaken the importance of maintaining the traditions of lineage and of the clan solidarity, and sometimes results in conflict between the non-Christian and Christian kinsmen."[318] Lineage responsibility is the single most important obligation of the children for their parents. It is the obligation of the children to care for their parents in their old age. Though this is universal for all cultures, for Hmong animists, it also means an obligation to sacrifice animals for their parents at their funeral, and worship and feed their spirits as ancestors. True, Hmong Christians do not sacrifice animals, worship, and feed the spirits of their

---

[317] Vang Vang, 110.
[318] Dia Cha, 3.

parents and ancestors, but they continue to respect and honor their parents long after their death. Lee and Tapp stated:

> The kinship-based clan or lineage is important in Hmong society at every level and there is a customary need to perform ancestral and shamanic rituals at times of life crisis and at particular points in the annual calendar to affirm and maintain that identity.[319]

This statement is very clear that Hmong traditional culture is animistic. When they engage in those rituals, they worship the spirits of their ancestors, the household demons, wild demons, natural and created objects, and Satan. Hmong Christians will not participate in those rituals because they no longer worship those things. Dia Cha, Gary Yia Lee and Nicholas Tapp tend to believe that Hmong kinship and clan system requires one to maintain the traditional Hmong animistic identity. That is a biased and completely one-sided perspective. They understand that maintaining clan solidarity means that one has to strictly observe and adhere to the tyrannical rule of animism handed down by their evil household demons. It is unfortunate that the majority of Hmong continue to remain slaves to these rules. For these reasons, it is very important for the Hmong animists to maintain clan solidarity. Hmong Christians continue to see the importance of kinship and clan solidarity, but from a different perspective. Hmong Christians believe that kinship and clan system do not have to involve animistic rituals. Hmong Christians continue to be involved in all aspects of kinship and clan matters, short of participating in the animistic rituals. For example, traditional Hmong funeral involves the sacrifice of animals to the dead, worship and

---

[319] Lee and Tapp, 42.

feed the dead, and many other rituals that are pure animistic, which Hmong Christians do not participate. But they attend the funeral, even help run the funeral, and give financial support. Even so, Hmong animists continue to accuse Hmong Christians of failure to meet the lineage obligations. For them, to fulfill the lineage obligations of kinship is to participate in all aspects of animistic rituals including the worship and sacrifice for the dead. The claims that Hmong Christians are unable to fulfill lineage and communal responsibilities for their Hmong animist relatives are a dishonest and one-sided perspective from the Hmong animists. While claiming that Hmong Christians have the lineage and communal responsibility for their non-Christian relatives, they deny having the same responsibility for their Christian relatives. Hmong animists not only refuse to attend the funeral of their Christian relatives, they sometimes force their Christian relatives to conduct animistic funeral for their love ones in order for them to participate. This does not only happen in Laos, China, Vietnam, and Thailand, but in the United States and also to a member of our church. As a new convert, he eventually bowed down to the demands of his non-Christian relatives and allowed his father's funeral to be conducted in traditional Hmong animistic way. As a Christian for over 40 years, a leader in the church, and a seminary student myself, I even was accused by my non-Christian relatives for not performing my mother's funeral the traditional way or at least some of it. Most of my non-Christian relatives did not even attend my mother's funeral. Most Hmong animists only see one side of the picture and only their way.

Dia Cha says:

> Lineage and clan solidarity are endangered by the message that all men are brothers, and that one's family, therefore, is inclusive of both relatives and all Christians. This places

an obligation upon a Hmong Christian, wherein aid of any sort is a necessity, to help his Christian non-relatives to be the same extend as his non-Christian relatives. When a member of these groups needs assistance at the same time, this obligation, born out Christian ideal, is difficult to fulfill."[320]

Giving assistance to others is part of human nature and it should not only limit to one's own kinship under the lineage obligation. Such understanding of one's obligation to the community is too narrow and only limited to one's own kinsmen. With the Christian message of love to humanity, Hmong Christians have adopted the broader perspective of lineage responsibility to include all Hmong and non-Hmong, Christians and non-Christians. The narrow perspective of lineage obligations that Hmong animists have is the root cause of fractions between the Hmong clans all the way down to the individual groups that do not share the same root of household demons. Dia Cha is trying to portray here that Hmong Christians are unable to fulfill their obligations of giving help to others. This shows how ignorant Hmong animists are of Hmong Christians. Hmong Christians send missionaries to several Asian countries and Africa. They raise fund to build churches, schools, give scholarships to students to attend college, organize and pay for revival conferences in Thailand for Hmong Christians and non-Christians in Asia to attend. Funds are also used to build water wells in Hmong villages, and build hostels in cities to bring Hmong children from Hmong villages to attend school and pay for staff to supervise and care for these children in most of Asian countries that have Hmong live in. Never mind what Hmong Christians have done to support Hmong kinship and

---

[320] Dia Cha, 3.

clan system, nothing is considered fulfillment of lineage obligation as long as if they don't sacrifice animals to their non-Christian relatives and feed the spirits of their ancestors. Hmong animists cannot think beyond the narrowest perspective of lineage obligation because it is part of the unbreakable centuries-old Hmong animistic religious boundary between clans that one cannot bridge, to offer assistance to another person who does not worship the same household guardian demons and share the same demonic rules (*thooj dlaab koom qhua*). These are the rules that no person can allow another person who does not share the same household demons to die in one's own house. This includes one's own daughter who has been married to another clan. If she comes to visit her parents or returns to live with them due to marriage problems and gets sick, she will have to be taken outside of the house before she dies.[321] Not only that she is not be allowed to die in her own parents' house, her parents cannot conduct a proper funeral service for her even when her husband's side of the family refuses to perform the funeral. It is a major violation of the household demonic rules if she is allowed to die in the house (*txhum dlaab qhuas*) because she is covered under her husband's demonic rules. No two people can worship two different sets of household demons in the same house. This happens when the father has passed away and the mother is remarried to a new husband of a different clan and brings her children, especially the son, to the new husband's house. He either has to adopt his stepfather's household demons or move out of the house in order to worship his biological father's household demons when he becomes of age. What a dreadful religion this is. Hmong animists also cannot allow their unmarried daughter who gives birth to stay at home the first 30 days after giving birth. In Laos where most Hmong Americans are from and possibly in Thailand, Vietnam,

---

[321] Symonds, 113.

China, and Myanmar, the parents have to build a temporary shelter outside of the family's house for their daughter to stay in for the first 30 days. But the building of a temporary shelter for the unmarried daughter rarely happens because any daughter who is pregnant is forced to marry out by her parents before the child is born. In the United States, they either have to rent an apartment or ask their Christian relatives to shelter her during that period. There are still other religious restrictions and boundaries that Hmong animists cannot cross. They are careful not to violate the demons, but when they violate them, they certainly will see disasters. This is the reason why Hmong have a proverb that says: "violate man is shame, but violate demons is death."

Dia Cha says that the "lineage and clan solidarity are endangered by the message that all men are brothers, and that one's family, therefore, is inclusive of both relatives and all Christians."[322] How wonderful this is that by the power of Jesus Christ, the unbreakable centuries-old clan boundary that has imprisoned the Hmong for thousands of years by the household demons is broken so that everyone has the obligation to everyone else as brothers and sisters. Only by the power of the Lord Jesus Christ, now Hmong Christians can die in one another's houses without fear and they can perform funerals for anyone who is a Christian. Just as the power of Jesus Christ breaks down the centuries-old boundary marker that prohibits the Jews from sharing food with Gentiles,[323] the power of the Lord Jesus Christ breaks down the centuries-old clan boundary of the Hmong who turn to Him. They are no longer bound by the power of the household demons, but free to share responsibility with every other Hmong.

---

[322] Dia Cha, 3

[323] James D. G. Dunn, *The New Perspective On Paul*, (Grand Rapids: William B. Eerdmans Publishing Company, 2005), 105.

She claims that the devotion to Christian faith weakens the relationship between Hmong Christians and Hmong animists.[324] It is not the devotion to Christian faith that weakens the clan solidarity and relationships between Christian and non-Christian Hmong kinsmen. It is the oppression, coercion, put-downs, and forced choices that are placed on Hmong Christians as well as the resentful, blasphemous, and sometimes cursing words toward Hmong Christians and their God and Savior that create the breakage between Hmong Christians and Hmong animists. To live in harmony with each other, these oppressive attitudes have to be abolished. They are the causes that weaken the relationship and widen the gap between these two groups of people. This type of rhetoric against Hmong Christians represents the cause of oppression and persecution of Hmong Christians worldwide. Evidently, on November 25, 2014, Worthy News in Vientiane, Laos, reported that "six Hmong families who were converted to Christianity were forced to leave their village after authorities ordered them to renounce their faith. . .Refusing to revert to Laotian traditional animist beliefs, all six families were evicted from their homes in Ko Hai village in Khamkeut district to Hoi Keo near the town of Lak Sao."[325] Hmong Christians worldwide, especially those in the communist countries, are being persecuted, forced to vacate their houses and farmlands, jailed, murdered, and forced to recant their faith in the Lord not only because of the intolerant policy of the governments, but also because of the intolerant attitude of the non-Christian relatives. In 2012, my wife and I traveled to China and had the opportunity to

---

[324] Dia Cha, 3.

[325] Worthy Christian News, "Lao Hmong Evicted after Converting to Christianity," http://www.worthynews.com/18120-lao-hmong-evicted-after-converting-to-christianity (accessed November 27, 2014.)

visit two Hmong churches there. However, the visits had to be done secretly at night for the very reason that if the Hmong villagers who are animists knew that we visited the churches, they would report, not only us the foreigners but also the church members, to the Chinese authorities. A Hmong missionary to China recently reported that a Hmong Christian couple who had been married for more than three years still could not obtain their marriage license. He reported that they had attempted several times to apply for the marriage license, but the Hmong village officer, a relative of the married couple, who, by law, must approve their marriage application in order for them to receive marriage license, continuously refused to approve and process their marriage application simply because they were Christians. Not only did he refuse to process the necessary documents for them, he repeatedly ridiculed them by saying, "Why don't you have your *Yexus* (Jesus) do it for you?"[326] When news agencies report about the persecution of Hmong Christians in Laos, Vietnam, and China, they usually refer to the persecutors as the police, security forces, and military officers as agents of the governments.[327] But what is untold by the news is equally appalling; that is the persecution of Hmong Christians by Hmong animists who are the local and provincial authorities. In some cases, it's the family members and relatives of the converts who coordinate with the local and provincial authorities to persecute them, beat them,

---

[326] Due to sensitivity and safety issues, this author cannot provide name.
[327] BosNewsLife, "Vietnamese security forces have destroyed two churches of minority Hmong Christians in Northwestern Vietnam and threaten to tear down a third," www.bosnewslife.com/22254-news-watch-vietnam-destroys-churches-hmong-christians (accessed Dec. 30, 2013).

force them to vacate their houses and farmlands, and order them to relocate to other villages.[328] Dia Cha claims that the refusal of Hmong Christians to provide shamanic healing ritual and traditional funerary rites to their animist parents is a problem for the health care of Hmong animists.[329] All animistic rituals are demonic worshipping, which true Hmong Christians would not do even for their parents. If Hmong Christians continue to believe, provide, and participate in those animistic rituals then they are not real Christians. What makes them Christians is their ability and determination to refuse to provide and participate in those animistic rituals. This is the process of transformation from the old and dying self of an animist to a regenerated self of a Christ-like Christian.[330] What makes them Christians is the fact that they can refuse to participate in the worship of demons, ancestors, trees, rocks, and Satan. And again, what makes them Christians is the fact that they can stand firm in their faith and not waver to the pressure, even to the point of death, and they are willing to sacrifice their lives for their faith. What does the refusal of Hmong Christians to provide or participate in shamanic healing rituals or traditional funeral have to do with the health problems and well-being of Hmong animists? The refusal of Hmong Christians to provide or participate in those rituals is not the problem. The problem is the intolerant attitude of Hmong animists towards Hmong Christians, pure and simple. No one can worship two lords. If Hmong animists are forced against their will to worship the Christian God, they would definitely refuse and despise those who force them. However, Hmong Christians

---

[328] Reported by Hmong Christian workers who traveled to Vietnam and from Hmong Christians in Vietnam. For safety reason, no name is provided.
[329] Dia Cha, 3.
[330] Willard, 41.

never expect, let alone force, their non-Christian relatives to participate in or perform any Christian rituals. Highly educated Hmong animists like Dr. Gary Yia Lee, Dr. Dia Cha, and many others should be the foremost people who promote tolerance and acceptance of one another between Hmong animists and Hmong Christians. What they say about Christianity and Hmong Christians not only widens the gap between the two groups, but is also seen as poisonous seeds of hatred, divisiveness, and intolerance toward Hmong Christians. Tolerance is the ability to understand and accept that Hmong Christians will not seek or participate in any of the animistic rituals. Nothing is more divisive than religions, but everyone can learn to live peacefully with one another if everyone can accept the differences. Hmong will achieve communal harmony when Hmong animists cease all resentful, divisive, and accusative attitudes toward Hmong Christians and ceased blaspheming their God. Otherwise, Hmong Christians and Hmong animists will continue to live with one another under the pretension of harmony. As the older generation passes away, so does Hmong animism, and it will gradually become a thing of the past, but Christianity is the future of the Hmong.

BIBLIOGRAPHY

Bahnsen, Greg L. *Van Til's Apologetic: Readings and Analysis*. Phillipsburg: P&R Publishing Co., 1998.

Bertrais, Yves and Va Thai Yang. *Kab Ke Pam Tuag Coj Zaj (Funeral Rites and procedures)*. Guyane, France: Association Communaute Hmong, 1987.

Bohac, Joseph, J. Ph.D. *Human Development: A Christian Perspective*. Ramona: Vision Publishing, 1993.

BosNewsLife, "Vietnamese security forces have destroyed two churches of minority Hmong Christians in Northwestern Vietnam and threaten to tear down a third." Hanoi, Vietnam, June 27, 2012, www.bosnewslife.com/22254-news-watch-vietnam-destroys-churches-hmong-christians, (accessed December 30, 2013).

BosNewsLife, Breaking News: Laos Security Forces Kill 13 Christians in Major Crackdown, http://www.bosnewslife.com/3094-3094-breaking-news-laos-security-forces-kill-13, (access, December 30, 2013).

Bush, L. Russ. *Classical Readings in Christian Apologetics, A. D. 100-1800.* Grand Rapids: Zondervan Corporation, 1983.

Cha, Dia. "The Hmong 'Dab Pog Couple' Story and its Significance in Arriving at an Understanding of Hmong Ritual." *Hmong Study Journal* 4 (2003): 1-20.

_____. *Hmong American Concepts of Health, Healing and the Conventional Medicine.* New York and London: Rutledge, 2003.

Cha, Ya Po. *An Introduction to Hmong Culture.* Jefferson and London: McFarland & Company, Inc., 2010.

Clarke, Samuel R. *Among The Tribes in South-West China.* 1911. Reprint, London: Forgotten Books, 2012.

Conquergood, Dwight. *I am a Shaman: A Hmong Life Story with Ethnographic Commentary, Southeast Asian Refugee Studies Occasional Papers Number Eight.* Minneapolis: University of Minnesota, Center for Urban and Regional Affairs, 1989.

Dalman, Rodger. *Yahweh's Song: A Handbook for Understanding Old Testament Historical Theology.* (Unpublished handbook.) Newberg: Trinity College of the Bible and Trinity Theological Seminary, 2007.

Davis, Stephen, T. *Reason & Religion: God, Reason & Theistic Proofs.* Grand Rapids: Wm. B. Eerdmans Publishing Company, 1997.

Douglas, J. D. and Merrill C. Tenney. *Zondervan Illustrated Bible Dictionary*. Rev. ed, Grand Rapids: Zondervan, 2011.

DuBois, Thomas A. *An Introduction to Shamanism*. New York: Cambridge University Press, 2009.

Dunn, James D. G. *The New Perspective on Paul*. Grand Rapids: Wm. B. Eerdmans Publishing Company, 2005.

Fadiman, Anne. *The Spirit Catches You And You Fall Down: A Hmong Child, Her American Doctors, and the Collision of Two Cultures*. New York: Farrar, Straus and Giroux, 1997.

Frame, John M. *A Theology of Lordship: The Doctrine of the Christian Life*, Phillipsburg: P & R Publishing, 2008.

Fordham University, "The Code of Hammurabi, Ancient History Sourcebook." www.fordham.edu/halsall/ancient/hamcode.asp (accessed August 20, 2013).

Geddes, William Robert. *Migrants of the Mountains: The Cultural Ecology of the Blue Miao (Hmong Njua) of Thailand*. Oxford: Clarendon Press, 1976.

Geisler, Norman, L. *Christian Ethics: Options and Issues*. Grand Rapids: Baker Book House, 1989.

Falk, Catherine. "Upon Meeting the Ancestors: The Hmong Funeral Ritual in Asia and Australia." *Hmong Studies Journal* 1 (Fall 1996): 1-15.

Hee, Kong. "God in Ancient China: Discover the Similarities between the History of China and the Christian Scriptures," http://youtube.com/watch?v=1kkxUy-MAMXQ&feature=plcp (accessed June 28, 2014).

Her, Steven X. Ph. D. "Contextualizing the Gospel for Miao Animists." PhD diss., Western Seminary 1999.

Her, Vincent, K. "Hmong Mortuary Practice: Self, Place and Meaning in Urban America." PhD diss., University of Wisconsin – Milwaukee, 2005).

──────. "Hmong Cosmology: Proposed Model, Preliminary Insights." *Hmong Studies Journal* 6 (2005): 1-25.

Hillmer, Paul. *A People's History of the Hmong*. St. Paul: The Minnesota Historical Society Press, 2010.

Hmong Cultural Center, Inc., St. Paul, MN, http://www.hmongcc.org (accessed May 28, 2013).

Hmongism. "The Bylaws of Temple of Hmongism." http://www.hmongism.org (accessed September 18, 2013).

Jenks, Robert, D. *Insurgency and Social Disorder in Guizhou: The "Miao" Rebellion 1854-1873*. Honolulu: University of Hawaii Press, 1994.

Keown, Damien. *Buddhism: A Very Short Introduction*. Oxford: Oxford University Press, 2013.

Khang, Nhia Toua, interview by author, St. Paul, MN, June 21, 2014.

Khang, Wang Sher, interview by author, Minneapolis, MN, October 5, 2013.

Khang, Youa Hang, interview by author, Wisconsin Rapids, WI, October 9, 2013,.

Kolb, Robert. *Speaking the Gospel Today*. Rev. ed. St. Louis: Concordia Publishing House, 1995.

Kraft, Charles H. *I Give You Authority: Practicing the Authority Jesus Gave Us*. Grand Rapids: Chosen Books, 1997.

Kue, Cher Chou, Interview by author, St. Paul, MN, September 4, 2013.

Kue, Naolue Taylor. *A Hmong Church History*. Thornton: Hmong District, 2000.

Lee, Gary Yia, and Nicholas Tapp. *Culture and Customs of the Hmong*. Santa Barbara: Greenwood, 2010.

Lee, Gary Yia. "Diaspora and the Predicament of Origins: Interrogating Hmong Postcolonial History and Identity." *Hmong Studies Journals* 8 (2007): 1-24.

Lee, Yvonne, interview by author, St. Paul, MN, December 22, 2014.

Lemoine, Jacques. "To Tell the Truth." *Hmong Studies Journal* 9 (2008): 1-29.

_____. "Commentary: The (H)mong Shaman's Power of Healing: Sharing the Esoteric Knowledge of a Great Mong Shaman," *Hmong Studies Journal* 12 (2011): 1-36.

Lo, Teng. "Kev Ntseeg Vajtswv Hmoob Yuamkev Lawm (Hmong Are Wrong In Believing In God." CD Rom, (2013).

Lindsley, Arthur, John Gerstner, and R.C. Sproul. *Classical Apologetics: A Rational Defense of the Christian Faith and a Critique of Presuppositional Apologetics*. Grand Rapids: Zondervan Publishing House, 1984.

Lewis, Paul and Elaine Lewis. *Peoples of the Golden Triangle*. London: Thames and Hudson Ltd, 1984.

McKinnon, John and Wanat Bhruksasri, *Highlanders of Thailand*. Oxford: Oxford University Press, 1983.

Morrison, Gayle. "The Hmong Qeej: Speaking to the Spirit World." *Hmong Studies Journal* 2 (1998): 1-17.

Penn-Lewis, Jessie. *Soul & Spirit: How to find Freedom from the Tyranny of the Soul*. New Kensington: Whitaker House, 1997.

Pollard, Samuel. *The Story of the Miao*. London: Henry Hooks, 1919.

Quincy, Keith. *Hmong History of a People: The Spirit World*. 2nd ed. Spokane: Eastern Washington University Press, 1995.

Reymond, Robert L. *The Lamb of God: The Bible's Unfolding Revelation of Sacrifice*. London: Christian Focus Publication, Ltd, 2006.

Richard, Ramesh. *Preparing Evangelistic Sermons: A Seven-Step Method for Preaching Salvation.* Grand Rapids: Baker Book, 2005.

Smedes, Lewis, B. *Mere Morality: What God Expects from Ordinary People,* 1983. Reprint. Grand Rapids: Wm. B. Eerdmans Publishing Co, 2002.

Symonds, Patricia, V. *Calling in the Spirit: Gender and the Cycle of Life in a Hmong Village.* Seattle and London: University of Washington Press, 2004.

Tapp, Nicholas. *The Hmong of China: Context, Agency, and the Imaginary.* Boston: Brill Academic Publishers, Inc., 2003.

Tapp, Nicholas, Jean Michaud, Christian Culas, and Gary Yia Lee. *Hmong/Miao in Asia.* Chiang Mai, Thailand: Silkworm Books, 2004.

Tozer, A. W. *The Purpose of Man: Designed to Worship.* Ventura: Regal, 2009.

Vang, Chia Koua, Gnia Yee Yang, and William A. Smalley. *The Life of Shong Lue Yang: Hmong "Mother of Writing,"* trans. Mitt Moua and See Yang. Minneapolis: University of Minnesota, Center for Urban and Regional Affairs, Southeast Asian Refugee Studies, 1990.

Vang, Paul. Personal testimony, Lake Elmo, MN, November 23, 2013.

Vang, Tchuyi, Interview by author, St. Paul, MN, November 4, 2013.

Vang, Timothy, T. "Coming A Full Circle: Historical Analysis of the Hmong Church Growth 1950-1998." PhD diss., Fuller Theological Seminary, 1998.

Vang, Vang. "Hmong: From Animism to Christianity." PhD diss., Vision International University, 2002.

White, Kenneth. *Kr'ua Ke (Showing the way): A Hmong Initiation of The Dead*. Bangkok: Pandora, 1983.

Willard, Dallas. *Renovation of the Heart: Putting On the Character of Christ*. Colorado Springs: Navpress, 2002.

Wilson, Ralph F. *Lamb of God: Jesus' Atonement for Sin*. Loomis: JesusWalk Publication, 2011.

Wommack, Andrew. *Spirit, Soul & Body*. Tulsa: Harrison House, 2010.

Yang, Dao. *Hmong at the Turning Point*. Minneapolis: WorldBridge Associates, Ltd, 1993.

Yang, Gao Xee and Doua Yang, Personal Testimony, Blaine, MN, 2011.

Yang, Kao-Ly. "The Meeting with Guanyin, the Goddess of Mercy: A Case Study of Syncretism in the Hmong System of Beliefs." *Hmong Studies Journal* 7 (2006):1-42.

ABOUT THE AUTHOR

I, Long Khang (*Swm-Looj Khaab*), was born in Xieng Khouang Province, Laos; grew up during the peak of the Vietnam War and saw the fall of Laos to Communism in the spring of 1975. In 1979, at the age of 14, I realized that it was not safe to live under the totalitarian government of Communism anymore, so I started to think about ways to flee Laos for freedom. However, I believed that God already had plans for me to escape the Communism. I lived with my family in the village of Pahoi, but was away from home to attend school in Ban Tha Ban Don, a city at least three hours walk away. In early April of 1979, during the week of the

Lao New Year celebration, some of the students and I went home for the week because school was on break for a whole week. When we arrived back in the city to attend school again, we discovered that the small house that we lived in to attend school was gone. I asked the cousin who lived in the house next to ours that stayed over during the holiday what happened to our house. He said that there was a storm during the week and the wind blew our house away. What amazed me until this day was the fact that the month of April in Laos was in the dry season and that part of the country never experienced any strong wind. But our house and our house alone was reportedly blown away by a strong storm during the unlikely season. He gave us our belongings and said that we could stay with him, but his house wouldn't have enough rooms for the four of us because there were already three of them living in his house. So we decided to quit school and return home. A week later three of us left for freedom. The walk for freedom was not an easy one. Many did not make it through the month-long walk through the thick of the jungles crisscrossing the trails of the enemy soldiers. Some died of starvation and illness, but others were shot and killed or captured by the Lao Communist soldiers, and still others drown while swam across the Mekong River. I was forced to make such a major decision at that young age. A decision that once I left the door of my house, I could not turn back. And it was a decision that I had to gamble my life for. But I put my trust in the Lord my God and took the leap of faith and left my family to search for freedom – freedom, not only for how I wanted to live my life, but also for my belief. I said goodbye to my mother with tears filled in both of our eyes. I left her that day and never knew if I would ever see her again. She watched me walked away until I disappeared into the thick of the woods. I did not even have the chance to say goodbye to my older brothers and sister-in-law because they weren't home. I wondered how they would feel when they

About the Author

came home only to learn that their youngest brother had left for a distant country.

I spent eight months in Ban Vinai, a refugee camp in Thailand, and came to the United States at the age of 15 and arrived in Minnesota on a cold winter day on December 23, 1979 with a pair of slippers and no winter coat. Arrived in Minnesota I was half the world away from my family and the chance to see them became dimmer. But with God's grace, they followed my path, first were my brothers and sister-in-law and several months later came my mother. They arrived in Minnesota in July 1980, seven months later. The torn apart family finally reunited again by God's grace. I graduated from high school in 1984 and went on to college. I spoke very little English when I started college, but managed to graduate with double majors in Political Science and Sociology of Criminology of Law and Deviance at the University of Minnesota in 1990. I received my Master Degree in Public Administration at Hamline University in 1996. I had heard the Lord's call for me to serve Him, long before I started college, but kept procrastinated it. Even when several bible colleges had accepted me, I still refused to attend. However, I could not ignore anymore the voice that kept whispering to me that God wanted me to go into ministry, so in 2007, I decided to enroll at Trinity College of the Bible and Trinity Theological Seminary. One month later, my wife became very sick and continued to struggle with her health even today. I lost my beloved mother in 2008. Then in 2009, I became very sick myself. There were times when I thought that I might not live to see another day. Several times, I gathered my family and we cried together, not knowing how long I would live. I was in the bottom of a pit and so was my wife. Our only hope was to trust in the Lord our God. I had to suspend school for over a year. But when I resumed classes, I would become very sick during exams. Many times, I thought about quitting and had discussed about it with my wife. She said to me: "If it is the worldly knowledge that you are pursuing then you should quit, but it's the knowledge of our Lord God, so you should not quit." With God's grace and my wife's encouragement, I persevered. In early 2015, after many long delayed years, I received my Ph. D Degree in Pastoral Ministry. I hope that God will use me and my wife for His Kingdom work. My accomplishment is not for me, but it's for my Lord, and it's all for His glory. I praise my God for His grace and unceasing mercy on me and my family. Amen.